A WOMAN OF SIGNIFICANCE

ALSO BY DONNA MORLEY

Choices That Lead to Godliness

A
WOMAN
OF
SIGNIFICANCE

Discovering Your Value and Purpose
in the Eyes of God

DONNA MORLEY

CROSSWAY BOOKS • WHEATON, ILLINOIS
A DIVISION OF GOOD NEWS PUBLISHERS

Cover design: Cindy Kiple

First printing 2001

Printed in the United States of America

Unless otherwise designated, Scripture quotations are taken from the New American Standard Bible® copyright © The Lockman Foundation 1960, 1962, 1963, 1968, 1971, 1972, 1973, 1975, 1977, 1995. Used by permission. (www.Lockman.org)

Scripture taken from the Holy Bible: New International Version® is identified NIV. Copyright © 1973, 1978, 1984 by International Bible Society. Used by permission of Zondervan Publishing House. All rights reserved.

The "NIV" and "New International Version" trademarks are registered in the United States Patent and Trademark Office by International Bible Society. Use of either trademark requires the permission of International Bible Society.

Scripture taken from *The Bible in Today's English Version* is identified as TEV. Old Testament © American Bible Society, 1976; New Testament © American Bible Society, 1966, 1971, 1976.

Library of Congress Cataloging-in-Publication Data
Morley, Donna, 1959-
   A woman of significance : discovering your value and purpose in
the eyes of God / Donna Morley.
     p.   cm.
   Includes bibliographical references.
   ISBN 1-58134-263-2 (alk. paper)
   1. Women—Religious aspects—Christianity. 2. Christian women—
Religious life. 3. Morley, Donna, 1959-   . I. Title.
BV4527.M65   2001
248.8'43—dc21   00-012351
                                          CIP

15	14	13	12	11	10	09	08	07	06	05	04	03	02	01
15	14	13	12	11	10	9	8	7	6	5	4	3	2	1

Contents

Acknowledgments

I would like to express my appreciation and gratitude to all those who have helped me on this book:

To my husband, Dr. Brian Morley, who joined me in burning the midnight oil as we edited the manuscript during the final days before it was due. As always, I am grateful for our in-depth conversations and your theological insights, such as on the image of God, which contributed greatly to this book.

To my editor Lila Bishop. Thanks for helping me sharpen the writing and make the manuscript the best it can be.

To Dr. John Street, professor at The Master's College. Thank you for giving me some of your precious time to share with me your penetrating insights on the concept of self-love.

To Dr. Robert Thomas, professor at The Master's Seminary. Thank you for your thoughts on the sacrificial life. I not only appreciate what you have to say, but I was honored that you would entrust to me chapters from your then-unpublished manuscript "Christian Self-Concept: A Death-Life Paradox" (Scotland: Christian Focus Publishers, forthcoming). Your biblical insights are so rich.

To Dr. James Rosscup, professor at The Master's Seminary. Thank you for your thorough and practical work in *Abiding in Christ* (Zondervan, 1973). It helped me a great deal personally and provided ideas for chapter four.

To author and cult expert, Professor Emeritus Dr. Ed Gruss. Thank you for your timely notes on the unorthodox teachings of Emanuel Swedenborg.

To author and editor Steve Miller. Thanks for your encouragement and assistance in getting this book started.

Introduction:
A Feeling of Insignificance

I can't believe I'm here, I thought to myself as I drove into one of Los Angeles's most prestigious movie studios. Who would have believed I would get to come here to interview a big-time celebrity—and a Christian one at that?

I wanted to soak it all in—the huge glass windows, the bronze Emmy statue, countless glossy pictures of stars from the past, the fancy cars, and most of all, the galaxy of stars I might run into. *If only my friends could see me now*, I thought.

As I entered the back door of the studio, I felt like a fairy tale princess entering the world of make-believe. After asking for directions to the starlet's dressing room, I walked down a long corridor of bright white doors with gold stars plastered on each one. My heart started to beat rapidly as I felt a heightening sense of intimidation.

When I came to the right door, I stood for a moment, wondering about how I should knock. Should it be soft or loud? Two knocks or three? Praying a quick, "Lord, give me strength," I decided on a hard, confident-sounding double knock.

A man opened the door and gave me a warm smile. I immediately felt at ease. I introduced myself simply as Donna and said, "I have an appointment to interview Marsha Mills" [name changed].

"Certainly. Please come in," said the gentleman. He then closed the door, extended his hand, and said, "I'm Marsha's agent—Charles Blair" [name changed].

"Nice to meet you." Beginning to feel uncomfortable again, I wasn't sure what to say next.

Mr. Blair took me to a couch where Marsha sat chatting with several of her friends, who were eagerly puffing their cigarettes. He said, "Marsha, this is Donna. She's here to interview you."

Without smiling or saying a word, Marsha just stared at me. My feelings of insecurity intensified. I felt that I was an unwanted interruption.

Marsha and her friends were dressed "to kill." They all stared at me silently, sizing me up. While I had made an effort to look nice, they were gloriously fashionable, and I appeared quite plain by comparison. I wondered if they thought I was some garage-sale jockey barging into their world of glamour and glitz.

While I stood waiting to be offered a seat, Mr. Blair explained that Marsha's friends were also "in the biz." Sensing that he thought I should know who they were, I smiled and said to all of them, "It must be so exciting to offer entertainment to millions of people."

No one said a word. No one smiled. No one acknowledged even hearing me.

Feeling more uneasy than ever, I said. "Well, how about we start the interview?"

Before I could ask the first question, the phone rang. Mr. Blair went to answer it, and Marsha and her friends whispered and giggled among themselves. I wondered if they were talking about me.

At that moment my world suddenly seemed dark and hollow. I was overwhelmed with the feeling that, compared to them, I was a nobody. I felt as if I needed an excuse for living. And unfortunately at the time, I didn't have one to give.

Putting down the phone, Mr. Blair said, "Girls, you are wanted on stage."

Turning to me, Mr. Blair said, "Donna, the girls are rehearsing for the upcoming Grammy Awards. Why don't you sit with me in the theater. We can talk and watch the girls perform."

Smiling, I replied, "I would like that."

As everyone sashayed out of the dressing room, I shuffled behind them, sensing nonverbally that I was at the bottom of an unspoken pecking order. As a mere college student from the sticks somewhere north of Los Angeles, I was last out the door. I clearly belonged last, and no one waited to walk beside me or say anything casual or friendly to me.

Mr. Blair and I sat in the darkened theater, and he rattled off the many accomplishments that made Marsha Mills the star she was. But as soon as Marsha stepped out on the stage, Mr. Blair became silent. His eyes were fixed on the beauty queen. Her performance was such that it seemed to demand the adoration and applause of the entire world. Proudly Mr. Blair said, "Isn't she great?"

By this time my heart had sunk into my stomach, and my excitement had turned to disenchantment. I didn't feel like acknowledging Marsha Mills's greatness. Instead, a lot of questions were whirling through my mind. I had arrived at the studio thinking I was about to meet a person who was significant because she was famous and popular—she was a rapidly rising star who had money and power.

It dawned on me that if . . .

fame

popularity

power

money

and a prestigious title

were the traits that made a person significant, then I, little Donna, was truly insignificant, for I had none of those things!

But was that really true?

Feeling much less like a fairy tale princess, I stood up and said, "Mr. Blair, I've taken up so much of your precious time. Thank you for allowing me to see Marsha."

Mr. Blair stood as well, shook my hand, and gave me his business card. "Though you didn't get the interview you wanted, I hope you were able to observe enough to write something," he said. "Call me if you need more information about Marsha."

I thanked Mr. Blair again and rapidly walked toward the exit. I couldn't get out of there fast enough. When I got to my car, I sat deep in thought for a while. Only mass popularity had value inside that peculiar little world of the studio. Everybody else and everything else were insignificant—not worthy of notice.

Driving away from that island of beautiful celebrities, I wondered, *Am I really insignificant? Just because no one has ever heard of me, and my life isn't glamorous or exciting, does that make me a nobody? And as a Christian, because I'm not a great singer, missionary, scholar, or evangelist, does that mean I have less value to God?*

I knew that couldn't be true. I knew that surely, in God's eyes, I was significant. Or was I? After all, I had no real idea of how He measured significance. I was surprised to see just how much my perception of significance lined up with what the *world* values rather than with what *God* values.

I began to wonder what exactly God *does* value. If significance isn't found in fame, fortune, and my position in life, where does it come from? As I continued my drive home, I had to admit I really didn't know the answers.

Even now as I write this, I vividly remember many other struggles with feeling insignificant. As a college student, I seldom participated in class discussion because I didn't think of myself as very smart. I thought that only intelligent students had the "right" to ask questions or speak in class. As a single woman, I felt insignificant when I didn't have what some classified as a "significant other." As a career woman, I had frequently compared myself with others who seemed more successful, more popular, and better paid. As a married woman raising children, my life at times seems to consist only of a vicious, never-ending cycle of mopping floors, changing dirty diapers, ironing shirts, cleaning toilets, dusting furniture, washing dishes, and doing laundry. When my husband gets home, I wonder if there is anything about my day worth sharing with him.

Moreover, as a citizen in this society, there have been times when I have felt, well . . . socially clumsy. Why? Because it seems the general populace is attracted to those who can keep a conversation going. They are "smooth." They always have the right thing to say in every circumstance. They are interesting, and they have great personalities.

Perhaps you've faced some of these same struggles. Perhaps you've been through those times when you've allowed your sense of significance to come from what *others* think of you. And you've therefore suffered the double insecurity of being uncertain how much people like you and whether whatever popularity you have attained will last.

Yet all that changes dramatically when we discover what makes us significant to *God*. From that we gain a joyful confidence and security that can never be taken away! What's especially exciting is that God's kind of significance far outlasts the temporal significance found in the world.

Little had I anticipated that my visit to that movie studio in Los Angeles would have such a profound influence on me. Since that day, the Lord has graciously continued to help me understand and pursue His kind of significance.

If that's what you desire for your life as well, then won't you come journey with me on God's path to becoming a woman of significance? Though a lot of people have embarked on this journey in recent decades, most never reached their destination. The advice they navigated by said only to think more highly of themselves while ignoring their genuine shortcomings and personal limitations. But groundlessly puffing ourselves is really a form of self-deception.

Rather than merely trying to change our feelings about ourselves, we will rely on the sufficiency of Scripture and discover what God thinks of us, the significance we *already* have in His eyes apart from our achievements. That will be the foundation for building certain character traits by which we can, through His strength, also *become* significant in the unfolding of His will.

As we shall see, our concept of ourselves must be formed not by putting on rose-colored glasses and looking within ourselves, but by looking to God and seeing in His eyes our reflection, which includes who we now are by His grace and who we can become through His power.

So our journey will lead us not back to ourselves, but to what God has done for us, to what He can do through us, and ultimately to God Himself.

Ready for the journey?

PART ONE

Why Don't I Feel Significant?

How many of us have ever asked the question, "Why don't I feel significant?" I think we all have at one time. We look at such things as our appearance or our mental, physical, and social limitations, and think, Why can't I be like _____? Why can't I be . . . well, more significant?

Some of us strive to change ourselves and be successful, but our efforts don't seem to pay off. They can lead to frustration and a sense of failure. With thoughts and feelings like these, we can easily end up with wrong opinions of ourselves.

In the first three chapters, let's discover how we can develop a true sense of who we are. We can be encouraged by some powerful truths.

One

IF ONLY I COULD CHANGE WHO I AM!

$\mathcal{M}$any times in my life I have wished I could change who I am. One time especially I wished it more than anything! Brian (my husband) and I had just broken up our fifteen-month dating relationship. Why the breakup? He wasn't quite sure I was "the one." So I suggested that we stop dating and that he begin to date others. After such a crazy suggestion, I prayed that God would put another woman in Brian's life so he would be able to pinpoint exactly what he was looking for. (I was selfishly hoping he would discover I was what he was looking for!)

Days after my prayer, it seemed as if women were falling from the sky like manna! Seven, to be exact, were interested in this "bachelor till the rapture."

"Lord," I pleaded, "I asked for only one woman, not seven!"

So, as the Lord most faithfully does, He answered my prayer. He chose for Brian one woman he was to get to know. Gloria was her name. She had the intellect of a professor, looks that would intimidate Barbie, a personality that glowed, and she came from wealthy stock. So much for answered prayer!

It was during this time that my feelings of inadequacy surfaced as I thought that the whole world considered Gloria ideal for Brian. I made unfavorable comparisons galore and ended up feeling as ugly and unwanted as a toxic waste dump.

Fortunately for me, about six months later Brian stopped spending time with Gloria and soon afterward came to see that I was the one he was to spend the rest of his life with. We married a year later.

I had been looking at Gloria as a person who "had it all." But Brian told me that he wasn't looking for someone who had it all. He wanted someone who was striving *to be all* that God wanted her to be. I was moved by his view of me—but, of course, even years later I know I have not arrived. I still keep striving!

I learned something valuable during Brian's courtship with

Gloria: we shouldn't compare ourselves with others. That is hard to stop, especially if we have been doing it since childhood. We can get quite good at it, like practiced fruit graders. They would rate an apple, for example, according to weight, sugar content, skin thickness, number of worms, and so on. We look at ourselves and grade our beauty (hair color, complexion, weight, and shape), our intelligence (special intuition, vocabulary, memory, education, etc.), or even our status (financial, social, career, and so on).[1]

Why do we tend to compare ourselves with others? There could be a variety of reasons, but I do it when I am too focused on myself. Maybe you've found this to be true for yourself. Think for a moment. Have you ever found yourself making one of the following remarks?

"I wish I had what she has!"

"Will I ever measure up?"

"I wish I were good at something!"

"I think my boss likes her work better than mine"

"They're probably talking about me behind my back."

"Why did he ask her out rather than me? What's wrong with me?"

"I can't believe he would ask *me* out. What's wrong with him?"

"I doubt that my life will ever amount to much."

"Why did God make me this way?"

The frequency of comments like these shows how easy it is to succumb to self-absorption. Why do we fall into it? Because we are tempted to get our sense of value from our appearance, from what other people think of us, or from how we perform in life.

OUR APPEARANCE

By the time missionary Amy Carmichael was three years old, her mother had taught her that "God was a hearer and answerer to prayer, One who could change water into wine."[2] Amy decided to test God's power by praying for something she had always wanted—blue eyes. The next morning she jumped out of bed and rushed to the mirror, only to see the same brown eyes looking back at her. She was quite puzzled as to why God wouldn't answer her prayer.

Years later, as a missionary to India, Amy became very concerned about the little girls being taken into the temples, never to be seen again. She not only wanted to know what occurred in these temples, but she had hopes of rescuing some of the temple children. Yet Amy had one thing against her. She was a foreigner. Foreigners were forbidden to enter the temples. Her only alternative was to disguise herself. With coffee she stained her skin a dark color; then she dressed in Indian clothing. It was during this time of disguising herself that she came to see God's wisdom in giving her brown eyes.[3] Amy could finally express her thankfulness "for the brown eyes she had once besought God to exchange for blue ones."[4]

God may give some people their looks for a certain reason. Scripture, for instance, mentions Job's daughters as having extraordinary beauty (Job 42:15). Because beauty has always been highly valued in the East,[5] the Lord might have given Job this special blessing to comfort him after his terrible trials. Then, of course, there was Esther. We know exactly why she was given beauty. Her appearance won for her the position of queen (Esther 2:2-20). Had she not been the queen, the Jews would have been slaughtered.

God may use our particular appearance in the outworking of His plan. Take Christ, for example. Isaiah prophesied that Christ would have "no stately form or majesty that we should look upon Him, nor appearance that we should be attracted to Him" (Isaiah 53:2). Because the eye admires what the heart adores, a worldly individual would never follow Christ. Only the pure in heart were attracted to the beauty of Jesus and the message He brought.

God also uses appearances to teach valuable lessons. Remember Samuel? Being so impressed with Eliab's outer appearance, the prophet thought, "Surely the LORD's anointed is before Him" (1 Samuel 16:6). Immediately the Lord corrected the prophet, "Do not look at his appearance or at the height of his stature, because I have rejected him; for God sees not as man sees, for man looks at the outward appearance, but the LORD looks at the heart" (1 Samuel 16:7).

And who can forget Jezebel? The scriptural description of her is quite sobering. She was as pretty as a wax doll, but she could likely have shown even the devil a dirty trick or two. Just before her death, even knowing that men were coming to kill her, she made herself up and adorned herself (2 Kings 9:30). How much did it matter? In a short while the sight of her would have made even the strongest stomach queasy. After being thrown out a high window, she was eaten by scavenger dogs who left only her skull, feet, and palms (2 Kings 9:33-37).

By spending her last moments beautifying herself, Jezebel used up precious time better spent on her soul. It is the soul—one's inner beauty—that Scripture focuses on (Proverbs 31:30). Peter said, in essence, don't go overboard on your appearance (1 Peter 3:3-4). That doesn't mean we need to utterly neglect our outer appearance; it's just that our emphasis by far should be on inner beauty.

Do we ever focus on our outer appearance a bit too much?

How Much Is Too Much?

A few days ago I saw a documentary about several people who were not happy with their outer appearance. One woman especially fascinated me. Since childhood, she had had a fixation on her Barbie doll. By high school she was completely dissatisfied with herself, all because she couldn't measure up to her plastic doll. As an adult, her dissatisfaction intensified.

After receiving an inheritance, she began her quest to look *exactly* like Barbie through plastic surgery. That began a string of over twenty operations, some of them radical and painful, though in my opinion she never needed any of them.

Two hundred thousand dollars later, she got what she wanted. She looked just like Barbie. But she admitted, she was still not content. This lack of contentment was stirred up in her soul when she didn't get the acceptance and affirmation she sought while at her twenty-year high school reunion.

Sad to say, our worldly society uses inappropriate standards to determine true beauty. And sometimes we apply them to ourselves, hoping, like that real-life Barbie, to gain the affirmation we crave.

THE AFFIRMATION OF OTHERS

A few years ago my own twenty-year high school reunion took place. Unfortunately, I wasn't able to attend, but a friend who helped organize it told me how it went. "Donna, it was great to see the ones who came," she said, "but there were many people who even live locally who didn't attend." When I asked if she knew the reason, she supposed that many of the men felt ashamed that they had not "arrived" career-wise. And the women were too embarrassed to be seen because "they had put on too much weight." She added thoughtfully, "It's sad that they want us to remember them the way they were and not the way they are now."

It occurred to me that a number of the ones who stayed home that night were the most popular in "their day." They had received a lot of affirmation for their looks and personality. Could it be that they didn't want to shatter the image that once made them so popular?

I'll never know the answer, but I do know that feeding off the affirmation of others can do strange things to us. Not only does it allow us to be controlled by what we continually guess others think of us—most likely people who really couldn't care less what we look like anyway—but it tempts us to be continually dissatisfied with our appearance. We can become a slave to our own image. For instance, we can strive to lose weight and exercise like mad, not because we want to be healthier, but because we want the approval of others. All too often this leads to deeper insecurity. Why? Because once the affirmation dies down (and it always does), we will most likely feel worse about ourselves and go back to our old eating patterns and sedentary life.

My friend Beth has allowed me to share with you that during her days of courtship she was constantly striving for positive affirmation from whatever man she was dating at the time. She would do whatever she thought would keep him (within moral limits). For some boyfriends she would let her hair grow long; for others she cut it short. For one she changed her hair color as often as the seasons changed. And for all of them she rigorously exercised and dieted. Then one day a guy she was getting to know jokingly called her "thunder thighs." This devastated her and prompted her to become obsessed with weight reduction. Eventually she became a borderline anorexic.

Beth's reason for all this? "I used to think that if people knew what I was like on the inside, they wouldn't like me."

Have you ever felt like Beth, that if people knew what was inside you, they wouldn't like you? I certainly have. The Lord had to deal with me on this one. You see, in my early college years I focused too much time on my appearance, trying to find approval and acceptance. Having become a Christian at the age of twenty-one, I had become accustomed to focusing upon the outer life. I considered it "safe." There were still a lot of things I had to work out in my inner life, and, I admit, it was easier to simply work on the outer stuff. But as the novelist Aldous Huxley points out, "beauty for some provides escape."[6]

I was escaping until one evening in the quietness of my apartment, the Lord convicted me. I came to see how shallow an outward focus is and that it will never bring fulfillment and contentment. Also I came to realize that a person with an outward focus usually attracts friends with that same focus, which means that their relationships—and to some extent their whole lives—lack depth.

I remember getting down on my knees and tearfully asking the Lord to forgive me for focusing on the wrong things. *I also acknowledged that no matter what benefits I could get from the use of things like makeup, diet, and exercise, none of these things would attract a godly man, bring nonbelievers to Christ, or please God Himself.*

I then asked the Lord to help me with my inner beauty. As I saw it, I was ugly inside because I had not focused on developing spiritual beauty, which belongs to the soul. The woman who focuses on her inner life has a greater influence in the lives of others because she has more depth, joy, and happiness.

When I finished praying, I determined that I was going to quit wasting so much time on my appearance while hiding my inner self. I determined that my goal would constantly be to work on my heart. I knew that would mean ending my quest for the affirmation of others, trusting God's love for me, and focusing on gaining His praise.

What about you? What are your motives for working on your appearance? *Is it to be happy with yourself?* Of course, even if you achieve the look you want, it won't make you truly happy. Some of the unhappiest people in the world have a very beautiful exterior.

Is it personal affirmation you want? If so, then you will discover that a makeover will not bring it. There is, of course, a sense in which it's appropriate to try to be acceptable to people. We should not neglect our appearance. A reasonable effort on our appearance shows respect for others and maintains the credibility we need to minister to people. What is crucial here is our motive.

I have discovered that personal affirmation can be a special gift from God when it comes to us from others and is based on our character, our choices in life, and our ministry to others. We can thank God for the kind words we may receive from others as we serve Him. But it's *nearly impossible* to feel affirmed when we get compliments on our physical appearance. That is because God is the artist, and He deserves the credit for the way He made us. Scripture compares Him to a skilled potter, and we are told that we have no right to be critical of His work (Romans 9:20). Instead we should be content with ourselves as He has made us.

Contentment refuses to try to measure up to society's standards of beauty. It refuses to seek affirmation from others based on appearance. Rather, it sees life through the eyes of God. In His eyes there are no ugly people. We are all an expression of His workmanship and creativity. And yet, despite this glorious truth, for some of us it still may be difficult to accept the way God made us.

HOW COULD GOD HAVE MADE ME THIS WAY?

Gigi was born with an abnormality that left over half of her face reddish purple. Self-conscious about her looks, she rarely went to church. She was understandably uncomfortable with the constant stares she got everywhere she went. She eventually went on welfare because she could no longer handle going out into society.

One day Gigi asked me, "How could God have made me this way?"

While God may use our particular appearance to accomplish unusual things, that idea was hard for Gigi to understand. Maybe you have a hard time understanding how God may use your appearance or limitations. Maybe you, too, struggle over your outer appearance or a certain disability, abnormality, or disorder. Maybe you feel limited in your intellect. Maybe what you consider to be your personal limitations prompt you to say, "If only I could change who I am!"

If you've ever struggled with accepting yourself as God made you, you're not alone. For as long as I can remember, I wished I had normal hearing. I am completely deaf in my right ear and have to make up for it with my left ear. I grew up dealing with the cruel comments of other children and with teachers who didn't understand how to deal with a person with a hearing problem. As an adult I have to try to read lips whenever I'm in noisy rooms, and I have to guess which direction a siren is coming from when I'm driving.

Whatever struggles I've had, which are minimal compared to many other people's, I know the Lord does not want me to regard myself as some sort of victim. There's a popular tendency today to claim "victimhood" or play the "blame game." One expert player at this game was a woman with a birth abnormality who sued her parents for allowing her to be born. Blaming others creates tidy categories of oppressors and victims. Sometimes people are tempted to make God an oppressor because of the way He created them.

Do you remember back in 1990 when the Americans with Disability Act was passed by Congress? I'm sure the bill has been genuinely helpful to many who are "differently abled," as it is called in the new lexicon.[7] But humorist and political commentator P. J. O'Rourke attended the signing of the ADA on the White House lawn and wrote the following observation: "People in wheelchairs were yelling at the deaf to sit down and the blind were bumping the palsied with their dogs. In a crueler age some onlookers might have laughed, but we never laugh at misfortune today. In fact we're all trying to get in on it."[8] Public policy scholar Charles Sykes added, " . . . the reality outpaces even O'Rourke's satire."[9]

We as Christians shouldn't settle for seeking victim status. We can easily fall into victimhood if we begin comparing ourselves with others—or contrasting what we have with what someone else has. Or we can fall into pride when we have more than others.

While we all struggle with something, not one of us deserves what God gave us. We can't say, "God should have been more gracious." Nor should we as Christians think that God cheated us out of something.

Certainly it isn't wrong to seek understanding as to why God gave us certain limitations; but when there is no understanding, we should accept God's creativity. We know that He can reverse our limitation, our birth abnormality, or whatever it is we reject about ourselves. Yet He usually doesn't. That is not necessarily a consequence of our lack of faith, contrary to what I have been told by some sincere Christians in regard to my hearing. I firmly believe that God can heal me; I have no doubts. But so far, in His perfect wisdom, He has not.

God never removed Paul's thorn in the flesh (2 Corinthians 12:7-

9). Nor did He heal Trophimus, who had to be left sick at Miletus (2 Timothy 4:20). And even faith-healer Benny Hinn admitted that he doesn't understand why his Christian parents weren't healed. His father died at the age of fifty-eight of cancer, and his godly mother still struggles with diabetes. Hinn explains in regard to his parents and others, "I can't explain why not all are healed."[10] It was Solomon who said, "Just as you do not know the path of the wind and how bones are formed in the womb of the pregnant woman, so you do not know the activity of God who makes all things" (Ecclesiastes 11:5).

While we don't understand the activity of God, especially when it concerns ourselves, I do believe there is a deeper reason God allows limitations. It is found in Christ's answer to the disciples' question about why a man was born blind. They supposed the root cause was sin, similar to some Christians today who believe that all suffering is rooted in a lack of faith. But Jesus replied that "it was so that the works of God might be displayed in him" (John 9:3). Christ refocused on the higher divine purpose of God revealing Himself. In this case God's purpose was to grant healing, but God may be glorified in other more hidden ways.

For instance, a few miles from our home is a small ranch with a yard that pens in several ostriches. If you've ever watched these birds, you know that they are awkward animals, with their tiny heads atop thin necks and large bodies; their knee joints even seem to bend backwards. They aren't particularly aware of what is going on around them; nor do they care much.

Job talked about the apparent irrational behavior of these odd creatures: "She abandons her eggs to the earth, and warms them in the dust, and she forgets that a foot may crush them, or that a wild beast may trample them. She treats her young cruelly, as if they were not hers; though her labor be in vain, she is unconcerned" (Job 39:14-16).

From all appearances, the ostrich seems to be quite deficient in intellect, as the Arabs recognize by their proverb: "As stupid as an ostrich." Yet God in His wisdom has given them very practical instincts. In places with sand or soft dirt, the ostrich can bury her eggs about a foot down, which is deep enough to keep them from other animals but close enough to the surface that the sun can warm them. During the day the female keeps alert for beasts of prey, and at night the male keeps the eggs warm.[11] So what appears senseless to observers actually shows God's wisdom, even if the ostrich works more by instinct than intelligence.

Like Job, we can be unaware of the deeper reasons for God's designs and His hidden wisdom. Job was unaware, too, of God's plan for his own life, of the part he was playing in a cosmic battle between the Creator and the chief rebel, Satan. Like Job, we can agonize over what we don't understand, wishing God would change us, that He would work differently in our lives, or that He would remove some limitation. But what if He doesn't? What if God wants to be glorified through our limitations? Can we work within them?

WORKING WITHIN OUR LIMITATIONS

Venita Schlotfeld is a woman who has mastered the discipline of working within her limitations. At the age of nineteen and newly married, she was in a car accident that left her a quadriplegic. Thinking Venita would be a burden, relatives told her husband to quietly divorce her and put her in an institution.

Fortunately her husband looked beyond her outer appearance. He helped his wife adjust to her new way of living, and they even became missionaries in Latin America. She also had three children while out on the field (Venita was told she would never have children). Now, many years later, they serve here in the United States, and Venita, with the limited use of her hands, uses her computer to translate the Bible and other materials into Braille.

God could have prevented Venita's accident, or He could have healed her. But for reasons hidden (Deuteronomy 29:29) He has allowed her to live with the limitations. As well, He has glorified himself through Venita's life and testimony.

When you struggle to deal with some unwanted limitation, you can think of Venita's example—and of the apostle Paul's. His life was full of limitations. The most obvious one was his thorn in the flesh. The thorn may have been some physical problem, such as difficulty with his eyes or malaria; it may have been some demonically inspired enemy.[12]

Despite these limitations, Paul did a lot of public speaking.

However, he was not the kind of polished orator that fit the ideals of the Greek society in which he ministered. He knew what people said about him: ". . . his personal presence is unimpressive and his speech contemptible" (2 Corinthians 10:10). His opponents tried to use his lack of skill to discredit him as a leader. In addition they even tried to take advantage of the fact that Paul spent a good part of his life in jail (Philippians 1:15-17).

In all, Paul had a lot of limitations that God did not remove. But we can follow his example in that he learned to work within them. Can you imagine having to travel on roads all the time without being able to see clearly? Or having to stay in people's homes and having recurring malaria, which makes a person miserably sick? Or being excruciatingly proper about the Law and being taken for a criminal? Or having to preach and evangelize with people snickering at your presentation?

Paul shows us how to carry on in the face of embarrassment and frustration with our limitations. Whatever our limits, we can still swallow our pride and get going, knowing that our goal is to glorify the Father. It's okay if our skills aren't perfect or if we sometimes fall on our face trying. It's okay if we use a wheelchair instead of our legs, if we use a guide dog for our eyes, or if we read lips to hear. It's okay if our clothes aren't the best and we have to deal with people far richer than we are. It's okay if we have no college education and have to work with those better educated. God still wants to use us. It may be to sing or to teach a Bible study or to reach someone by teaching that person English, or whatever.

Without having some of Paul's willingness to work in spite of limitations, we will never do anything significant. With that said, it is possible that as we step out in faith, God will reduce or remove some of our limitations.

WITHERED HANDS AND CRIPPLED FEET NO MORE

Like so many who met Jesus, the lives of two men were forever changed. Jesus told one man who had been crippled for thirty-eight years to "get up, pick up your pallet and walk" (John 5:8). The other man had a withered hand, and Jesus told him, "Stretch out your hand!" (Matthew 12:13). Both men were healed; their burdensome limits were removed.

The blessing did not come without cost, however. First, they needed a certain amount of faith to do what Jesus told them to do. That faith led them to obey, and God did the rest.

The man with the withered hand may have had to overcome some embarrassment and emotional pain to do what Jesus required. His natural tendency was probably not to display his hand to the whole synagogue.

Both men needed a great deal more of something besides faith and obedience. They had to overcome enormous pressure from peers and society. You see, in both cases it was the Sabbath.

The man with the withered hand knew he was right in the middle of a hot controversy between Jesus and the Pharisees about keeping the Sabbath. He no doubt realized that to stretch out his hand and be healed (this was considered work) risked the wrath of the religious authorities. They had the power to excommunicate him from the synagogue, which would make him an outcast from society (cf. John 9:22).

The crippled man had to make the same decision. Taking up his pallet and walking with it amounted to working on the Sabbath, a violation of the traditional rules. It was no small matter.

I'm realizing that before I can do something significant in God's plan, I must make these same choices. I need to demonstrate a certain amount of faith and obedience; there may be some embarrassment to overcome, too. As well, God's will may go against the grain of society and carry the risk of making me something of an outcast.

But the other side of this is that God just may choose to remove our limits. For a while I had a young woman come with me to evangelize and teach women at retirement homes. She was quite hesitant because as she put it, "I don't think I can do it, yet I know God wants me to." As she trusted, obeyed, and overcame embarrassment, God reduced her limits by developing her abilities. I've seen shy women come out of their shells and women who have felt socially awkward become polished—all because they obeyed. They were willing to put out their withered hands, to take up their pallets and walk.

Are you willing to step out? You may not be healed physically or intellectually, but you may be healed from the worst limitation we could possibly have—self-consciousness. I personally am working on this in my own life, learning the importance of being willing to go against the grain, even among Christians, especially when it comes to the Christian mold.

THE CHRISTIAN MOLD

We all recognize the secular mold for women—you know, the voluptuous figure, gorgeous hair, the radiant smile, and perfect teeth. If we try to fit into such a shallow mold, our insecurities will run high. But we can also run into insecurity problems if we try to fit into the Christian mold. You might be thinking, *Could there really be such a thing?* I believe there is. It has to do with how some Christians believe other godly Christians are *supposed to act*.

The other day while some friends and I were watching our children play kickball, we had a lively discussion about this very topic. Here are a few observations we made.

In order to fit the Christian mold, it's important not to appear too "outgoing." You will be seen as shallow or even flaky, as opposed to quiet and thoughtful.

Too, you should be cautious when voicing your opinion, or you will be seen as lacking appropriate meekness.

Also, stay away from that "high-voltage" look. There is an unspoken belief in an inverse relationship between beauty and brains; it is thought that the more attractive you are, the smaller your brain must be. Recommendation: Go easy on the makeup, wear serviceable but not overly stylish dresses and shoes, and go to a hairdresser of indifferent skill.[13]

It's also important to stay away from bold colors, which make you look worldly, rather than pure and chaste. A high collar and bland colors add the sort of distinction that could qualify you for the deaconess board.

Now if you are single and over thirty, you should be married unless you have some highly demanding ministry. Otherwise the Sisters of the Christian Mold will try to "rescue" you. They'll want to find you someone—virtually *anyone*—who has prayed the sinner's prayer. And if you point out that there's not much fruit in his life, they remind you of his main asset: he's breathing.

If, on the other hand, you are married with no children, something's got to be wrong—don't you like children?

Christian molds don't end at the front door of your home. Inside, your home must always be in tiptop shape—unless, of course, you have young children. In that case having a home that is too orderly makes it apparent that you aren't spending enough time with the youngsters.

It's also important to say yes to any ministry-related demands. This is one of the fastest and surest ways to appear spiritual. (Of course, if you have young children, you'll need to plan ahead what to say when, as teenagers, they rebel against God and the church, which they'll see as robbing them of their parents.)

We will know we've arrived in the good graces of the Sisters of the Christian Mold when we are mistaken for the Proverbs 31 woman.

Please don't misunderstand. All of us at that kickball game would love to be exactly like Mrs. Proverbs. She's our role model. But she's also—

- the role model of every man—*looking for a wife*
- the role model of every husband—*wishing it were his wife*
- the role model of every pastor's sermon—*for the wives*

Despite the fact that so many Christian women, single and married, strive to be like Mrs. Proverbs, we can't seem to shake the feeling that we are somehow missing the mark. Ever feel that way? Ever wonder how you can compete with all that she did in life? What a tall order!

THINKING IT OVER

1. When is the affirmation of others a good thing? When is it not?
2. What limitations do you struggle with? Starting today, in what ways will you work within them? How might God reduce or eliminate your limits by your obedience?
3. What are the risks of judging others based on appearances?
4. Can you add anything to the Christian Mold list?

Two

HOW CAN *I* COMPETE WITH
MRS. PROVERBS?

*S*everal years ago when I began writing, my friend Glenda said, "Whatever you write about, don't mention Mrs. Proverbs!"

Laughing I asked, "Why not?"

With a seriousness that surprised me she said, "I'm sick and tired of hearing about her! She's perfect! What woman can ever compete with her? All Proverbs 31 does is make the average woman feel guilty. How can we ever measure up?"

Thinking for a moment, I replied, "Well, we hear about Christ every Sunday, and no one can ever measure up to His perfection."

Glenda said, "That's different. Men and women in the body of Christ strive to live the Christlike life. Everyone understands how difficult it can be at times to imitate Christ. For some reason, although we fall short of His example, we are lifted up and encouraged. But when I fall short of being the Proverbs woman, I feel like a failure. And the only encouragement I'm given is information on the latest craft seminar, as if I need some skill at doing something in order to be like her. I want to *scream* every time I hear how that lady was able to sew, make things and then sell them, buy land, and buy food from afar. What is she—Wonder Woman? When I read Proverbs 31, I'm asking myself, along with the writer, 'Who can find a woman like that?'" Glenda ended with, "Unlike Mrs. Proverbs, no one is going to praise my works."

After getting off the phone, I thought a lot about what Glenda said and decided she had a point. Many of us think that we simply can't be as industrious, as godly, as perfect as Mrs. Proverbs seemed to be. On her own she bought a field. And she did more—she planted a vineyard, helped the poor, clothed her family with scarlet, and worked late into the night. Because of her works, she was praised in the gates (Proverbs 31:31).

Do you ever feel, like my friend Glenda, that you simply can't compete with all that? What should we do about this dilemma? Wouldn't it be great if we could sit down with Mrs. Proverbs for a little chat and share with her our true feelings about how difficult she has made things for us ordinary women?

A CHAT WITH MRS. PROVERBS

Interviewer: Mrs. Proverbs, how does it make you feel, knowing that every Christian woman, single and married alike, strives to be like you?

Mrs. Proverbs: Women need role models. It's a God-given desire. I'm flattered.

Interviewer: The difficult part about having you as a role model is that you appear "so perfect."

Mrs. Proverbs: We know the only perfect one is God. I have my struggles and shortcomings. You just don't read about them.

Interviewer: Despite your humanness, you seem like a "superwoman." Many of us believe it's impossible to accomplish all the things you did.

Mrs. Proverbs: It's kind of you to point out that I was industrious. I did work hard because of my concern for my family. What Christian wife or mother today doesn't have the same concerns? And what single woman isn't as hard-working? Though modern women may not be doing exactly what I did, they are doing things I didn't do.

Interviewer: Well, with all due respect, many women, unlike you, aren't given the opportunity to see that their work is profitable (v. 18). Therefore, they feel quite inadequate.

Mrs. Proverbs: When each day came to an end, I did consider my work as profitable, and I had no second thoughts about how I spent my day. How am I any different from all the many other women who can go to bed without regrets about how they spent their day? They, too, should feel that their day's work was profitable.

Interviewer: That's a good point, but let's take this one step further. You are shown to be a businesswoman. There are many women who feel inadequate to make things, sell them, and run a home business.

Mrs. Proverbs: I would like to make two points in regard to your comment. First, the proverb says I did those things "in delight." The issue isn't the trading and selling. It's in doing the things God calls us to—with delight. In doing so, a woman will be doing the business God gave her, just as I did the business He gave me. Secondly, I did make money to help my husband. Not all women can do that. To feel that they must do exactly as I did is misleading. The underlying issue here is that I was a helper to my husband, in my case, by making money. Other women help meet their family's goals by living frugally.

Interviewer: You are making yourself sound as if you are much like the Christian women of today.

Mrs. Proverbs: That's right. You see, we can all be proverbial women in our own right. *I say this not based upon what we do but upon who we are.*

Interviewer: But much of Proverbs 31 is about what you do.

Mrs. Proverbs: Today's woman is caught in a trap that I never had to contend with. It's called "the performance trap." So much of a woman's sense of worth in your culture seems to be wrapped up in what she does, and she is judged by that. Having a career or a successful ministry appears quite significant, whereas being a wife at home or having a job that is "not worth talking about" makes a woman insignificant by your society's standards. I just don't understand this. No wonder so many women desire to change who they are! No wonder many feel so insignificant!

Interviewer: What do you suggest for women of today?

Mrs. Proverbs: I suggest that they live life at the bottom. The bottom is the place of humility, where we are free to regard the spiritual success of others as more important than our own. It's where we can never feel threatened by the abilities and talents of others. It's a place that saints of the past have occupied, where great rewards are found. Those who live at the bottom come to discover that it's really living life at the top.

Interviewer: Any last words?

Mrs. Proverbs: Yes, it's important for each woman to realize that God has given her a specific personality, talents, and giftedness—a unique beauty—that can be used to fit into His plan and accomplish His will. *Real change—and may I include true significance—comes from the inside out.*

Interviewer: Mrs. Proverbs, thank you for your time and helpful insights. You are absolutely right about the emphasis in my society on what people do rather than on who they are. And that focus really is a trap.

THE PERFORMANCE TRAP

What is significance from the inside out? Perhaps we can understand this concept better by looking at its opposite—significance from the outside in.

One day while boarding a train en route to a celebration, Ella Wheeler (later Ella Wheeler Wilcox) heard someone crying. She turned and noticed a woman dressed in black. Approaching her, Ella asked what was wrong and came to find out that the grieving woman had just lost her husband. Ella's remaining time on the train was occupied with listening to the woman and trying to comfort her as best she could.

That evening while getting ready for her joyous event, Ella looked at her own beaming face in the mirror and suddenly thought about the sorrowing widow. At that moment, she came up with the opening line of her poem *Solitude*: "Laugh, and the world laughs with you; weep, and you weep alone. . . ."

Little did Ella know when she first put those words down on paper that she would have to fight for them the rest of her life. A man by the name of John A. Joyce produced in 1885 the second edition of his book *A Checkered Life*, based on his own personal reflections. In that book he wrote a poem titled "Laugh, and the World Laughs with You." It was identical to the poem Ella claimed she had written.

Ella challenged John Joyce to produce evidence of his authorship, offering to give $5,000 (then a sizable amount) in his name to any reputable charity of his choosing. All he had to do was prove that Ella was not the actual author of the poem. John Joyce refused her offer.

Years later, perhaps as a parting gesture, Joyce had the first two lines of the disputed poem engraved on his tombstone, where it has been since 1915, in Oak Hill Cemetery in Washington, D.C.[1]

It's no surprise that Ella Wheeler Wilcox wanted to defend her claim to this poem; her integrity was at stake. And if she is to be believed, John Joyce spent his life trying to cash in on her success—a worldly success that was all too fleeting.

While Ella was well known in her day, as evidenced by a contemporary article about her in the *Appleton's Cyclopaedia of American Biography* (1889)[2], few people know of her now. Far less do we know who John Joyce was.

It's understandable that most of us wouldn't know or think much about the successful people of a century before us. But what about those over the centuries who are still remembered as great?

In Shakespeare's *The Tragedy of Julius Caesar*, Mark Antony stood at the coffin of Caesar and said, " . . . yesterday the word of Caesar might have stood against the world; now lies he there, and none so poor to do him reverence."[3] The once-feared and all-powerful Caesar, whom Romans literally worshiped as an incarnation of God, was in a moment cut down to the stature of ordinary mortals, his body reduced to a crumbling relic of history.

Cemeteries are filled with faded relics. They give mute testimony to whole lives caught in the performance trap—people wanting to be "somebody," pursuing notoriety, fortune, and respect. Yet all of those glories are now reduced to the barest line on a tombstone. Absent from that final remembrance of their lives are even their most cherished accomplishments. Tombstones, as we know, never read:

> *Trudy Thompson 1932-1999*
> *Top Amway Salesperson from 1985-1990*
> *Won the State Fair Contest for Best Apple Pie 1987*
> *Home displayed in* Better *Homes and Gardens,* Spring Issue, 1996
> *Drove a late-model Lexus*

And whatever material possessions the deceased acquired get scattered; no hearse ever pulled a trailer. No matter how high people climb in life, they all end up six feet below ground. One thing matters: Did they leave anything besides a weathering grave marker? Did they do anything of eternal value? To what extent were their lives a true success?

What is your estimation of a successful life? I am sure God rejects many of our opinions on the subject. In His estimation, human standards are foolishness. All too often our view of success is determined by the wrong things. For instance, many believe that the significant life consists of what we do outwardly. Aren't we often judged by that? Because we are, we can make the mistake of believing that our worth is based upon our accomplishments.

ARE YOU IN THE TRAP?

Prior to becoming a Christian, I based my worth on the approval I could gain from others through my appearance, and I tried to prove myself by the things I did. Since junior high school I had an interest in nutrition and pursued a career in it, planning either to work in a hospital or to do research. While in college I met the president of a cancer research firm and told him of my goals and desires. He handed me his card and invited me after graduation to give him a call (recently I stumbled across that twenty-three-year-old card!). I was thrilled and a bit prideful.

Shortly after that conversation, my ego got even more puffed up when I was selected to be part of a special dietetics program with an internship at a renowned hospital. Having such an internship on my resume was for me like going from the minor leagues to the major leagues in baseball. This was "big stuff!"

Even before the internship, I was already working in a hospital. I was amazed and delighted over the respect I gained from others. Though the job wasn't anything worth writing home about, as a twenty-year-old I felt I had proven myself to those who thought I would never amount to anything. People who didn't know me seemed to think I was important as I walked the floors of the hospital, wearing my white jacket and carrying a clipboard full of information.

I think any one of us can be viewed as important but for all the wrong reasons. People seemed to view me as somebody because of my lab coat. Maybe others consider you important because of the material possessions you have or the diplomas on your wall, the prestigious school you attended, your career or your spouse's work, the things your children are doing, or some famous person you know. Possibly you are in the ministry limelight.

Maybe others consider you to be somebody because you are making your job, your goals, or your connections sound a little more important than they really are. Maybe you yourself base your sense of importance on one of these outward things. Or perhaps the opposite is true—you're a bit disappointed that there's nothing tangible that makes you look important to people. If so, you are just as entangled in the performance trap as the person who *has* found something external to base her identity on.

There are many reasons why some of us can end up having an unnecessarily low view of ourselves. Let me just say here that when we strive to be someone we are not, or we want to be known strictly by things that are external to us, we are seeking acceptability in the wrong way. This path has no forks, and it's all downhill. What can get us on that downward path? For one thing—a fear of failure.

Fear of Failure

In the classic movie *Michelangelo*, the pope expresses the unspoken thoughts of a lot of people. Reflecting over his life, he said to the great artist, "It's a sad thing to strive all your life only to realize at its end that you're a failure." Imagine—someone who has the attention, even the admiration, of millions can still feel like a failure.

What could make us feel like a failure or at least fear we're a failure? There could be many causes, but I think the most common one is that we focus on ourselves, which makes us want to see something tangible that will make us feel better about ourselves or makes others think better of us. For instance, when I was first asked to speak to a group of women, I wanted to say no. Why? Because I thought I would fail. I didn't want to make a fool of myself. I knew I wouldn't be as polished a speaker as other women they had heard. The Lord convicted me on this, showing me that I was focused on myself rather than on the women I needed to serve.

Focusing on ourselves can give rise to some pretty awkward behaviors. For example, we can become perfectionists. Such people are unwilling to fail—whether at work, with house-cleaning, in appearance, in promptness, in hobbies and skills, and many other things. While it's good to strive for a job well done, perfectionists will do whatever possible to avoid the low self-appraisal they would experience should they fail.

Sad to say, extreme perfectionists will likely put their standards of perfection upon their children. Because the parent mustn't fail, neither can the child. Imagine what this does to the child who must go through life thinking that in order to gain the parent's acceptance, he or she has to be perfect in everything. That's impossible. Later as a grownup, this person will become overly discouraged in times of failure because of associating his or her identity with performance. What a burden to carry, always needing to be perfect in order to gain acceptance from others, always depending on that acceptance to confirm personal worth.

Avoiding Risks

Then there is the woman who won't take risks. If this is your tendency, you know all too well that you are willing to be involved only in those things you are good at doing. Risk-averse people, however, limit their service to God; they limit the role they could have in this life. They are afraid to try new things, fearing the disapproval or criticism of others should they fail.

Taking sensible risks isn't the same as jumping into something without thinking it through. Christ showed us the importance of prudence when He said, "For which one of you, when he wants to build a tower, does not first sit down and calculate the cost to see if he has enough to complete it? Otherwise, when he has laid a foundation and is not able to finish . . ." (Luke 14:28-29).

It's wise to think through our actions, but it's wrong for us to shrink from doing something good based on the opinions of others. To have a right attitude toward risk we simply have to realize that even our efforts to accomplish good cannot control all the outcomes once we start something. We cannot be absolutely sure how something will end. Just realize that you may be keeping back some beautiful gifts from others if you won't take reasonable risks. Think of the hidden talents you may find as you step out, or of how much more you will be used by God as you consider His will more than your reputation—and of how much more fulfilling life can be when you refuse to fear failure.

I recently listened to a nurse talk about her experiences in working with dying patients. She said that the majority of them shared one regret. That is, they lamented that they had lived with a fear of failure. They came to realize that their fear had kept them from doing many things in life. If we are consumed with a fear of failure or feel down over a past failure, we are not only kept from doing a variety of things in life, but we are kept from fulfilling God's significant plan for our lives.

Consider how the world worships success—or what it calls success. Many of the great prophets—Elijah, Jeremiah, Ezekiel, Isaiah— would be classified as failures if we were to look at their lives with a worldly point of view. These men saw little or no fruit in their endeavors. Elijah not only saw little fruit, but toward the end of his life on earth, he was depressed (his enemies wanted to kill him), and he was very much alone (1 Kings 19:10, 14). What did the Lord do? He didn't allow Elijah to sulk or feel sorry for himself. God didn't allow the prophet to focus upon himself at all. Rather, He gave Elijah a command (1 Kings 19:15-16). This helped him get his mind off himself and back onto others so that he could continue to do the ministry God had called him to.

For us it is the same. We will never be imprisoned by a fear of failure, or even feel like a failure, if we keep our minds off ourselves and on the work the Lord has for us to do. You might be wondering, "Will I *see* success in my endeavors?" No one can predict. It is God who decides who will see the fruit of their work and who will have to wait until heaven. But it is possible for every Christian to *be* successful by following the advice God gave Joshua.

Remember when Joshua had been given the command to take the place of Moses and lead the rebellious and grumbling Israelites into the promised land (Joshua 1:1-4)? This would be no easy task. Joshua was in direct verbal communication with God, but this is not what would keep him from failing. What then would be the key to his success? Saturating his mind with the Word of God. God told Joshua he was to stay in it and meditate upon it continually: " . . . then you will make your way prosperous, and then you will have success" (Joshua 1:8).

Being in the Word is God's simple formula for a successful life. That's because it is the foundation for obedience—born of a renewed mind—transformation from the inside out (Romans 12:2). And since obedience to God meets His criteria for success, we can have the confidence that our lives are successful in the truest and best sense regardless of how things appear. To the extent that we are deeply transformed by the Word, our lives will have practical significance in God's eyes. So a woman of the Word never fails and needn't ever feel like a failure. Incidentally, *it's when we are away from the Word that we focus upon ourselves and develop self-centered thoughts, such as fears of failure.*

Being in the Word does something else for us. It reminds us that we don't have to be the "best" in the eyes of others.

I DON'T HAVE TO BE THE BEST

While we want to be all we can be for the Lord, we don't have to be the best in other people's eyes. In Galatians when Paul was being accused of preaching a cheap form of admission to God's kingdom, he replied, "For am I now seeking the favor of men, or of God? Or am I striving to please men?" (Galatians 1:10). When Paul and some others were being accused of improper conduct, he said, "We speak, not as pleasing men, but God who examines our hearts" (1 Thessalonians 2:4).

Pleasing God is all that counts, and to be acceptable to others, we don't need to perform. For instance, our sense of who we are when we are with our guests doesn't depend on our being the world's best hostess or cook. We can think of ourselves as being loved by God and valued apart from the cooking (or anything else we are attempting to do). As long as we base our acceptance on God's acceptance of us, we can work as hard as we like to be a good cook. If we never reach perfection—so what? Perfectionism is just one type of bandage to cover a wounded ego. Our identity is based on who we are before God, and that is a matter of who we are in Christ. We do not have to be successful in terms of the world's standards; nor do our husbands or children. Nor do we have to be pleasing to others in order to gain a healthy sense of worth.

Christ addressed imbalances in this area. For instance, clothing meant a lot in ancient times. Because everything was handmade, finer clothing was expensive, while burlap was the cheapest material one could wear. So people's economic status was very obvious. Christ challenged those who worried about their apparel and what others thought of them. He compassionately asked, "Why are you worried about clothing? Observe how the lilies of the field grow; they do not toil nor do they spin, yet I say to you that not even Solomon in all his glory clothed himself like one of these" (Matthew 6:28-30).

By pointing to the lilies, Jesus was assuring the people of His day and us today that we can trust our need for clothing to a gracious God. Because our wardrobe is His provision, we need not be embarrassed or concerned with the opinions of others.

Among the religious leaders of the day, concern over human opinion led to a far worse problem. They were notorious for seeking honor from men. They loved respectful greetings in the market-places, the front seats in the synagogues (Luke 11:43), and places of honor at banquets (Luke 20:46). They even used their prayers as a way to impress people (Matthew 6:5). Jesus revealed that it was their focus on man that caused them to reject Him: "How can you believe, when you receive glory from one another and you do not seek the glory that is from the one and only God?" (John 5:44).

When we focus on what others think of us, we are seeking approval from them rather than from God. And when we fear human opinions, there are consequences. For instance, in Christ's day, fear of human opinion discouraged people from coming to Christ (John 9:22), and it kept believers like Joseph of Arimathea from openly admitting that they followed Him (John 19:38; the wrath of the Jewish leaders could have cost him his life).

We cannot serve two masters; we cannot serve God and human opinion any more than we can serve God and wealth (Matthew 6:24). We must choose whom to please. As the expression goes, we have to play to an audience of One.

We must remember that our worth is given to us by God alone. Rather than focusing on what others think of us, we can focus on the love relationship we have with God (1 John 4:9-11), the forgiveness we receive from Him (Colossians 2:13-14), the eternal life He has given us (John 5:24), the fact that He lives in us (Colossians 1:27; Revelation 3:20), and the truth that we are fully accepted by Him (Colossians 1:19-22).

When I am focusing on these truths, I find I don't need to be in every way like Mrs. Proverbs; nor does my husband have to be like Mr. Proverbs, who was well known because he had a high position (Proverbs 31:23). We don't need to measure up to anyone else or gauge ourselves by what anyone thinks in order to have a proper sense of worth.

My goal is to be like Christ, and I'm sure it's your goal, too. Because of our love for Him, we can strive to be like Him. And with God's help, we can be godly women like Mrs. Proverbs—without the burden of trying to gain a sense of significance from what others may think about us.

How wonderful it was when I surrendered all my pursuits to the Lord, including those things I had been trusting in to give me a sense of significance. In the process of giving it all to God, I made a grand discovery: When we shed that outer shell, something wonderful happens. The Lord changes our desires.

A CHANGE IN DESIRE

In what ways did my desires change? I began to have an insatiable interest in the Bible and anything else pertaining to growth in Christ. Nothing could distract me. I remember being in a university library and stumbling across Charles Spurgeon's *Lectures to My Students*. I should have been studying organic chemistry; instead I spent the entire day reading that book. I couldn't put it down. It was that day in the library that I started to think that perhaps God was changing my deepest desires.

Another change, a dramatic one, was that I no longer cared about trying to prove myself to others; I wanted only to please God with my life. There was such a sense of freedom in this. About a year later I went to Central America as a short-term missionary, and I was offered the position of dietician in a Honduran hospital after completing my degree. While I was tempted to finish my education and take the job (which also offered a lot of opportunities to share the Gospel with patients), accepting it as a way of feeling significant was not even a thought.

In due time my interest changed completely from nutrition to Christian education. I still remember the reaction of one Christian when talking to him about my newfound pursuits. He looked me straight in the eye and said, "Are you kidding!? Why in the world would you walk away from all your previous education and hard work to major in a degree for Sunday school teachers?"

Knowing this guy wouldn't understand, I simply replied, "I am now in God's will rather than my own."

All he could do was shake his head and say, "I just don't get it!"

Other people, too, didn't "get it." My boss at the hospital had told my coworkers that I had gone "completely nuts!" But I understood what God was doing. While He was freeing me from the performance trap and what it brought—a false sense of importance—He was testing me as well, seeing whether my first love was Him or nutrition. As I've come to see, *the performance trap can lead us to loving what we do more than we love God.*

When we come to love God more than anything we do in life, we discover that it doesn't really matter what we accomplish in our own strength. What matters is what God accomplishes through us, whether that impresses people or not. His will is certainly better than our own. And part of that will, as we "live and move and exist" in Him (Acts 17:28), is to help *others, rather than ourselves,* become successful—successful in finding the Lord, successful in growing in Christ, successful in whatever God has called them to be and do.

Some women have asked me if I've ever been tempted to get back into the trap—especially as it involves ministry. I have been able to respond that I haven't—only because I constantly examine my ambitions, making sure they never become misguided.

MISGUIDED AMBITIONS

We've all been taught since childhood that ambition is a good thing. And it is. A teacher can't help a child who is satisfied with getting low grades. That's the purpose for motivating children with spelling bees and other drills—some of which give out prizes. We want to challenge our children, and we ourselves want challenges in life too. That's how the Lord gets some of us up and going.

But some of our more ambitious goals may actually be unrealistic and unattainable. These goals can create distractions or consequences that keep us from our main priorities. How do we keep ourselves from becoming misguided? By discerning our motives when we are about to begin a new venture:

What are my reasons for pursuing this goal?

Do my actions seem to be self-serving?

Is this pursuit based upon wanting the affirmation of others, to prove something, or to gain a sense of worth?

Will this pursuit sever my daily dependence upon God?

Will my ambitions hurt my family or anyone I'm committed to?

If the Lord wanted me to change directions, would I?

Asking questions like these has helped me stay out of the performance trap, and I am truly thankful for that. God has helped me unload that heavy burden.

> *He emptied my hands of my treasure store,*
> *And His covenant grace revealed;*
> *There was not a wound in my aching heart*
> *But the balm of His breath had healed.*
> *Oh! tender and true was the chastening sore*
> *In wisdom that taught and tried,*
> *Till the soul that He sought was trusting in Him*
> *And nothing on earth beside.*[9]

Can you trust in God—and nothing on earth beside? You can—I can, as we forget the externals, those things we use to manipulate and build up our sense of worth. Instead we can focus more upon being a servant. *Choosing God over human opinion is choosing the role of a servant.* Paul used the imagery of slavery to describe our position as Christians. We were slaves to sin (Romans 6:20), but Christ purchased us out of the slave market (Galatians 3:13; 4:5). The price He paid was His blood (Revelation 5:9).

Professor David Field explains, "The main point of emphasis is not the freedom of the redeemed . . . but their new status as slaves of

God, bought with a price to do his will."[10] Paul the apostle understood this. He used the main word for slave (*doulos*) to refer to himself.[11]

So what does it mean for you and me to be a slave to God? It means thinking much less of worldly success and much more of Christian virtues and character. It means being less concerned about status in this life but more concerned with our standing before God. It means forgetting about feeling better about ourselves and instead working for the approval of God and the good of others. And for those who have status, popularity, or riches, it means we aren't to make them an issue in our lives, something to cling to. They have nothing to do with the significant life.

Significance has to do with recognizing our positional worth—that we are already significant in God's eyes—and then working that out on a practical level in service to God. That service takes us to the "bottom" rather than to what society considers the top.

LIFE AT THE BOTTOM

Many people in Scripture show us how to live at the bottom of society. John the Baptist's whole life played out on that level. Prior to Christ's coming on the scene, John had a ministry as an evangelist. Multitudes crowded around him, followed him, listened to his every word. How did he respond? Certainly not with the pride of someone who had "arrived" in life. He showed that he had the right perspective on his gifts and opportunities when he said, "A man can receive nothing unless it has been given him from heaven" (John 3:27).

John recognized that it wasn't his personality, demeanor, or celebrity status that brought the multitudes. Rather it was a work of God. It's clear that he did not think more highly of himself than he ought to think (cf. Romans 12:3).

At the proper time Christ came on the scene, but John didn't feel threatened when the multitudes left him to follow Christ. And he didn't concern himself with what others might think about his fading influence or shrinking following. He rejoiced at Christ's appearance and pointed people to Him (John 3:28-29). His motto was, "He must increase, but I must decrease" (John 3:30).

Are we able to make John's motto ours? That depends on whether we can ignore all the externals of life and keep our eyes on Jesus, remaining ever mindful that all we have and all we have done comes from God.

Honor follows the great. And the greatest are those like Elizabeth of Braunschweig (1510-1558). While living in Germany during the time of the Reformation, she risked her life for the cause of the Gospel rather than fill her days with worldly pursuits. Then there was Pandita Ramabai (1858-1922), born to parents of the high caste of priestly Brahmins in Southern India. After her conversion she became concerned about the young widows who had become outcasts. Indian society believed that a widow was the cause of her husband's death. Rather than live at the "top," in the lifestyle she had been raised in, Pandita went against the system to help these widows. She said, "Depending altogether on our Father God, we have nothing to fear, nothing to lose, nothing to regret." Through her bold ministry, thousands of widows came to Christ.

How could women like Elizabeth and Pandita get to this point in their lives? The answer is through *kenosis*. What?

THE FINE ART OF PRACTICING KENOSIS

Kenosis is the Greek word for emptying. Paul explains that Christ was the supreme example of emptying Himself: ". . . although He existed in the form of God, did not regard equality with God a thing to be grasped, but emptied Himself, taking the form of a bond-servant, and being made in the likeness of men" (Philippians 2:6-7).

It's hard to grasp even a little of what our Lord did on our behalf—but let us try. Think of it. Christ possessed full Godhood; He was "the radiance of His glory. . . . and at the right hand of the Majesty on high . . . [with] a more excellent name" than all the angels in heaven (Hebrews 1:3). Yet with all the splendor, glory, omnipotence, and all the attributes of deity, He took on human flesh.

If our souls could be reborn into the body of the lowest creature that crawls—let's say an ant—that would not even compare to the descent Christ made in order to be in the likeness of humanity. What's more, as if the transformation were not enough, He came from glory to be abused and to suffer the cross.

While outwardly He became one of us, He never ceased to be God. He never made an issue of the loss of His position—His divine glory, His power, His equality with God the Father. He made submission to the Father and our welfare, our helplessness, our peril, and our need of a Savior the issue. He left everything. He never concerned Himself with titles. He never felt the need to prove Himself or perform for others. His ambitions were not focused upon Himself but on the Father and His glory. Because He lived out the fine art of *kenosis*, He was able to live at the bottom, which entails a life of humble service. So well did Christ live out this humility that He is known as the servant of servants. Is it even possible for you and me to imitate His *kenosis*? Yes, and Paul shows us how.

Paul said, " . . . *We do not preach ourselves but Christ Jesus as Lord . . .*" (2 Corinthians 4:5). Paul shows us that the first thing we must focus on is not ourselves and our own reputation but God and His reputation. This focus certainly is the opposite of striving to gain a reputation, of climbing to the top.

"*But we have this treasure in earthen vessels, so that the surpassing greatness of the power will be of God and not from ourselves*" (2 Corinthians 4:7). Paul knew that God is best glorified by working through unadorned vessels, and that is all he wanted to be. He didn't expect that God would make him an object of admiration, and he didn't serve people in order to become one.

"*Always carrying about in the body the dying of Jesus, so that the life of Jesus also may be manifested in our body*" (2 Corinthians 4:10). Paul understood that difficult trials only helped him to be more like Christ (2 Corinthians 4:7).

"*For all things are for your sakes . . .*" (2 Corinthians 4:15). Paul worked for other people's gain. They, along with God, were his focus. He considered serving people a privilege in itself, but he also realized that he would share in their spiritual success when we all appear before God (2 Corinthians 4:14). Imagine what it will be like to someday see our efforts for others crowned with success!

"*For momentary, light affliction is producing for us an eternal weight of glory far beyond all comparison*" (2 Corinthians 4:17). Paul could see trials and setbacks in an eternal perspective, which made any hardship fade into insignificance. It allowed him to stay focused upon serving.

By following Christ's *kenosis*, we can successfully live at the bottom. Paul chose to live that way because it made him effective, gave him the freedom to serve, and helped him to be like Christ and to know Him (Philippians 3:8-10). However, Paul realized that even if he were to stop desiring a life of humble service, God would make sure he kept true to his calling. He wrote, " . . . I am under compulsion; for woe is me if I do not preach the gospel" (1 Corinthians 9:16).

UNEXPECTED REWARDS

While many of us would gladly serve the Lord to the fullest without expecting anything in return, He is always faithful to reward His servants. As Paul said, "Whatever good thing each one does, this he will receive back from the Lord" (Ephesians 6:8).

Consider the many ironies we have here. First, while there are people in this world who strive to gain good things for themselves, who strive for things even if it means keeping their children at daycare until late, even if it means spending money they don't have, who pursue the things they think will bring them pleasure—the servant doesn't need to do any of this to attain blessings. Why? Because the Lord has given her good things, things that bring lasting pleasure simply because she serves a God who is "not unjust so as to forget" (Hebrews 6:10). What peace we can have knowing that we don't need to strive to attain any good thing!

The second irony is that worldlings pursue "greatness." They desire recognition, reputation, and notoriety. The Pharisees sought the limelight in their day. Yet Christ says that people on the top are not the great ones. Then who is? Christ says it's the servant (Matthew 23:11) . . . the one who is last (Matthew 20:16) . . . the one at the bottom (Matthew 23:12).

The third irony is that the people who strive for the top never really get there. That is because the real top is reserved for those at the bottom. You see, those who strive for the bottom are raised up by God. James says, "Humble yourselves in the presence of the Lord, and He will exalt you" (James 4:10). God exalted Solomon because the king asked for wisdom to rule well, instead of asking for wealth or long life. God graciously granted him "both riches and honor . . ." (1 Kings

3:13). It's no surprise then that the ultimate example of exaltation is the ultimate example of humility: Christ becoming man and dying on a cross. For this God "bestowed on Him the name which is above every name" (Philippians 2:9). God has given Christ the ultimate honor, and He promises to all: "Those who honor Me I will honor" (1 Samuel 2:30).

Striving for the bottom by shunning the world's values in order to be a servant like Christ, we honor God. Living on the bottom is a matter of trust in God, trust that you do not need to be consumed with your own interests because God is consumed with them.

Lastly, living at the bottom brings true significance, which is an inward thing, a matter of the spirit and soul. Our worth reveals itself best when it comes from the inside out. Our true value before God is permanent and outlasts all changes of time, pain, and death. If the inner life isn't cultivated, we will end up cultivating a false sense of significance. *True significance comes from the inside out, a truth foundational for the rest of this book.*

THINKING IT OVER

1. In what ways must we be like Mrs. Proverbs, and in what way does it not matter?
2. Why is it harmful for us to seek our sense of significance in the outward things in life?
3. How can we ensure that our ambitions aren't misguided?
4. Do you have a fear of failure? In what ways can you overcome it?
6. Read Mark 9:35. Christ said if we are "to be" anything, what are we to be?
7. What rewards are gained from being a servant?
8. What makes being at the bottom so special, and why is the bottom really the top? How can you strive for the bottom?

Three

THE "100 MOST IMPORTANT WOMEN"...
THEN THERE'S ME

*T*oday at the grocery counter I saw *Ladies' Home Journal*. I usually overlook it, but today I was interested. The entire month's issue featured the "100 Most Important Women of the 20th Century."[1] Intrigued as to whom they had selected as the "most important" rather than simply the best known, I bought a copy.

While skimming through the magazine, I quickly saw that these women were celebrated for the highly visible things they did. The list included entrepreneurs, activists and politicians, writers and journalists, doctors and scientists, artists and entertainers, athletes, pioneers, and adventurers.

I was glad to see women such as Mother Teresa honored for her kind heart, Helen Keller for overcoming her limitations, and Margaret Thatcher for her insight, but I must admit I was scratching my head in puzzlement a lot of times. I wondered why some of the women were selected—for instance, Margaret Sanger (1879-1966).

Sanger first found notoriety when she wrote and published the magazine *The Woman Rebel*. *Ladies' Home Journal* mentioned that she published it as a way to speak openly about contraception and that she was considered to be in violation of the postal code. But *Ladies' Home Journal* failed to mention the other things Sanger wrote about.

With the slogan "No Gods! No Masters!" emblazoned on this magazine, Sanger advertised her eight-page publication as "a paper of militant thought." The first issue denounced marriage as a "degenerate institution," capitalism as "indecent exploitation," and sexual modesty as "obscene prudery."[2] An article titled "A Woman's Duty" proclaimed that rebel women were to "look the whole world in the face with a go-to-hell look in the eyes."[3] In another article she said that "rebel women claim the following rights: the right to be lazy, the right to be an unmarried mother, the right to destroy . . . and the right to love."[4] In later issues she wrote on sexual liberation and defended political assassinations.[5]

Though Sanger married and became the mother of three, as time went on, she advocated free love. She eventually left her husband to follow this philosophy. It was at this time that *The Woman Rebel* got the attention of the postal service. Sanger was indicted on three counts for the publication of lewd and indecent articles in violation of the federal Comstock Laws, which were passed in 1873 to keep "obscene and lascivious" material from traveling through the postal system.[6]

If convicted, Sanger could have gotten five years in jail. Rather than face prison, she fled to England where she lived as a fugitive. In later years, desiring to return to the U.S., she pulled off a cunning public relations campaign that forced authorities to drop all charges against her.[7] Once back in the U.S., Sanger remarried and assured her lovers that her "marriage would make little or no difference in her life—apart from the convenience of money, of course."[8]

While continuing on with her free sex, Margaret became closely associated with the scientists and theorists who put together Nazi Germany's "race purification" program. She had openly endorsed the euthanasia, sterilization, abortion, and infanticide programs of the early Reich. She published a number of articles in her new magazine, *The Birth Control Review,* that mirrored Hitler's Aryan-White Supremacist rhetoric. She even commissioned Dr. Ernst Rudin, the director of the Nazi Medical Experimentation program, to write for *The Review* himself.[9] It was Nazi ideology that influenced Sanger to found the Planned Parenthood Federation of America in 1941.

The same woman who gave us Planned Parenthood wrote the book *The Pivot of Civilization*, where she calls for the elimination of "human weeds," for the cessation of charity, for the segregation of "morons, misfits, and the maladjusted," and for the sterilization of "genetically inferior races."[10]

I wonder if *Ladies' Home Journal* would salute Margaret Sanger as one of the "most important" women if they knew the rest of the story. It probably wouldn't have made a difference. But . . . how dangerous to look only at selected "achievements," forgetting the inner person of the heart!

THE INNER PERSON OF THE HEART

Cultivating the inner life cannot begin without two things: hope and mercy. Do you have these two anchors of the soul? We need mercy—God's forgiveness of our sins despite the fact that we do not deserve it. Hope is the confident expectation of something quite wonderful. Regardless of whatever life may bring of disaster, tragedy, or pain, Christians hope—that is, they confidently expect—the opposite. They can know they will someday experience the deepest pleasure and happiness, peace and love. The foundation of that hope is Jesus Christ (1 Peter 1:3). As the apostle Paul said, we look "for the blessed hope and the appearing of the glory of our great God and Savior, Christ Jesus" (Titus 2:13).

If you are without God's hope and mercy, it is probably because you are without other things as well. You may not have a personal knowledge of Christ (Philippians 3:8); His righteousness in place of your own (Philippians 3:9); His power, fellowship, and glory (Philippians 3:10-11). If you are devoid of these, you have not experienced God's salvation (Acts 16:31). As the Word of God bids us, "The time is fulfilled, and the kingdom of God is at hand; repent and believe in the gospel" (Mark 1:15).

Those of us who are certain of our hope must continually cultivate the inner life. We have been crucified with Christ, which means that our old, self-centered nature is "dead." The self that built up a false sense of significance no longer lives. The new self can seek to glorify God and make everything revolve around Him.

Look at Christ. When I think of His life as Scripture reveals it, I can remember many occasions where He received very little respect. People threw rocks at Him, argued with Him, and mocked Him. Many people thought He amounted to nothing. And amazingly this never bothered Him.

Christ didn't concern Himself with fulfilling other people's expectations—the Pharisees, scribes, and other Jewish leaders. But neither did He define Himself merely by trying to be unique from all others. So while He wasn't a slave to anyone's opinion, neither did He try to establish Himself as a rebel. He did not let other people determine who He was. He let His relationship to God determine and define Him (John 10:15, 38). *His goal was to please the Father, not to fit in with public opinion.*

For us, cultivating the inner life is a matter of wanting to live the Christ-life, pleasing the Father, and being more concerned about His opinion than that of others. It involves being in prayer and in the Word daily. And, just as important, cultivating the inner life involves being controlled by the Holy Spirit.

THE SPIRIT-EMPOWERED LIFE

The other day I got out the paints for my children and decided to join in the fun. Hoping for a bold effect, I thought I would try for something similar to Claude Monet's painting *The Artist's Garden at Giverny.* When I finished, the end result looked absolutely awful. Unlike Monet's work, my painting was sloppy, lifeless, and, to put it bluntly, more like a blob rendition of a junkyard than a French garden.

I wish I could paint like Monet, but in this lifetime that will never be. Like him I have eyes and hands, but the only way I could ever come close to Monet's talent is to have the actual spirit of the artist enter my body and control my eyes and hands. But even then, I would only be reproducing Monet. As impossible as that is, there is a mysterious presence in all believers. They have been bodily filled with God's Spirit.

Miraculously, Christ by the Spirit dwells within us as a divine life, able to image forth Himself from our inner life to the outer. This is how our significance is worked in us spiritually from the inside out.

Possibly it's difficult for you to work on your inner life because you haven't seen a power higher than your own working in you. The reason for this might lie in the nature of your belief. Is it a second-hand belief that knows next to nothing of a day-by-day relationship with God? If so, you should consider whether you are truly a follower of Christ.

Possibly you don't have the Spirit mightily at work in you because you are grieving Him by sin in your life (Ephesians 4:30). From personal experience I can tell you there is absolutely no spiritual power where there is known, willful sin. The best way to keep the Spirit mightily at work is to keep short accounts with God. Quickly ask forgiveness the moment you realize your transgression. Ask in faith for the Spirit to revive you and give you once again a true love for God. Even if there aren't any known sin issues in your life, you still may not see the Spirit powerfully at work. Do you know why that is?

MAKING THE MOST OF THE POWER

There are many Christians who don't see the Spirit's power working within them, nor do they take advantage of such power simply because, well—they don't think about it. When we depend more upon the Spirit's power, marvelous things can happen:

First, we see more clearly God's love for us in that He not only saved us, but He chose to reveal Himself to others through us.

Second, we forget about the performance trap because we are more concerned about those who are in other traps, such as the "lost trap."

Third, we have the spiritual power to worry much less about what others think of us. We are consumed with serving God and building His kingdom—which paradoxically is the stuff of a significant life.

We can become more confident that as children of God, we aren't mechanical robots obeying His orders, but we are unique individuals whom He longs to bless with all spiritual things (one of which is the Spirit's power).

When we depend on God's Spirit rather than ourselves, He blesses us with growth in our inner life. As God, His Word, and His plan come more sharply into focus, we become less attached to the world's views and values. Being confident of our true significance before God, we no longer strive to achieve it with artificial externals. We are then free to give ourselves to expressing our significance from the inside out, *from who we are inside and before God, to what we are to do for Him outwardly in building up His kingdom.*

Along with living a life pleasing to God, an important factor in keeping ourselves Spirit-energized is to be daily in tune with the Spirit's work. He is always ready to work in and through every situation. Are we? We can be ready, by praying for God to work mightily in and through us. While our prayers don't produce power—since it's already there—our lack of prayer, our lack of alertness, our failure to cultivate the inner life neglects the power to which we already have access.

Let me share with you an incident that happened in my single days, after I had prayed for the Spirit to work powerfully through me. One night an old college friend named Theo was passing through my area solely for the purpose of driving his friend Mike, who had visited Theo, to the airport. They had a few hours to spare, so they came by my house for a visit.

I invited them in and immediately prayed in my heart, "Oh, Lord, may Your Spirit powerfully lead me!"

As Theo and Mike sat on the couch, I was focusing on Theo. I figured Mike lived out of state, and I would never see him again. Despite my shallow thinking, the Spirit of God strongly got through to me that I was to focus on Mike. So I did, starting with light questions such as how he enjoyed his visit to California and how he had met Theo.

After a few minutes, I could tell something was really troubling Mike. So I said, "I guess you're quite anxious to get back home." My question stirred up a hornets' nest. Mike unloaded! He shared with me how much he loved his wife and children, but revealed that his family was breaking apart because his wife wanted a divorce. With great sorrow he said he didn't really have a home to go to.

As I listened intently, I knew that there was only one source of help for him. So I began speaking about Christ. I told Mike that Jesus understood his pain. The Lord, too, had been rejected by those in his own hometown, by family members, and even by His closest friends—His disciples (Mark 6:3; Matthew 26:56, 74).

As I began telling Mike how Christ could help him during this difficult time, Theo got noticeably uncomfortable. I was able to understand his discomfort. Theo had only known me as an unbeliever, so I am sure he was squirming out of shock. Standing up, he looked at his watch and said to Mike, "We've got to go."

As Theo and Mike were heading toward the door, my eye caught a small twenty-page booklet lying on a table near the door. It was called "My Heart, Christ's Home." Grabbing it, I said to Mike, "I'll give this pamphlet to you if you promise me you will read it on the airplane."

Mike promised.

A few days later I got a call from Theo. He said, "Mike called me last night and has asked me to give you a message."

I sensed Theo was looking for something, and, sure enough, he said, "Mike insisted I write down his message word for word. Hmmm . . . now where is that slip of paper? Ah, here, I found it."

"Well, what does it say?" I asked anxiously.

Clearing his throat, Theo read: "'I've repented of my sins. Christ is now in my heart. He's my Lord and Savior! I'll see you in heaven.'"

Now you might think that this is the end of the story, but it isn't.

One week later Theo called me and in a very solemn voice said, "Donna, Mike died last night of a massive heart attack."

Consider the ramifications had I not been in tune with the Spirit and His power. Consider what would have happened had I kept my mouth closed because of fear of Theo's opinion of me. Either one of these things could have easily occurred had I been in the flesh and had the Spirit not worked so dynamically.

The Spirit of God is the dynamic behind the significant life. We are told that it is through the Spirit that we will do great things for God—things that change lives (John 14:12). It could be sharing Christ, molding a child for Christ, or lifting up the downtrodden. These things and more come as we cultivate the inner life and draw on the Spirit's power.

And draw on the Spirit's power we must, especially as we examine ourselves in the light of the next two chapters. It is the Spirit's job not only to confront whatever wrong views we may have of ourselves, but also to help us to correct them and think accurately. Are you ready for the challenge? I certainly am. But before we move on, allow me to encourage you with one last thought.

While your life lived from the inside out may never attract the attention of *Ladies' Home Journal*, it will catch the attention of the Almighty. He, too, has a book with a list of names—not just any names, but the names of the most important people who ever lived throughout time. It's called *The Book of Life*.

If you are living your life from the inside out, you are a person of significance. Your name has been written in the heavenly book and will be confessed before the Father and before His angels (Revelation

3:5). Such an honor hasn't even been given to the cherubim, the seraphim, the angels, and archangels. *But to you it has been granted.*

THINKING IT OVER

1. What roles do hope and mercy play in your life?
2. What does it mean to live from the inside out?
3. Do you see the Spirit powerfully working in your life? If so, tell about a situation(s) in which the Spirit worked through you. If you haven't noticed the Spirit's power in your life, what steps will you take to activate that power?

PART TWO

Gaining a Sense of Our Significance

In the last section we saw how easily we can feel insignificant when we base our sense of who we are on the outer stuff of life. But we can feel insignificant for other reasons as well. We can, for instance, allow wounds from the past to keep us down. We can be hindered by a parent's view of us or by a friend's rejection. We can nurture the memory of cruel words that were said to us and even believe them. We can allow ourselves to be intimidated by another person, believing him or her to be better than we are. We can be so focused on what other people can do that we fail to see our own potential and abilities.

On the other hand, we can fall into the temptation to see ourselves through pride's rose-colored spectacles. Pride always gives us a distorted view of ourselves and conveys a wrong impression to others.

When we view ourselves in an unbiblical way, we forfeit a knowledge of our true significance by failing to grasp our own God-given worth. Together let's look at these views (and more) as we gain a sense of our significance in the eyes of God.

Four

GETTING RID OF FEELINGS OF UNWORTHINESS

*O*n January 30, 1968, the Viet Cong moved into a mission compound and carried out a bloody massacre, killing five American missionaries, including a four-year-old boy. Less fortunate than the dead were Betty Olsen and two others, who were taken captive. For eight months they suffered indescribable torture and humiliation before Betty gave her life as a Christian martyr.[1]

Betty had been a missionary all her life, having grown up on the field in Africa. Yet those who knew her best had doubted her usefulness as a missionary. They thought that the role of heroine simply didn't fit the image they had of her.

While Betty's days in Africa had been relatively happy ones, they were also filled with turmoil. Her earliest recollections were of her parents consumed by their work, often leaving her for days at a time while they visited African churches. When she was eight years old, she was sent away to a boarding school where on most nights she would cry herself to sleep. For eight months each year she would be separated from her parents. Because of her deep sense of rejection by her parents, Betty rebelled against the rules of the school and resisted close relationships with others. She feared the hurt that would inevitably come when separations occurred. Her insecurities as a teenager heightened when her mother became ill and died of cancer just prior to Betty's seventeenth birthday.[2]

The troubled missionary kid completed high school in the United States and then went back to Africa. She was still struggling with emotional insecurity, craving love and attention from a father whose hectic schedule and plans for remarriage diverted his attention from her. After he remarried, Betty returned to the United States and undertook nurse's training at a hospital in Brooklyn. Then she enrolled at Nyack Missionary College to prepare for a missionary career.[3]

In spite of her achievements and increased stability, Betty found no real happiness. She desperately wanted to get married and have a family of her own, but the relationship she hoped for never developed. The feelings of rejection deepened.

After graduating in 1962, Betty's view of herself was at an all-time low. So convinced that the mission board representing Vietnam wouldn't accept her as a candidate on her own merits, she went back to Africa on her own to work with her father and stepmother. It was difficult, however, for Betty to get along with them, and eventually with anybody. She had been suppressing an unbearable amount of bitterness and rebellion that could no longer be controlled. She became so irritating and difficult to work with that she was asked to leave the field.[4]

At the age of twenty-nine, Betty found herself in Chicago working as a nurse and feeling thoroughly defeated in her Christian life. Plagued by a lifetime of rejection and insecurities, she contemplated suicide. Fortunately, she met a young man whose principles for Christian living would change her life. Taking a special interest in Betty, he listened as she shared the heartbreak and frustration of her walk with the Lord. He gave her scriptural principles to help her deal with her feelings of inadequacy.[5]

Then some great things happened in Betty's difficult journey. She made those biblical truths a part of her thoughts and feelings, putting into perspective the rejection she had felt over the years. She focused on the depths of God's love and acceptance for her. She grew to be willing and even eager to serve God as a single woman. And in due time she was accepted by the Christian and Missionary Alliance (C&MA) to serve in Vietnam. She also became a productive and sacrificial missionary, once risking her life by going through a dangerous area to get an injured girl to a hospital.

Betty's counselor, Bill Gothard, went on to develop seminars to promote his scriptural principles for life. He said he developed his ministry "based largely on the questions Betty Olsen had asked."[6]

While Betty's story is both disturbing and inspiring, it's also revealing. It shows that the view we have of ourselves cannot help but be seen by others, for whatever is down deep eventually comes out.

A DEEP SPRING

When I was a teenager, my great-uncle Robert used to take me and my other siblings hiking on some property that our English ancestors had settled in the 1800s. Our goal was always the same—to hike over the property until we reached a waterfall, the most beautiful that our young eyes had ever beheld. A highlight of the trek was always to drink water from the natural springs flowing from the rocks. I was always curious about the origin of the water, the resource that gave life to everything in those mountains. I was told that the water came from deep underground, hidden in the rock. No one had seen its origin, and no one ever would. It was down too deep.

Scripture uses the metaphor of an underground spring to explain the inner life of the heart and mind: " . . . the heart of a man is like deep water" (Proverbs 20:5). Each of us has a deep spring hidden where no one can see it; yet it flows out for all the world to see. Though we believe our thoughts are hidden and secret, they do flow out and show what is in the depths of our being. Even if we can't see it, others can, especially the wise (Proverbs 20:5).

For instance, Nathan the prophet understood all too well the type of person David was, though David couldn't admit his sins (2 Samuel 12:5-7). And, of course, through her very negative thoughts, everyone saw what type of person Betty Olsen was. Sad to say, for much of her adult life no one wanted to be around her.

What thoughts do you have of yourself?

If we think too highly of ourselves, we are giving ourselves the glory that belongs to God (1 Corinthians 4:7). If we have too low an opinion of ourselves (which we can have if we view ourselves apart from the grace of God), we may not only become distant toward God, possibly even challenging His wisdom (Romans 9:20), but we can become a paralyzed spouse, an ineffective parent, an unproductive missionary, an ineffectual teacher, an incapable helper, or a person jealous of almost everyone.

I've known some women whose insecurities have led them to make rules such as, "Don't commit yourself to anyone and don't allow anyone to come close to you." It is a simple yet pivotal rule. It is uncomplicated, and yet it will lead to profound loneliness. It is easy to carry out but an unfruitful way to live.

So how does one begin to descend into a sense of worthlessness? In many ways, but first and foremost, through our sin.

FREE FROM OUR DARKER SELF

Sin is everywhere! I can't go one place on planet earth without finding it. I can't watch the news without being confronted with it. I see it in my enemies, my friends, and, worst of all, in myself.

Now does recognition of my own sin mean I have low self-esteem? Some people would think so. One pastor believes that the "one reason many Christians have behaved so badly in the past 2,000 years is that we have been taught from infancy to adulthood how sinful and how worthless we are."[7]

I must respectfully disagree with such a comment. Seeing how sinful we are is good in the sense that only as we come face to face with our sin—and deal with it rather than ignore it—can we begin to think rightly about ourselves, live to the fullest in Christ, and know His mercy and grace.

While some make the mistake of avoiding any thought of sin, others can't stop thinking about their sins and won't leave them behind. Despite the fact that our sins were confessed and forgiven, we can find ourselves drawn back to the their graveyard. In our minds we revisit the day of our sin, where we were, what we did, and the gloomy consequences. In so doing we invite those dark memories of dead and buried sins to haunt us.

Sometimes we bring dead sins to life by seeing judgment for them in every unwanted turn of events. The widow of Zarephath, for instance, must have been haunted by some past sin. When her son was taken ill and died, she assumed her sin was the cause (1 Kings 17:18).[8]

Our memories can work against us, not only recalling past sins and imagining that they exceed God's forgiveness—that He holds a grudge against us—but causing us to feel worthless. Instead of focusing on the grace of God's forgiveness, we wallow in shame and regret over what we have done.

Now there may be sorrow if God is disciplining us (for our

good) in order to bring us to repentance. But once we repent, we must embrace the truth of divine forgiveness. That is, we must be convinced that God forgives and will never hold our forgiven sin against us (Jeremiah 31:34). If we fail to believe this truth, the sense of God's displeasure further tempts us to withdraw from Him into our mind's shadows. There our focus on ourselves likely becomes a downward spiral.

The key to clearing our mind of our past and present sins is by daily having a firm grip on God's forgiveness. In this sense we never leave the foot of the cross. We do not start with the cross and then go on to something else. Maturity involves having an ever deepening understanding of what the cross means for our lives. It is the foundation of who we are. We are in Christ—we belong to Him. We've been bought with a price; we no longer live, but Christ lives in us (Galatians 2:20).

REJECTION

In addition to a sense of sin, rejection can cause us to descend into a sense of worthlessness. Like Betty Olsen, the missionary, each of us has experienced rejection. Think back long enough and you can remember an episode. Many of us can vividly recall incidents of rejection that occurred when we were in high school, where social life was dominated by a hierarchy of cliques. The popular, beautiful people belonged to one group, the athletes belonged to another, and the brainy people to another. If you had an average high school experience, you may have thought that you were outside every elite group.

How a person feels in that situation is best described by singer Janis Ian, "love was just for beauty queens, with clear-skinned smiles." Those of us who felt overlooked concluded we were among those with "ravaged faces, lacking in social graces." After those experiences fade into the background, we can continue to feel rejection, even decades later. Perhaps it's because we were sensitized in our formative years by those vivid experiences of being somewhere down the pecking order.

Others suffer from more devastating rejection, such as when a husband leaves for another woman. A few women who have been through a humiliating abandonment have told me that it would have been far easier had their husbands died. Children can feel a deep sense of rejection, too, when a parent leaves a marriage. Unable to understand the situation, they think that Mom or Dad has left them rather than the marriage. Those early wounds can become scars in adulthood.

A majority of single women have at one time or another been rejected by a boyfriend. This is difficult to take, especially when you see that boyfriend clinging to his new flame.

Perhaps you are like some women who have become reluctant to get close to other women. In the past you felt rejected when a close friend wasn't loyal, steadfast, and unwavering. Possibly you think that it's because your friend got to know the "real you" that she walked away from the friendship. Hurt and disappointed, you have made it a goal not to let others come close.

Yes, relationships can become a source of rejection. We know that people can hurt us without really meaning to. Sometimes they can be deliberately cruel. But the answer is not to stay away from people or to avoid developing close relationships.

I believe there are four steps we can take when we feel rejected. First, we can gain comfort from drawing near to a Savior who experienced a lot of deep rejection. He was "despised and forsaken of men, a man of sorrows and acquainted with grief; and like one from whom men hide their face He was despised, and we did not esteem Him" (Isaiah 53:3).

Second, we can refocus away from what others think of us and onto what God thinks of us. That means letting our Creator, not others, define who we are. It means turning away from thoughts such as, *That person knew me well and rejected me; I must not be worth much.* Instead we can think: *I was made by an infinitely loving and skillful Creator, and His Spirit is helping me become all I can be.* Catching unbiblical thoughts and making them biblical is a part of what Paul meant when he told us to be transformed by the renewing of our minds (Romans 12:2).

Third, we can develop a dynamic prayer life that involves forgiveness of those who hurt us. Remember the wounding words Job received from his friends? Part of God's healing process for Job required that he pray for those friends. Scripture records:

"The LORD restored the fortunes of Job when he prayed for his friends . . ." (Job 42:10).

As we can see, Job was blessed *after* he prayed for those who had hurt him. So it can be with us. We can forgive those who hurt us (Matthew 6:14). We can also trust that ultimately all things, including our deep hurts, can be used for good (Romans 8:28) and for God's glory.

While wallowing in our hurts—and thereby possibly becoming bitter against those who have hurt us—keeps us from being effective, prayer strengthens us and enables us to have an impact. Rather than dwell morbidly on our situation, praying about it makes us open to God's comfort. We, in turn, are able to comfort others who are hurting (2 Corinthians 1:3-4).

And fourth, we can refocus on truth, on all that is good, and on God by dealing with our painful memories.

DEALING WITH OUR MEMORIES

Memories are powerful. They can bring back the best times of a close relationship or a great victory God helped us achieve. But they can also make us relive insults, embarrassments, cruel words, or our past failures and sins.

Some people have never recovered from harsh words that continually haunt them. Others have been affected by the corrosive attitude of a parent's unreasonable expectations or unfair criticism or the deep wounds of physical or mental abuse. Abuse can make a person feel unwanted and unloved—that he or she is deeply flawed as a human being.

The Lord's way of dealing with painful memories of the past is not necessarily to make us forget them but to refocus our thinking. We are told: " . . . whatsoever things are true, whatsoever things are honest, whatsoever things are just, whatsoever things are pure, whatsoever things are lovely . . . think on these things" (Philippians 4:8 KJV). We must be very careful what we think about, which must include what we think about ourselves. We can, for example, dwell *for years* on the hurtful comments of others, or we can think about what God says is true of us.

Possibly you were told by a parent or someone else that you are ugly, or a failure, or stupid, or that you will never amount to much in life. I can still remember my fifth grade teacher proclaiming before the class that I was a scatterbrain. At that impressionable age I believed her. Since that time, many other hurtful comments have come my way. If I'm not careful, those comments can creep back into my thought process and actually shape what I think of myself. Fortunately, you and I can eliminate those hurtful, untrue thoughts because they fail the test of "whatsoever things are true."

We must dwell on things that are "honorable." That rules out fruitless brooding over our weaknesses and failures. We must also dwell on what is right or true—that is, on what lies behind appearances and conforms to reality. This rules out any refusal to face the truth about ourselves or any attempt to hide it from others. Our sense of who we are has to be based on just that—who we are.

While we must face what is imperfect in ourselves, as Christians we have the advantage of seeing ourselves through the eyes of God. His perspective includes not only our immaturity and what remains of sin, but He also sees us as forgiven and knows where His power is at work to transform us.

We must think about things that are "pure" and undefiled. Doing so rules out dwelling on our weaknesses in a way that accomplishes no moral good—a way that is not part of the process of repentance, does not help us change some specific behavior, or does not help us deal with pride.

Insofar as there is anything "worthy of praise" in us—or anything good for that matter—we can give the credit ultimately to God. In fact, Philippians 4:8 does not tell us to be continually absorbed with thoughts about ourselves or even to dwell on the good things about ourselves. But since it tells us to dwell on good things, we ought to discipline our thoughts about ourselves to conform to that verse. Ultimately, because the source of all goodness is God, it's most helpful to be absorbed in thinking about Him. That's what 1 Corinthians 3:18 indicates we should be doing.

In thinking about God, we can come full circle in that we become aware of His thoughts about us. We can dwell on the fact that He loves us (Jeremiah 31:3) and that His love is unconditional. There is nothing we can do that will make God stop loving us. In that sense He is unlike the people from whom we may be tempted to try to gain acceptance.

While some rejections cannot be avoided, others we set ourselves up for.

MISREADING THE ACTIONS OF OTHERS

A while back I realized how easy it is to read something into the action of others. A publicist lined up for me countless radio interviews about my book *Choices That Lead to Godliness*. As you might imagine, entering into the "radio biz" was quite intimidating to me, realizing that on some programs I could be speaking to several million people "live."

Well, one day I was to do a forty-five-minute telephone interview for a Christian radio station in another state. Because it was one of my first interviews, I thought I would call the interviewer beforehand to find out what he would ask me. He said, "I don't know what questions I'll ask you." I asked him if he had read the book. His answer was a casual no.

With a nervous laugh I asked, "Are you going to read the book or at least skim through it?"

He said, "I'll just let the Spirit lead."

Sensing my increasing jitters, the interviewer said, "Hey, don't worry about it. I have yet to lose an author."

The hour of the interview arrived. As the unpolished questions came haltingly from the interviewer, I answered the best I could. But ten minutes into the conversation, the interviewer ended it abruptly.

I was stunned. Staring at the phone, I thought to myself, *Wow, I guess I'm the first author he has given up on! Was I that bad?*

After recovering, I called the interviewer's secretary and asked her, "What happened?" She had no idea but said she would call me back that day.

She never called back. It was a Friday, so I had the entire weekend to fret and brood, thinking of myself as a big failure. I imagined that I must have been so boring that the station knew instinctively that their ratings were crashing. I contemplated canceling all future interviews, but I realized that I had promised to do whatever interviews came my way. With growing desperation I became convinced that my promise would condemn me to national humiliation as I flopped on one interview after another. I imagined that after a couple of public disasters, the publisher would decide never to do another of my books.

That Monday I called the radio station back and found out the real reason the interview had ended. The state's senator happened to walk into the station during my interview. The interviewer understandably made use of the rare opportunity.

So I had wasted a beautiful weekend emotionally knocking my head against a wall, denigrating myself, feeling as if I had really blown it, and generally thinking of myself as a total failure. Having misread the situation, I had needlessly developed a low opinion of myself—all for nothing!

Are you prone to misread situations? You might be if you base your perceptions on inadequate information. Do you read a lot into a fleeting look on someone's face, thinking, for example, that the person is mad at you? Do you ever think someone is avoiding you because he or she doesn't return a phone call quickly? Are you convinced that someone is rejecting you because the person turned down one invitation or failed to greet you? Might you be misreading your friend's intentions or possibly misconstruing those of people who don't even know you?

I've been on the other end of this kind of rush to self-judgment. People have accused me, for instance, of ignoring them when I simply hadn't heard what they said. They felt hurt for nothing. Usually it isn't until quite a bit later that they bring up the incident, and I discover that they had said something into my completely deaf ear. I've learned that it's quite easy for any one of us to misjudge. Remember when Eli the priest mistook Hannah's praying for drunkenness (1 Samuel 1:10-14)?

Where might you be vulnerable to misjudge? Have you ever, for instance, misread your husband's actions? If so, you could end up questioning your mate's love for you. In such situations some women keep trying to get acceptance from their husbands, constantly asking, "Do you love me?" Never fully sure of that love, they become possessive of their husbands, expecting something from them that they, as mere human beings, just can't give. Christ told His followers that He alone is the true vine (John 15:1). Nothing and no one else can fulfill us. When a wife forgets this important truth, a wedge can come between herself and her husband as she needlessly feels rejected. She can feel threatened (he's more loyal to his job than to me), jealous (perhaps there's another woman), and driven to accuse him (you don't love me like you used to).

If we aren't careful, misreading the actions of others can lead us to another problem—manipulation. When we try to manipulate someone else to fulfill our need for constant approval, praise, and love, we can become incapable of giving to a spouse, a child, or a friend. Again Christ said that only as we draw life from Him, the vine, can we bear fruit (John 15:5). We cannot be a blessing to others or have a significant impact on their lives, nor can we serve God, without staying close to Him and looking to Him as our only source of real life.

If you are depending on someone other than God to meet your every need, you are sabotaging your relationships. I've seen this in women who were incapable of forming deep relationships with anyone because no one could possibly meet their expectations. In turn, they ended up thinking that no one would ever love them. And because they themselves do not love unselfishly, without wanting something in return, they cannot comprehend anyone loving them in an unselfish way. They feel inadequate and undeserving to receive love. Thus, their relationships have become a source of rejection.

I think of the account of Joseph. His brothers who had sold him into slavery met him later as Egypt's prime minister, second only to Pharaoh (Genesis 41:44). They were at his mercy. Being selfish schemers, they had trouble understanding Joseph's love and forgiveness ("they were dismayed," Genesis 45:3—that is, they were terrified). Several times they interpreted Joseph's actions in light of their own unloving motives (Genesis 44; 50:15), but Joseph's steadfast love won their trust (Genesis 50:21-22).

It's so easy to misread the actions of others by supposing they have the same motives and thoughts we do. We can see rejection where it doesn't exist. And if we are looking to anyone but Christ for our fulfillment, we can be devastated. Abiding in Christ as our true vine will keep us out of this downward spiral.

Now let's look at another manifestation of an inaccurate low view of ourselves. The true sense of who we are can be eroded when we believe others are better than we are and when we succumb to self-pity.

ARE OTHERS BETTER THAN I AM?

Remember Mephibosheth, the fourteen-year-old grandson of King Saul who was handicapped in both legs? When King David invited him to eat regularly at his own table, Mephibosheth replied, "What is your servant, that you should regard a dead dog like me?" (2 Samuel 9:8).

While Mephibosheth may have been trying to emphasize that he was no threat to David's throne (the death of the boy's father, Jonathan, meant that Mephibosheth would have been next in line to rule), I do think there could be something else that prompted his self-denigrating attitude. It seems that his crippled feet (2 Samuel 9:2-8) had become the focus of his insecurities. His handicap not only kept him looking inward but convinced him that everyone was better than he was.

Many of us think that others are better than we are, and we try to deal with the discomfort by desiring to be someone we're not. When we feel this way, we can think as little of ourselves as Mephibosheth did, believing we have nothing to offer. But this attitude only takes away our motivation to discover and appreciate the good and unique qualities God has given us and wants to further develop in us.

How do we get into this sad state? Simple. We dislike the abilities we see in ourselves. But as seminary professor James Rosscup points out, our dissatisfaction may simply be the result of not going far enough in our Christian walk. We don't allow enough time for God to bring out our hidden and unrealized potentialities. We wrongly assume that what we are in our present condition is all we will ever be. However, "when God wants to make a life a monument of His grace, it is not His usual method to throw it up shantylike, overnight, or in a week, or even in a year. God is in no hurry."[9]

We have to keep in mind that God has not given us each the same endowment. We each have, for example, a different family heritage, personal background, and mental makeup.[10] Ignoring what God has made us to be and wanting instead to be someone else altogether is inconsistent with some basic Christian attitudes.

First, such thinking rejects the wisdom, love, and power of God.[11] We are in effect saying, "Lord, I guess I'm stuck with the way You've made me. Look at me. What abilities have You given me? None of value. I guess I'm not going to amount to much in this life, unlike so many others You have blessed."

Even a well-meaning Christian can fall into this lack of respect for God and His wisdom. And when we do, we communicate our lack of faith in God's love for us, our disbelief in His fairness. We ought to be saying, "Lord, right now I can see only little in myself that is of value. However, You are altogether wise and intelligent in Your good purposes, and I know that You have given me the potential to be worthwhile and to bear much fruit. I'm confident that You will graciously work in my life in a way that will enable me to fulfill Your plan for me. Thank You, Lord."[12]

Second, we must deal with our desire to be like others because we can become covetous, jealous, and unloving if we don't.[13] Years ago a woman I barely knew (and haven't seen since) came up to me after church. She pointed out a woman she envied and said in a very disturbed tone, "Why is it that she is so knowledgeable about God's Word and is doing great things for God, when I have been a Christian so much longer than she has?"

Because of her attitude it wasn't difficult for me to guess the answer to her question. God warns us of the seriousness of jealousy: "Wrath is fierce and anger is a flood, but who can stand before jealousy?" (Proverbs 27:4).

Jealousy can surface unnoticeably in many of us when we wish we were in the shoes of someone else. We feel somehow cheated that others have had better lives or that God has gifted others more than us. These sorts of feelings can lead us not only to a low view of ourselves, but, worse, we may stay away from the people we consider more blessed. Why? Because we don't like what we see in ourselves when we are with them. A smart woman can make us feel a little dense, a beautiful woman can make us feel ugly, an articulate woman can make us feel tongue-tied, a nicely dressed woman can make us feel shabby, a Mrs. Proverbs can make us feel like a Mrs. Job.

Years ago I was feeling intimidated by a woman who is very intelligent, probably the most articulate woman I know. You might say I was in awe of her. Her manner is poised. Each word is thought through. But my admiration of her made me feel as if I couldn't measure up. After spending time with her, I would find myself evaluating our conversation. I would say to myself, "Oh, I should have explained my point this way" or, "Why can't I come across as more intelligent when I'm around her?"

Obviously I was self-conscious around her, so I didn't pursue a relationship with her. Actually I avoided her. But as time went on, I thought, *Whose fault is it, mine or hers, that she intimidates me?* It was mine, I concluded. She can't help it that she is much more gifted than I am. Though I couldn't change my level of giftedness, I had to stop thinking about my vanity and just start appreciating the way God has wonderfully blessed this woman. Rather than withdraw from her, I decided to be around her more and learn from her. And I have!

When we compare ourselves to others in an unfavorable way, believing they are somehow better than we are, we can't help but develop feelings of unworthiness, a sense of inferiority, and a strong desire to stay away from them. And when we avoid such people, we forfeit so much. We miss out on a friendship, we miss out on enhancing our own abilities, and we fail to minister to that person.

Is there someone whose great giftedness intimidates you? How might you begin with this person anew?

By the way, in case you struggle with wanting to have much greater abilities, giftedness, or ministry, think again. A lot of people wish they could have the gifts or ministry of an apostle Paul, but they wouldn't want to experience what he did to have his gifts and ministry. He had a thorn in the flesh and endured considerable persecution that kept him humble (2 Corinthians 12:7). In our day many people look at Joni Eareckson Tada and wish they had her giftedness as an artist, singer, and communicator. But the trials of her life are obvious. Just as Paul accepted his trials, she accepts hers so others will benefit.[14]

What we often miss when we are envying another person's gifts is that each of us is accountable to God for the use we make of what He *has* given us. Are you sure you would like to give account to God for a far greater giftedness?[15]

SELF-PITY

For much of America's history people were proud of the difficulties they overcame. Popular stories told of those who started with nothing, or even with special disadvantages, and did the impossible to accomplish their goals and dreams. But most of that has changed. As I briefly mentioned in chapter one, in so much of popular culture people want to be seen as victims of forces they can't overcome.

For instance, some people want to be known for what they *can't do* in order to get sympathy along with privileges they have not earned. Others want us to feel sorry for them because of their situation in life. Still others, because of their sense of worthlessness, may even fabricate something to make another person look bad and make themselves look good. What such a person wants is pity, not respect.

When we indulge in self-pity, we are trying to give others a reason for treating us kindly, for thinking we have it rough. When we don't get the response we are looking for, we can play a game with ourselves, thinking that we really deserve better treatment—because we have somehow suffered. As biblical counseling professor Dr. John Street points out, people absorbed in self-pity are miserable—not because they think too lowly of themselves, but because they think too highly of themselves, being self-centered. A person wrapped up in self-pity has forgotten what God has done for him or her.

Self-pity is closely related to the anger and bitterness people may have when they don't get what they think they deserve. We can see it in the depressed housewife who tries to continually draw sympathy from her friends because of her terrible situation. She may be sick and tired of a husband who treats her rudely or who comes home and sits in front of the TV with a newspaper blocking his face. Frustrated because she is convinced that she deserves better from life, she nurses her resentment. Rather than focus on pleasing God by serving others, she wastes her days absorbed in self-pity.

Self-pity can be more subtle, as in the case of the person who feels slighted because she has fewer talents and spiritual gifts than, say, her friends. Or a person can simply be unsure of how she is gifted and resentful that her gifts aren't obvious and grand. A person may sink into self-pity because she is not physically attractive or lacks material possessions, or simply because things aren't going well. Possibly she got fired from a job or flunked a college course.

Living in self-pity has yet to create a better person, a more fruitful person, a godlier person. As long as we indulge in it, we cannot discover and develop all that God has planned for us. Eventually, we cannot help but feel that we are failures. We don't appreciate the way God has made us and the opportunities He is bringing our way, and we do not grow to fulfill the significant role He *has* planned for us. Also we can even lose sight of the great biblical truths about ourselves, those things that are true regardless of our response: We are forgiven, loved by Him, bound for heaven, and indwelt by the Holy Spirit.

Rather than struggling with a sense that God doesn't care about our situation or that we don't count for much, we need to be open to the idea that God may change our direction.

GOD'S REDIRECTION

By all accounts King David was one of the most gifted men in history. Not only was he a godly man, but he was a great king, a general, a theologian, and even a musician. Yet he prayed, "O Lord, my heart is not proud, nor my eyes haughty; *nor do I involve myself in great matters, or in things too difficult for me*" (Psalm 131:1). A secret to his success was a clear sense of his limits.

When it comes to gifts and talents, we are each "deficient" or "inadequate" compared to someone. It's most apparent when we venture too far outside our abilities. If you were fired from a job, for example, it may be that the work was outside your capabilities. If so, look for one that requires what you do well, and then work hard at it. If you failed a college class only because it was outside your abilities, don't give up on school. Try taking a different class that you can pass; get into a different major if you need to.

It's not always easy to know when something is outside your giftedness. If you are not succeeding at a ministry, it could be because of spiritual attacks or simply lack of training. Also, it is possible to get into the wrong ministry by mistaking the need for the call. Just because something needs to be done does not mean God is calling *you* to do it. If after a lot of effort over a long period of time, you are still miserable and unsuccessful, it's possible that you are in the wrong ministry. After prayer and counsel from others you may wish to seek a change.

Some people fear change from one ministry to another because it implies failure, as if the change must have come because they were not successful. Some, too, fear that several changes in rapid succession imply that they are irresponsible. One friend, through no fault of her own, had several changes in ministry within a few short years. She confided to me, "I appear as if I haven't got my act together." I was able to encourage her by reminding her of the apostle Paul's ministry. He never saw change as failure.

Paul had such a sense of security about his ministry because he simply worked at those things for which God had equipped him. He never fretted that he was not gifted in other areas. That freed him to focus all his attention on what he was gifted to do. Just as important was the fact that Paul carefully followed any leading he got from the Spirit. Remember when Paul was ministering in the church at Antioch? God didn't keep him there; He and Barnabas were supernaturally called to leave the church and go into missions (Acts 13:2).

During their first missionary journey, God didn't tell them which cities to go to; they just did what seemed best. But at one point they were trying unsuccessfully to go into southern Turkey. Paul then received a vision and concluded that God was calling them to set a course for Macedonia (Acts 16:10). Paul's sensitivity to what the Holy Spirit wanted to do in and through him prevented the sort of humiliating failures a lot of us experience.

Another source of Paul's seemingly inexhaustible strength was his confidence that " . . . God causes all things to work together for good to those who love God, to those who are called according to His purpose" (Romans 8:28). This confidence helps us see God's purposes where we might otherwise see only failure. David Brainerd, for example, dropped out of Yale for a while because of illness, but shortly after his return, he was expelled.[16] Had he not been forced to leave school, I doubt that he would have become a missionary to Native Americans.

Faith that God can work in any circumstance helps us focus on ultimate spiritual victory. It's a victory won in spite of and even through our inadequacies. In fact, consider this: Our true significance is grounded in our inadequacies. *Who we are positionally in Christ is founded upon God rescuing us from our sinfulness. Who we are practically in God's plan is founded on personal inadequacies that God divinely empowers.* What a liberating truth!

So the bottom line is, let's work to overcome an unbiblical view of ourselves. Instead of dwelling on our past hurts, failures, and inadequacies, let's strive for a deeper understanding of God, seek to know Him better, worship Him for who He is, and strive to understand the world He put together and how we fit into His divine plan. In company with Paul the apostle, let us proclaim, " . . . by the grace of God I am what I am" (1 Corinthians 15:10).

THINKING IT OVER

1. How can sin keep us feeling unworthy?
2. Have you ever perceived rejection where it did not exist? How can you avoid this problem in the future?
3. How might we deal with the memories that plague us?
4. Do you ever feel intimidated by the looks, the "smarts," or the personality of another? Read Jeremiah 31:3. What matters most? How should you regard the person who intimidates you? How might you reach out to this person?
5. Think of a time when you thought you had failed in some endeavor. Was it really failure, or was it God's redirection? Explain.

Five

THE THIRD BEATITUDE, HEAVENLY BEAUTY

*M*any historians agree that the most significant as well as the most dramatic event in the history of the American West took place on May 10, 1869. On that day the Union Pacific and the Central Pacific Railroads met and were joined at Promontory Point, a desolate spot in the Utah desert (forty miles northwest of Ogden).

A painting was made of this momentous event, and it hangs in the California capitol in Sacramento. The canvas depicts an assembly of about seventy respectable-looking citizens, all in formal attire, all witnessing the Central Pacific Railroad's President Leland Stanford drive a golden spike into the ground. Among those looking on are a number of important men of the day, including the Reverend John Todd and Theodore Judah, Central Pacific's founder.

As dramatic as the scene appears, the painting does not represent the facts. It is considered nothing more than a fanciful re-creation of American history. Comparing the painting with an actual photograph of the event reveals the unglamorous truth. In the photograph the two chief engineers are in the center of the scene, shaking hands while champagne bottles are brandished above their heads. Around them are not dignified citizens in their finery, but scruffy-looking workmen, uncouth and a bit boozy. Also on hand for the occasion were several prostitutes.

And who was in the painting but not in the photograph? The honorable Leland Stanford and the imported man of God, Rev. Todd. Also in the painting, though not at the actual event, were three other top executives of Central Pacific Railroad and the prestigious Theodore Judah, who had died six years earlier.[1]

Why the discrepancies between the photograph and the painting? Leland Stanford considered what really happened at the event to be most unfortunate. Therefore he commissioned painter Thomas Hill to clean up history—just a little.[2] And so he did.

Portraits often distort the truth. Look at the famous portrait of Napoleon on a mighty stallion rearing up. You are viewing a sheer fabrication. Napoleon ordered that the painting make him look heroic and royal. In the actual scene he was riding on a donkey and was a muddy mess.

Since the Fall, people have had a dual temptation to see themselves either as worms without benefit of God's grace and empowerment, or conversely as those who are a bit above others. Yet both views fail to represent us as we are, in proper relation to God; both fail to give God the credit due Him.

At first it would seem that too low an opinion and too high an opinion of ourselves could never connect in the same person. Yet when we view ourselves without Christ and cannot face our weakness and sinfulness, pride can tempt us to show a bold face—covering up the truth about ourselves and making people think we are better than we are. Thus we have a low view of ourselves and cover it up with a false front. Or we can genuinely be unaware of our weakness, sinfulness, and unworthiness apart from Christ, and thus have an opinion of ourselves that is higher than what we deserve. Either way manifests pride, and in both cases, we have an untruthful image of ourselves.

AN UNTRUTHFUL IMAGE

After years of faithful and courageous leadership in the Exodus and in the wilderness, Moses was not allowed to enter the promised land. Neither was his brother Aaron. Why?

One fateful day the people of Israel were very thirsty and began to complain and rebel (Numbers 20:2-5; Psalm 106:32-33). The Lord told Moses and Aaron to speak to a rock in front of the congregation, and it would yield water (Numbers 20:8). But rather than speak to the rock as God commanded, Moses struck it in anger twice with his rod. Then with Aaron at his side, Moses said to the people, "Shall *we* bring forth water for you out of this rock?" (Numbers 20:10).

Moses not only disobeyed God by not following His instructions, but he took credit for providing the water, when the glory belonged to God alone. Moses' disobedience, it seems, bore a touch of pride. And for a moment Moses' pride got the best of him as he portrayed himself in an untruthful way before the people. As a result, God was not honored before the people of Israel.

Commentators Keil and Delitzsch remark that Moses acted "as if it depended upon human exertion, and not upon the power of God alone."[3] Winterbotham, another commentator, tells us that Moses' statement that he and Aaron ("we") would bring water from the rock "showed how completely he was carried away." In reality, "he and Aaron were the merest instruments in the hand of God."[4] This mistake would haunt Moses the rest of his life.

Moses isn't the only person in the Bible who had this problem of a puffed-up view of himself. The disciples argued over which of them was the "greatest" (Mark 9:33-34). And the Corinthians boasted of their spiritual pedigree (1 Corinthians 1:12; 3:4, 22). Have we ever done this? We can be proud about our denomination or church, our education, or our spiritual gifts. We can even boast of our service to God, like Jehu, who said, "Come with me and see my zeal for the LORD" (2 Kings 10:16).

Paul challenged the Corinthians who were strutting their stuff: "What do you have that you did not receive? And if you did receive it, why do you boast as though you did not?" (1 Corinthians 4:7 NIV). Paul tells the spiritually superior that "if anyone thinks he is something when he is nothing, he deceives himself" (Galatians 6:3 NIV).

The lesson I have been learning while writing this chapter is that there is something pitifully self-serving about seeking respect and honor for myself. Also I've come to realize that success can be a very dangerous thing. If we don't handle it carefully, we can become puffed up, and God will limit or end our opportunities for service, just as He did with Moses and his brother Aaron. The Lord warns us that He "opposes the proud" (1 Peter 5:5; cf. Proverbs 3:34; James 4:6). If you are proud, God will block you, hinder you, oppose you. How would you like to have God as your opponent?

We must face pride as an enemy within us and defeat it. Unlike many other sins, it can threaten us more when we are spiritually the most successful, when our ministry is expanding, when God is doing great things in our lives. It can torment us when we are young and ambitious; it can test us when we are old and able to look back on a long record of victories. Most of all, at any age it can cause us to stumble and fall (Jeremiah 50:32).

Pride short-circuits the Holy Spirit, probably because God will not give His glory to another (Isaiah 42:8). He will not work in such a way that the credit for what He alone can do goes to someone else. So we shouldn't expect to have the Spirit's power and thus to have a significant part in God's work if we are not truly humble.

On a more positive note, God "gives grace to the humble" (1 Peter 5:5 NIV). In other words, God bestows His favor upon the humble, and they find acceptance in His sight.[5] Would you rather have God as your helper or as your opponent? That all depends on whether you trust Him or yourself, whether you put yourself above others or take a servant's place, whether you try to fool people or let them know the real you—weaknesses and all.

Needless to say, when it comes to our sense of who we are and our significance in life, we want to avoid pride at all costs. How do we avoid it and get a right perspective on ourselves?

GETTING THE RIGHT PERSPECTIVE

The road that leads away from pride and toward humility is the road to the throne room of God. When we are focused on ourselves, pride is a very real possibility. We can remember our accomplishments and conveniently forget our failures. We can inwardly compare our strengths with other people's weaknesses. We can try to display our strengths while hiding our weaknesses from others. But none of these things can happen in the dazzling light of God's presence.

Even the flickering light of our lives—our wisdom, strength, and righteousness—seems bright in a dark room. But in the presence of God our light pales like a candle in the noon sun. God's infinite wisdom, power, and holiness dwarf ours and put everything in proper perspective. When I compare myself to God, I bring myself down to size.

Whenever Scripture gives us the smallest glimpse of His presence, the scene is always overwhelming. The Lord is surrounded by His holy angels; elders sit clothed in white garments with golden crowns on their heads. And from the throne proceed flashes of lightning and peals of thunder. Imagine seeing seven lamps of fire burning before the throne—the seven Spirits of God (Revelation 4:5-6; 7:11). All around Him are living creatures, thousands and thousands of ministering spirits, and ten thousand times ten thousand angels standing before Him (5:11).

God's awesome majesty rises before me, powerfully and impressively, revealing how little I am, how altogether unholy I am, especially when I consider that the seraphim hide their faces before His indescribable glory.

If we could observe such a sight this moment, each one of us would see ourselves as smaller and more sinful than we could grasp. But God does not leave us there. He accepts and clothes us in His own righteousness (2 Corinthians 5:21). He affirms the significance we have as His children, which is a birthright that cannot be taken away. And someday He will affirm the importance we have had in the outworking of His plan. We will each appear at the judgment seat (2 Corinthians 5:10) where every believer's praise will come from God (1 Corinthians 4:5). And as the twenty-four elders testify by throwing their crowns at the Lord's feet (Revelation 4:10), all that we have earned ultimately came from God, and the glory for it is His (Isaiah 42:8). This is true humility, which is easiest to attain when we have two attitudes—poverty of spirit and mourning for our sin.

Consider the beatitudes, that centerpiece of the eloquent and powerful Sermon on the Mount. Those simple blessings build upon one another. The first two beatitudes appear sad and negative—but for good reason.

The Lord first spoke of the "poor in spirit" (Matthew 5:3). These people are sorrowful because they see their emptiness and recognize their deficiencies. They "mourn" (Matthew 5:4) because, unlike others, they have gained insight into how far they fall short. We can't help but be deeply stirred when we come to see our pride and where we are in relation to what we could be.

Fortunately, we do not need to stay sorrowful because to do so would be to stay wrapped up in ourselves; God wants us to get beyond thinking about self. And we can, by going to the third beatitude, which gives us something very positive to work on—a humility born of meekness (Matthew 5:5). This humility, according to theologian H. H. Esser, "is to know how lowly we really are before God."[6]

Humility requires nothing more than accuracy. A humble woman is one who has a true view of herself. Paul admonished the church, "I say to everyone among you not to think more highly of himself than he ought to think; but to think so as to have *sound judgment*" (Romans 12:3, italics mine).

BEING TRUTHFUL ABOUT OURSELVES

The Bible chronicles the lives of many people of integrity, and many of them were quite humble. Nehemiah was such a man. God empowered him in a very special way. Nehemiah did not alter or embellish the events of his life, and without any pride he includes the good deeds he performed. For example, he records how, during his entire twelve years as governor, he did not accept any salary or allowance from the impoverished people, unlike former governors (Nehemiah 5:14-15, 18). He worked hard on the city wall and did not take advantage of opportunities to make money off the desperate citizens (v. 16). Furthermore, he spent his own money to supply food for 150 families (vv. 17-18).

Why is it that Nehemiah didn't hesitate to record his good deeds? Because he never lost sight of his dependence on God (2:12; 7:5), his own weaknesses and sins (1:6), and the fact that he owed all success to God, whose glory (6:16) and pleasure he worked tirelessly to achieve.

Nehemiah wasn't the only one to speak humbly yet realistically about his life. Paul was simply telling the truth when he said that he "labored even more than all of them" for the Gospel. But he knew the source of his power, adding, "yet not I, but the grace of God with me" (1 Corinthians 15:10). He was also frank about the "surpassing greatness of the revelations" God had given him; yet he added that God had to give him a thorn in the flesh to keep him from exalting himself over others (2 Corinthians 12:7).

Jesus' mother, Mary, in her encounter with God, shows us how to grow in genuine humility. Her example is an unnoticed part of Luke's account of the greatest story ever told. We all know the account by heart: An angel appears to Mary and tells her she is going to have a son. He wasn't going to be any ordinary child for: "He will be great and will be called the Son of the Most High; and the Lord God will give Him the throne of His father David; and He will reign over the house of Jacob forever, and His kingdom will have no end" (Luke 1:32).

What a message! Mary has just been told she is going to be the mother of the Son of God. Does she struggle with a sense of pride? Not at all. Her response in a conversation with her cousin Elizabeth was, "My soul exalts the Lord, and my spirit has rejoiced in God my Savior" (Luke 1:46-47).

The angel Gabriel himself announces that Mary has found favor with God (Luke 1:30), who will use her to accomplish one of the most remarkable events of history. Yet in humility Mary doesn't rejoice over what it will do for her; God is the source of her joy (Luke 1:47). She never considers herself to be above other people. Rather she humbly recognizes God as *her Savior.*

After voicing her delight, Mary notes that God is mindful of her humble state (Luke 1:48). She neither overvalues nor undervalues herself. She doesn't say that God made the right choice, nor does she say that He made a mistake. She doesn't ask God to get someone else. To have any of these responses would amount to questioning God's wisdom. Though amazed, Mary doesn't blink an eye or say, "I can't do it." She does not say, "God can't do it." Why? Because her thoughts are heavenward. She knows her God is big enough to do such a monumental thing through a person such as her. She graciously accepts God's high honor because she knows that God accepts her. What simple humility!

Though Mary recognizes that "from this time on all generations will count me blessed" (Luke 1:48), she doesn't expect people to honor her or give her homage. Nor does she expect a prominent place in society. Instead she extols the Lord, speaking of His power, holiness, mercy, providential care for the needy, and faithfulness (Luke 1:49-55).

Obviously Mary went on to be used of God, bearing Jesus and raising Him. Do you think she would have been effective had she been absorbed in herself, her inadequacies, or painful memories? Could she have accomplished God's will if she had been proud and independent from Him? I doubt it.

Contrary to popular opinion today, a proper view of ourselves is not nurtured by becoming absorbed in ourselves, trying constantly to think better thoughts about ourselves. And contrary to some Christian opinions, humility (which, as we have seen, has a lot to do with a proper view of ourselves) is not developed by becoming absorbed in our inadequacies. As William Temple explains: "Humility does not mean thinking less of yourself than of other people, nor does it mean having a low opinion of your own gifts. It means freedom from thinking about yourself one way or the other at all. . . . The humility which consists in being a great deal occupied about yourself, and saying you are of little worth, is not Christian humility. It is one form of self-occupation and a very poor and futile one at that."[7]

Look at our greatest example of humility, Jesus Christ. He didn't just tell us to be humble; His life showed us how. And in so doing, He showed us the proper attitude toward ourselves: He spent little time thinking about Himself. He was in the business of fellowshipping with the Father and ministering to others (Matthew 20:28). He pitied those He came to save and met their great needs. He supplied their physical necessities, relieved their pain, and consoled their grieving hearts. Most of all, He met their deepest spiritual needs. He aroused the sinful, showing them the condition of their souls. He brought pardon to the penitent, hope to the downcast, and salvation to all willing to receive it. To those who sought wisdom, He freely gave. To those crying for His mercy, He reached out with His love. And to all who would be His children, He gave His Holy Spirit to enable us to live as He did.

Humility requires that, like the Savior, we focus on our relationship with the Father and the needs of others. It also requires that we never forget God's mercy and forgiveness, and that it is to Him that we owe our lives.

Humility reminds us that our lives are grounded in and sustained by God. Therefore we can resist pride and all the while accurately assess our abilities and maturity because we do so in the light of God's glory and grace.

Humility is valued in heaven, but also here on earth as we, like Mary, offer praise to God for using us in His loving and significant plan.

And so may we keep the third beatitude active in our hearts, displaying heavenly beauty, for truly, "Happy are those who are humble; they will receive what God has promised!" (Matthew 5:5 TEV).

> *She that is down need fear no fall;*
> *She that is low no pride;*
> *She that is humble ever shall*
> *Have God to be her Guide.*[8]

THINKING IT OVER

1. What are characteristics of pride?
2. How can pride result from an unbiblical view of ourselves?
3. How does William Temple's idea of humility differ from the modern view?
4. What things, good and bad, would you include in an honest appraisal of yourself?
5. What changes would you need to make in order to focus on God instead of on yourself?

Six

TRUE DIGNITY, OUR BIRTHRIGHT

Court papers don't do justice to Sarah Johnson's life. They record only that she was born on the eastern shore of Maryland in 1742 and died in 1845. That's it. But there was so much more to Sarah's life. She endured nearly 104 years in the shadow of hatred and bigotry over the color of her skin.

Imagine yourself as a slave, as someone's "property," and regarded as nothing more than a "savage." Imagine your husband[1] and children being sold off like cattle. Imagine that the only keepsake you have of your baby are memories of his cries for you.

Imagine, too, prejudice breeding a conspiracy, a conspiracy to create public distrust in some good thing you are trying to accomplish. A group of sympathetic white women open a school for black women who are eager to learn. A mob of whites protest outside the school doors, demanding that it be shut down. Frustrated that they can't do anything about it legally, white men spread false rumors that the black people are going to burn down the city and massacre white colonists. Then see gullible white people respond by further restricting black social mobility.

Be puzzled as to why the colonists would give you, as a slave, a biblical name, but then exclude you from church membership and even discourage you from coming to Christ. Be stunned over the fact that before African women were imported to America, adultery and rape were legally punishable by death. After the African woman arrived, the law became soft. In 1640, for instance, a white man raped a woman slave. The man had to make a public apology while his victim received a whipping.[2]

Such treatment of the black community could have made Sarah Johnson bitter; yet she refused this attitude. She understood that she was a new creation (2 Corinthians 5:17). In this renewed state God adorned Sarah with a heavenly grace and beauty that allowed her to rise above the temptations presented by her potentially debasing situation. She looked at herself and her relationship with God, the giver of worth. She said, "I am sinful . . . but my Redeemer is all righteous, in myself I am lost, but in Him I am safe. I pray that I may be faithful to the end and that my Saviour may be my portion forever."[3]

Although dead now for more than 150 years, Sarah speaks so clearly to us today. She had a deep grasp of her true worth in the eyes of God—her true significance. Do you?

YOU ARE WORTH EVERYTHING!

King David was so in awe of mankind as the crown of God's creation that he asked God, "What is man that You take thought of him, and the son of man that You care for him?" (Psalm 8:4). Haven't we ourselves wondered this, too?

I find it hard to believe, and most likely you do also, that even before we were created, we were known by God (Jeremiah 1:5). He knows the exact number of hairs on our heads (Matthew 10:30). How special we are to Him! He considers us of such value that He calls us by name (John 10:3; Exodus 33:12).

Just as incomprehensible is the fact that God has given us something of His likeness (Genesis 1:26-27). That likeness comes with "glory and majesty" (Psalm 8:5) and includes the ability to think morally and spiritually. Because of that likeness we can be attracted to the things of God.

Obviously our origin as humans was no an accident, and we weren't derived from some knuckle-dragging ape. We were created by one who has eternal value, by one who stamped His own image on each one of us.

How marvelous the creation story is! It's not just about mankind coming from dust (miraculous though that is); it's about God creating our entire race, which includes each of us as individuals, to have great worth.

Sad to say, since being thrown out of the Garden of Eden, man and woman are mere shadows of that first unfallen pair. As theologian John Calvin (1509-1664) pointed out: "Even though we grant that God's image was not totally annihilated and destroyed in him [man], yet it was so corrupted [by sin] that whatever remains is frightful deformity."[4] However, we still bear something of the image of God. We still have our God-given capacities, though unfortunately people are prone to use them in sinful and disobedient ways.[5]

So here we have it—everyone is created in the image of God. The bag lady picking up cans as she pushes her belongings in a cart bears God's image. The drug addict who turns to prostitution to feed her habit bears God's image. Even the most corrupt dictator demanding a bribe from relief agencies that are trying to feed his starving people is made in God's image.

Because we were made in the image of God, our worth can't be taken away—only distorted. Distorted though it is, it is crucially important that we recognize that it is there and respect the Creator who put it there. When societies forget this crucial point, the results can be disastrous, as much of modern history has shown us.

THE EVE OF DESTRUCTION

My daughter Michelle is currently memorizing the Declaration of Independence. While she struggles with its length, I try to encourage her because of what the document means to every American.

The Declaration says that the United States was built on the idea that "all men are created equal" and that they "are endowed by their Creator with certain unalienable rights." The crucial idea is that God, not the state, granted those rights; therefore, the state can only protect them and can never legitimately take them away.

I wish I could tell Michelle that these rights will always remain, and yet I honestly wonder if they will. Before our very eyes some of these rights have deteriorated because our society's view of human beings is becoming debased.

Look at other nations in modern history, including Russia, Germany, and China. When the concept that mankind bears the image of God is ignored, things go terribly wrong. Even in the United States the Christian foundations have been crumbling, which has led to disaster.

So what has eroded the view of human beings as fashioned in the image of God? First, faith in the Creator eroded. During the Victorian age many Christians could see this trend unfold, beginning with novels of the period. One nineteenth-century Bible commentator said of those novelists that they "present model characters in social life on the basis of non-theism [no belief in God], and which depict it as a virtue to be without any fear of God whatsoever."[6]

Second, in the nineteenth century, the concept of man as made in the image of God eroded as he came to be viewed as merely a product of evolution—a higher animal.

It can be no coincidence, then, that the twentieth century saw more atrocities against humanity than any other century, perhaps more than all others combined. These brutalities came at the hands of governments that saw no inherent dignity in people and had no sense that the image of God in man ought to be respected. Hitler killed six million Jews and another six million people who were judged to be genetically inferior, including Gypsies and mentally handicapped people. Stalin killed over twenty million of his own people, whom he regarded as mere creatures of the state. Under Mao, too, millions died—we may never know how many. Stalin and Mao were guided by Karl Marx's atheistic philosophy that replaced God with the state.

And now all over the world there are millions of abortions each year. These deaths are not even for some high-sounding cause such as "genetic purity" or a Communist "workers' paradise." Infanticide is practiced for mere personal convenience and the maintenance of the mother's lifestyle. Just over the horizon, too, looms euthanasia, tempting society with an easy solution to the problem of the aging population.

Yes, the twentieth century was one long, tragic story, and if the human race continues to deny that mankind is made in the image of God, the twenty-first century promises to be no better. The psalmist warned, "Transgression speaks to the ungodly within his heart; there is no fear of God before his eyes. . . . He has ceased to be wise and to do good" (Psalm 36:1, 3).

Depressing as all of that is, look at what sin has done to you and me. Though we are all made in the image of God and should treat each other that way, sin has given us a negative value. If the *Mona Lisa* were slashed by a vandal, it would no longer be priceless. A fortune would be required to restore it. In the same way, sin has defaced the image of God in us, and we are worthy of wrath. In spite of the destruction caused by the darkest depravity, God reached out to us with divine love.

DIVINE LOVE

Consider that we are so loved by the Father that He gave us His Son (John 3:16); we are so loved by the Son that He left paradise to give us life (1 Thessalonians 5:10); we are so loved by the Father and the Son that we have been given the Spirit to dwell in us, "that we may know the things freely given to us by God, which things we also speak, not in words taught by human wisdom, but in those taught by the Spirit" (1 Corinthians 2:12-13). What love!

Divine love has *made* us worth more than other creatures (sparrows—Matthew 10:28-31) and has given us the greatest value (Matthew 16:26). Because of this great love and mercy, we are renewed in the image of God and given true dignity to the fullest.

Try to comprehend your value. You are completely forgiven (Ephesians 1:7; Romans 8:1); you have God's complete love and acceptance (Jeremiah 31:3). You have been personally chosen (Isaiah 41:9); you are an object of His grace (Ephesians 1:4, 6); you have been blessed with every spiritual blessing (Ephesians 1:3); you have become His heir (Ephesians 1:11); you can rest in His vigilant protection (Isaiah 9:10); you are part of God's great plan (Ephesians 1:9).

Because Sarah Johnson understood these things, not one of the white people who challenged her worth could change her sense of who she really was. They could not take away her dignity. You see, dignity allows us to get beyond ourselves and live in a significant way. Without it, I doubt that our lives could ever have the impact we desire. Let's look at dignity, first by exposing its counterfeit.

FALSE DIGNITY

A year before I gave my life to Christ, I was good friends with a fellow college student whom we'll call Farid. He was a Muslim and a member of a royal family in the Arab world. While Farid and I were from completely different worlds, we seemed to "click" and dated often. One day I called Farid and told him to meet me at one of the local restaurants.

The moment we met, Farid said, "So, Donna, would you like to go to dinner and a movie tonight?"

"Thanks, but, no, I can't." I further explained, "I've become a Christian."

I then began to tell Farid all about my newfound faith in Jesus Christ. I was so excited that I rambled on about God's promises of forgiveness, about how undeserving I was to receive it, and about everlasting life in heaven. I remember saying emphatically to Farid that we must repent of our sins, walk away from a sinful life, and follow Christ as our Lord and Master, walking in His ways.

Farid, taken aback, began to get defensive. He declared that he was not a sinful person but a rather nice one.

I explained as best I could that everyone has sinned (Romans 3:23). I told him that sin entails even those things that people think of as unimportant, such as losing our temper, gossiping, and having wrong thoughts.

Farid was beginning to look quite uneasy. So changing the subject—but only slightly in order to pursue a better angle—I said with a smile, "Farid, like you, I now belong to a royal family. I am now a child of the King of heaven! And I don't think any human being can ever be as rich as I am at this moment!"

Then with excitement I told him that he could have the same riches in Jesus Christ that I had. Along with being saved from the torment of hell, he could be a part of real royalty. He, too, would be called a child of God (John 1:12) or, if he preferred, an ambassador of Christ (2 Corinthians 5:20).

I went on to tell Farid that the Old and New Testaments point the way to Jesus Christ and that even in his religion Muslims believe that Christ was a great prophet. Christ, I continued, is the only way for us to get to heaven (John 14:6) and to have a truly meaningful life here as we live for Him.

For a while Farid politely listened, but finally in a condescending tone he said, "Donna, Donna, Donna, I'm already rich! I have everything I could possibly ever want. This Jesus of yours doesn't even have the prestige *I* have in my homeland."

Farid then started laughing, and in a high-pitched tone with his Arabic accent, declared, "If I were to tell others that I have accepted this Christ of yours and that I have become some sort of ambassador for Him, I would become a laughingstock, stripped of my reputation, robbed of my royalty, and treated worse than a 'common' man!" Then in a nervous tone Farid added, "No thanks, Donna. I have my dignity to think about."

Little did Farid realize that I was offering him true dignity. It was a dignity that reflects not earthly glory but God's own glory. As our conversation continued, I could see that Farid simply couldn't get beyond the fact that he would look foolish should he believe in Christ. Saddened by this, I finally got up from the table. Farid grasped my hand as if pleading for me to sit back down.

Looking into his eyes, I said, "Farid, you are a dear friend. I want you to have what I have, but first you must see how miserably poor you really are. Your prestige, your money, your family will never be able to fill your soul. Only Christ can."

Grabbing for the check, I said, "It's on me." I gave Farid a hug and told him, "I hope I see you one day in heaven."

After walking out of the restaurant, I could see Farid through the windows, still sitting at the booth with a blank stare on his face. Oh, he still appeared to have his "dignity" intact as he sat upright, well dressed, with an air of earthly royalty about him. And yet I never saw a lonelier, more lost, sadder-looking man.

Looking back, I realize that I could have reminded him of Saladin, who through great conquests became the sultan over Egypt and Syria during the Middle Ages. Wanting more to conquer, he seized numerous towns and retook Jerusalem from the Crusaders. But his great prestige has faded with time, and someday it will be no more. So it will be for all glory derived from earthly nobility, reputation, and success. But God offers us a dignity that will never fade because it is from God Himself.

Paul is an example of one who gave up earthly accomplishments and recognized the value of what is in Christ. He tells his audience that if anyone could have confidence in the flesh, he could. Beginning with his Jewish roots, He said he was circumcised the eighth day, showing that he was a pure Jew and not a proselyte.

He was of the nation of Israel. With regard to God's plan he was in a special ethnic group.

He was of the tribe of Benjamin, which had distinguished leaders.

He was a Hebrew of Hebrews, therefore a pure Hebrew.

He was at the very center of religious Judaism, being "as to the Law, a Pharisee."

Showing his zeal, he added that he was a persecutor of the church. All this was no mere show because he was "as to the righteousness which is in the Law, found blameless" (Philippians 3:5-6).

Paul certainly had an ethnic and religious pedigree. But he came to discount any standing it gave him. He said, "Whatever things were gain to me, those things I have counted as loss for the sake of Christ" (Philippians 3:7). Paul gladly gave up everything he had that in his world could be classified as significant. He gave it up in order to identify with Christ. Did he suffer some sort of identity crisis? Was he depressed and confused now that he was a nobody among the people who once considered him a somebody? No, he saw clearly that true dignity is not grounded in externals nor in the things of this life. True dignity is a birthright, and we grow into it as we mature in Christ.

Unfortunately, many Christians aren't living up to their spiritual dignity. It's not because they don't want to, but because something is holding them back.

WHAT'S HOLDING YOU BACK?

Early yesterday morning while ironing some clothes, I saw on television a short but interesting conversation between Fox News commentator Bill O'Reilly and author Dr. Vikki Ashley. Ashley recently wrote a book with the questionable title *How to Be a Bitch with Style*. Dr. Ashley told O'Reilly that her book is about women who are in total control. She tells how the rest of us women can follow their example. Some of the many role models she offers are Janet Reno, Hillary Clinton, Whoopi Goldberg, and Madonna.

O'Reilly admitted to Dr. Ashley that most of the women in her book aren't people he respects. He said that they are "drawn into themselves, self-assured, self-centered; having an 'I don't care who you are'" attitude. It seemed, he said, that the driving force of the book is hostility.

Dr. Ashley quickly excused the women, saying that many of them have been hurt in life, but they overcame it and determined never to be hurt again. You can do that, she said, by "being yourself and not needing anyone else."

To Dr. Ashley I would say that while there's nothing wrong with being yourself, there is something very wrong with adopting an "I don't care attitude" in order to protect yourself from being hurt. Let's face it, in a world full of sinners we all get hurt. And as long as we interact with people, we are going to get hurt. To build a wall that no one can penetrate is not the answer.

To be fair to Dr. Ashley, I haven't read her book (and, frankly, I don't think I ever will. I just can't get myself to buy a book with such an obnoxious title). But O'Reilly summed it up when he said that the one thing missing entirely from her book was dignity.[7]

Bravo, O'Reilly! But still, I would guess that even the dignity O'Reilly has in mind is but a shadow of the real thing. Bernard of Clairvaux said it well, "We are, but by His dignifying us, not by our own dignity."[8]

You and I have access to the greatest dignity possible because we are one with Jesus Christ (1 Corinthians 6:17). When we surrender our lives to Him, He becomes ours, and we become His. So complete is that identification that we have no spiritual identity apart from Christ. Paul confirms this when he said, "For to me to live is Christ" (Philippians 1:21 NIV). He also says, "It is no longer I who live, but Christ lives in me" (Galatians 2:20).

Because Christ lives in us, we don't need to be self-protective regarding emotional wounds from the past. We do not need to be self-centered, focusing on the problems in our life. Furthermore, we can refuse to be aggressive, hostile, and bitter toward others. These things definitely hold us back from living up to our true dignity. The dignity found in Christ allows us to live out a significant life that is not controlled by our emotions, our pain, or our flesh. Rather it is controlled by God.

CONTROLLED BY GOD

My friend Melanie has been through a nightmarish trial. She had been married for over fifteen years to Dirk, a police officer. In that marriage they were blessed with three wonderful children, whom they raised together in what she regarded as a Christian home.

All seemed well until Dirk met another woman. Shortly thereafter he left Melanie. That would be heartache enough, but Dirk and his new wife (with the assistance of a fellow officer) drummed up false allegations of child abuse against Melanie in order to take the children away from her and avoid paying child support.

Dirk then filed what could be called a false police report and showed it to the principal of the school where Melanie had recently gotten a job. (Dirk had stopped financially supporting Melanie as an at-home mom.) As a result, Melanie lost her job as a school nurse, lost the rights to her two sons, and faced the prospect of owing thousands of dollars in what looked like a new legal fight over her daughter. Though Melanie is innocent of the charges against her, she never resorted to being a "b—— with style." Rather she demonstrated the dignity of a godly life.

While Dirk tried every way possible to prove Melanie to be an unfit mother, she kept quiet. She firmly believed that as God's child, "no weapon that is formed against you will prosper; and every tongue that accuses you in judgment you will condemn" (Isaiah 54:17). She determined that no matter what others did to her, no matter how false the accusations or how much damage was done to her life and her children, she was going to respond with what is proper in the sight of God.

One day in court, for instance, Melanie was accused of threatening the welfare of the children by being part of a cult. That charge hurt deeply, especially because her husband had once professed Christ, and they had gone to church together. Yet she took the dignified way and determined not to be quarrelsome but to "be kind to all, able to teach, patient when wronged, with gentleness correcting those who are in opposition, if perhaps God may grant them repentance leading to the knowledge of the truth, and they may come to their senses" (2 Timothy 2:24-26).

I personally have learned so much from Melanie. She has stayed on course for over seven difficult years, never stooping to retaliate as she watched everything of earthly value dissolve. Melanie truly holds to Shakespeare's description of the good heart that "shines bright and never changes, but keeps his course truly."[9]

Are we holding our course regardless of what others may do to us, say about us, think about us? We are well on the way if we are praying for and forgiving those who have hurt us (Luke 23:34). Our goal must be that they "may know that the LORD is God; there is no one else" (1 Kings 8:60). The person with true dignity seeks to win others to Christ, trusting God for the outcome in every situation.

The person with dignity has a sense of calm, regardless of circumstances. He or she resists the temptation to run around without direction, concerned, worried, and irritated. This person rests upon the sovereignty of God.

Think how remarkable the truly dignified life is—it is a life that doesn't know the word *insignificant*. Sarah Johnson never felt insignificant in spite of being a slave and facing extreme prejudice. And Melanie never yielded to feelings of insignificance after her husband's false accusations and rejection.

Those women were unaffected by what others thought of them because they understood their own position before God and were willing to manifest it in the way they lived. A large part of grasping our position in Christ is comprehending how secure we are in it.

Remember Paul's words? He said, "If God is for us, who is against us?" (Romans 8:31). Paul was saying that for someone—such as an ex-spouse, a social worker, a gossiper, or a coworker—to spiritually vanquish us, he or she would have to be able to overcome God. He is for us, and no one can snatch us out of His hand (John 10:28-29). Do you know any person who can overcome God? Is there anyone in the universe who can revoke our "no-condemnation" status? Is anyone stronger or purer than God, with a higher standard than His?[10] The next time you go through a difficult time with someone, remember that dignity is your birthright.

True dignity makes for a stark contrast between those who have it and those who don't. Consider, for example, Scripture's starkest contrasts—Christ and Paul versus Caesar and Festus. Christ and Paul were both content to live humbly, to be thought weak, and to shun flashiness and any public relations orientation. They simply lived the spiritually dignified life that focused on giving glory to God.

Festus and Caesar were their opposites. These rulers maneuvered themselves politically to the top of their bureaucratic world. They used their power to bring trembling men to their knees and sentence them to death. Yes, status and power were their means to reach their ends and to gain the praises of man. They filled their courts with unbounded luxuries and lusts, and their earthly glory was to their shame. Now, centuries later, which of these people appear to have led more dignified and significant lives?

Christians and non-Christians alike have heard of Paul the apostle, but who is Festus? Though Caesar has been known throughout the ages, Jesus Christ has been far better known. Christ is the most prominent theme of art and literature. By contrast, very little is said of Caesar outside of historical works on that period.

Think of what all this means for you. It is not the person who attains a high position that gains lasting dignity; rather it is the godly person who seeks to glorify the Lord each day. Those who will reign with Him are the ones who bear witness for Christ and truth, who are willing to be despised, as was their Master, and who sacrifice earthly things of little value to gain a heavenly reward that will never fade. Christ's name is branded on their souls. His imprint is on their every step. Be encouraged.

We may be poor in earthly possessions, but we have inherited the treasures of heaven.

We may be marred with suffering, but we have a firm hope.

We may be "low class," but we have been fashioned with wisdom.

We may be impaired, but we have been given His holiness.

We may be foolish, but we have been crowned as wise.

We may be simple, but we have been adorned with heavenly grace and beauty.

We may be despised, but we have been blessed with dignity and worth.

And, while these things are important to consider, we don't want to stop here. *We are not simply significant for who we are now, but we are important for who we will become.*

WHO WE WILL BECOME

Modern liberal theologian Jurgen Moltmann commented that "Christ's resurrection is the beginning and promise of that which is yet to come."[11] While I thought I would never agree with a liberal on anything, I must say Moltmann is right about the future. He makes the point from his book *Theology of Hope* that our lives gain their significance and meaning not just from the past (what has gone before or who we have been), but from the future—what we will be.[12]

So in a sense the Christian is like a prince who is still a child. His significance is not so much in who he is currently, but in who he will become—the king. Like that prince, we wait and long for what we will become, since this life is but a shadow of what exists in heaven. The present is shaped by what we shall be in the future.

Can you even imagine what such a future will be like, knowing that our true identity has yet to be fully revealed? Bunyan reminds us that at the moment of our unveiling, "we shall be with Seraphims and Cherubims, Creatures that will dazzle your eyes to look on them: there also you shall meet with thousands, and ten thousands that have gone before us to that place; none of them are hurtful, but loving and holy, everyone walking in the sight of God, and *standing in His presence with acceptance forever.*"[13]

It is then that we will *fully know* what God has given us—true dignity and worth. What could be more significant?

THINKING IT OVER

1. What is the difference between the dignity unbelievers have and the dignity God offers? In what ways do people attempt to build a false sense of dignity? How should we build a true sense of dignity?
2. How can a sense of your true spiritual dignity help you in your current circumstances? In a recent difficulty you have experienced?
3. What are some of the ways God has shown that you are loved, valued, and very significant in His eyes?

PART THREE

Living Out Our Significance

Most of us have some heroes of the faith whom we admire. We look at their lives and think that we could never attain their level of significance either in this world or in God's kingdom to come. While we may realize that God loves us equally and that we all have the same position in Christ, we also know that some people have had an especially significant part in advancing God's plan here on earth. Yet, as I'm discovering, we, too, can attain the same level of practical significance by fulfilling our own unique, God-given potential.

From the beginning, God has taken what seem to be ordinary men and women and used them in extraordinary ways. They may have done very different things, using diverse gifts in various places on the globe, but it is likely that their lives had something in common. They had certain character qualities undergirding the use of their gifts and opportunities. Let's explore those qualities and how they contribute to a significant life.

Seven

FAITHFULNESS—IN THE MANY FACETS OF LIFE

Today, as on any other day, a child will be born in India. She will be expected all the days of her life to follow Indian customs faithfully, such as venerating cows and seeking favor with one or more Hindu gods.

Another child will be born in Arabia. From her earliest days she will be expected to revere Allah through the prophet Mohammed. She will faithfully repeat her prayers and verses from the Koran. And she will be expected some time in her life to make a pilgrimage to Mecca.

Another child will be born today, this time in Thailand. She will be taught to honor statues of Buddha in the temple and bring offerings of food, drink, flowers, candles, incense, or elephant figures (legendary symbol of Buddha) to spirit shrines.

It is expected that each child born around the world will form friendships and opinions and learn a code of conduct based upon the single fact that he or she was born to parents of a certain race, tribe, religion, or status. And each is required to live faithfully according to the customs and beliefs of his or her family.

Now let me tell you about one more child who will be born today. Her world is completely different from all the rest. It won't matter whether she is in India or Arabia, China or Tibet, or even of royal descent. Regardless of the nation, this child is "born again" (John 3:3). The twice-born child will not become captive to a religious system of mere traditions enforced by cultural and religious taboos. She is born into something much higher, an eternal family with a personal God.

Unlike most devotees of religions around the world, whose strivings are aimed at earning the favor of their gods, her devotion is a loving response to the God of heaven who loves her. She knows He is forever faithful to her—even when she fails (2 Timothy 2:13). Imagine—even if we are unfaithful, God still is faithful to us. As well, we shall forever be significant in His sight—regardless of what we do. How is that so? Through what Christ has done on our behalf. We are loved, we are forgiven, we were chosen before the foundation of the world (Ephesians 1:4). Nothing will ever change that. *In Christ we are significant.*

Now, with that said, do we play a significant part in the outworking of God's plan? It all depends.

LIVING SO IT COUNTS

Prior to becoming a Christian, I lived right on the beach and thought, *This is the life!* Between my classes at the local college, after school, after work, and even while jogging, I was on the beach. I simply loved having my feet buried in the warm sand, my eyes staring out toward the endless sea, and my lungs breathing in the misty salt air. During those years of young adulthood, I cared about many things, but I cared most of all about "life on the beach."

When I became a Christian, things began to change. While I will always enjoy the beach, I found that I could no longer spend so much time being a beach bum. Why? Because I wanted my life to count for something. I'm sure that's your desire, too. Otherwise you wouldn't be reading this book.

Since then I've learned to evaluate my life on a continual basis to see what, if anything, is wasting my time and keeping me from reaching my goals. I check myself: Am I being a couch potato? Am I chitchatting hours away on the telephone? Am I spending needless time at the mall? Or am I being active but without a goal or plan so that I'm wearing myself out and getting nowhere?

Sometimes feeling convicted by the answers to these sorts of questions, I have come to see that a significant life doesn't come out of thin air. It is achieved, as with all great men and women of the faith, when we are faithful.

Consider these faithful individuals in Scripture. Onesimus, the trusted companion of Paul, and Tychicus, both of whom were called beloved and faithful brothers, were sent to minister personally to the Colossian church (Ephesians 6:21; Colossians 4:7-9). Luke, as Paul's faithful comrade, had a part in establishing the church and writing the

New Testament. Epaphras was able to significantly help the Colossian church (Colossians 4:12-13), and Timothy ministered to Christians in a number of regions (1 Corinthians 4:17; 1 Timothy 1:3; cf., 1 and 2 Timothy, Titus). In part because of her obedience—a hallmark of the faithful person—Mary was given the significant role of being the mother of Christ. In the Old Testament Abigail was faithful to her very difficult husband, and upon his death the door opened for her to marry King David (1 Samuel 25:1-42; 2 Samuel 3:3).

In the Bible faithfulness constantly characterizes those who are given the chance to serve God in significant ways. This is true of everyone from Dorcas, who faithfully performed deeds of kindness and charity (Acts 9:36), to Priscilla who, with her husband Aquila, "risked their own necks" and were regarded by Paul as "fellow workers in Christ Jesus" (Romans 16:3-4).

What if all these people in the Bible and all the believers who have labored throughout history had simply sat on the beach, doing nothing but enjoying life's pleasures? Sure, they would have had positional significance as God's children, but they would not have played a significant part in the plan of God.

WHAT IS FAITHFULNESS?

Faithfulness—that distinguishing characteristic of the significant life—is what enables ordinary people to do extraordinary things. Unlike talent or giftedness, faithfulness is not a divine endowment unique to a particular individual. Unlike opportunity, it does not depend on circumstances. Faithfulness is the strength of will to be consistent over a long period of time. Faithfulness is required to accomplish anything significant in life and in God's kingdom.

A faithful person stays focused on God and the task at hand. Anyone trying to accomplish something can easily become distracted by setbacks, failures, personal rejections, and worries about the difficulties that lie ahead.

Imagine how easy it would have been for Paul to long for his pre-Christian life of respect and power or to sulk while in jail, bitter at his enemies and doubtful of God's support. Instead he rejoiced that his circumstances worked out to "the greater progress of the gospel"

(Philippians 1:12), and he took those opportunities to write the letters that became much of the New Testament.

Paul shared part of the secret of his consistency with his companion Timothy: "I thank Christ Jesus our Lord, who has strengthened me, because He considered me faithful, putting me into service" (1 Timothy 1:12). God kept on strengthening Paul because he kept on being faithful. Because he was careful to use the power and the opportunities God gave him, God kept giving him more power and more opportunities.

Paul knew God did not empower him because he was somehow better than other people. In fact, in the same context he was careful to point out that he was formerly a blasphemer and persecutor of the church (vv. 13-14), and elsewhere he confessed that he was the greatest of sinners (1 Timothy 1:15).

It is God's grace that made Paul, and makes us, worthy to be children of God. But whether we are worthy to serve Him and get greater opportunities to do so depends on how faithful we are with the things He gives us, great and small.

Faithfulness in the Little Things

One day the Lord told a parable about ten slaves whose faithfulness was about to be tested in a practical way. Their boss divided among them a total of ten minas so that each got an equal amount of money. For a nobleman, this was not a lot of money, perhaps a few hundred dollars.[1] He told them, "Do business with this until I come back" (Luke 19:13).

What a great opportunity for these men! They must have been thrilled at the chance to prove themselves to their boss and possibly to advance themselves in the world. As we see, two of the men made good with the money. One made ten times as much, the other five times. But the third man didn't do anything with his portion. He simply stored it.

When the nobleman returned home, he was pleased with those who had done something with what they were given. They were found faithful. Not so with the man who had stored the money. The nobleman asked the bystanders to take the mina away from the unfaithful worker and give it to the most faithful one (Luke 19:15-24).

Though the amount of money given to each person was not large, it was clear that on the nobleman's return he judged the slaves' faithfulness by how they used the money. The responsibility he then gave them was far out of proportion to the small thing he had entrusted to them. The one who made ten times as much was given authority over ten *cities*; the one who made five times as much was given authority over five cities.

Jesus was saying that God looks at how we handle the little things and decides how much to give us. He was not talking here about our various God-given spiritual gifts and abilities. That He dealt with in another parable (Matthew 25:14-30). In this parable each man got the same amount, so Christ must have been talking about something we each have in the same amount, such as the Word of God.[2]

Let's consider God's Word for a moment. Because it contains the message of salvation, when we share the Gospel, we are sharing the Word. And when we do what the Word says, such as love God and each other, we are using it faithfully. To be a faithful Christian, then, is to be faithful to the Word.

Commentator Lenski says, "The law in the kingdom of Christ is that everyone who has (by using the Word of God aright and by its getting gain for the Lord), to him shall be given (more and more by the Lord himself [*sic*]); but he who has not (by refusing to use the Word), by that very non-having he shall lose even what he has (the very Word itself which was originally given to him as it was to others)."[3]

Look at what Paul gained because of his faithfulness in the little things. He started out small, proclaiming "Jesus in the synagogues, saying 'He is the Son of God'" (Acts 9:20). After a while, the Holy Spirit called him into missionary work (Acts 13:1—14:28). As time went on, he began writing letters to the churches, teaching pure doctrine as an apostle (Romans 1:1). Truly, Paul's life illustrates the principle that he who is faithful with little shall receive more (Luke 19:26).

As for ourselves, we may think the "little" things aren't that important, but they are. The Lord looks closely at what is done with little things such as a cup of cold water (Matthew 10:42), and He commends other small acts of kindness (Matthew 25:35-40). We need to look at the little things in our lives, starting with seeming trivialities such as getting to our appointments on time, meeting deadlines, returning phone calls, and expressing appreciation to others.

Are we watching those larger daily things that matter, too, such as keeping up our home, taking care of the needs of our family, helping friends, being responsible to help with needs in our church or in other groups to which we have committed ourselves?

Over the years I have heard believers and nonbelievers alike say, "There are too many flaky Christians!" Why would they say that? Possibly because too many of us are committing ourselves to things and then dropping the ball. How? By not following through with what we said we would do. Perhaps we're being too impulsive, taking up things excitedly, but because of weakness of character, not showing any staying power.

Impulsiveness is a great way to prevent success in life. Remember Reuben, Jacob's son? He was very impulsive, and it was said of him that he was "unstable as water" (Genesis 49:4 KJV). His own father predicted his son's ineffectiveness. Interestingly, there would be no prophet, judge, or hero that would ever come from the tribe of Reuben.[4]

Maybe we appear flaky because we have not only made commitments, but we have overcommitted ourselves and have to keep backing out. Or, on a more basic level, possibly we are simply lacking two important qualities—energy and thoughtfulness.

So many women I know complain that they lack energy. And in a culture that doesn't emphasize the intellect, it doesn't surprise me that we often fail to use our minds to the fullest as well. As I've been learning, it's not just the spiritual things that matter as far as our faithfulness is concerned. Everything matters. Our lives are not made of little compartments. So what should we do? Be faithful with what we have been given, including our bodies and our minds. Lack of faithfulness in these areas keeps us from getting greater opportunities.

GETTING MORE ENERGY

Do you wish you had more energy? You can, but it has a lot to do with how you are taking care of your body. Are you eating the right foods? Are you controlling your appetite? Are you exercising? As the old saying goes, "Use it or lose it." I saw this happen to my friend Becky.

Becky was a sensitive and very loving Christian woman who often gave herself away by helping anyone in need. It may have been simply an encouraging word, assisting in outreach endeavors, or even typing college papers free of charge for students who didn't have typewriters. (Becky and I were college students in the "B.C. era," meaning "before computers.")

Becky enjoyed being a blessing to others and had an especially tender spot for abused children. She often spoke of how she would love to become a foster mom or a social worker who reaches neglected children with the love of Christ.

Unfortunately, as time went on, Becky gave up on her dream of helping children in need. Instead, she allowed one problem to take over everything else—her uncontrollable appetite. Though she had always had a weight problem, she got to the point that she didn't care anymore about controlling it. Within a few years, she became very unhappy with herself, especially when she noticed that she couldn't go anywhere without getting exhausted.

Rather than dealing with her depression or seeking the help of a Christian counselor, Becky decided to hide from view. She created a full-time typing business in her home. Her insecurities only mounted. Whenever she got new customers, she would warn them of her size before they came to her home to drop off work.

I told Becky that she didn't need to mention her size; it didn't matter. She was lovely inside and out, was loved by her friends, but most of all was loved by God. And it was in God that she needed to find her value. Fortunately, Becky came to see the tremendous value she had in God's eyes and knew she had to do something about her weight problem.

I remember being so happy when she told me she had decided to get serious about her health and see a doctor. She planned to meet with a dietician in order to get on a healthful diet. And she would start going to a fitness center, she said. She was not trying to find acceptance from others or meet any worldly standards of the "perfect body," but she simply wanted the energy she needed to live a long life of faithfulness to the Lord.

But Becky's plans to regain her health were too late. The night after she shared with me her hopeful goals, her heart stopped. She died in her sleep, at the age of twenty-six. While Becky's short life was a blessing, her failure to take care of herself caught up with her. Her dreams of reaching out to abused children died with her, too. Imagine what she could have accomplished had she taken care of her body.

Paul the apostle saw the extreme importance of taking care of every aspect of life, to do "all things for the sake of the gospel" (1 Corinthians 9:23). That included making sure he controlled his bodily appetites and that they didn't control him. He said, "I buffet my body and make it my slave" (1 Corinthians 9:27).

Today when many of us see the word *buffet*, we pronounce it differently. We think it means going to a smorgasbord. But Paul's definition means to be self-disciplined. Think what would have happened had Paul been indulgent and thus ineffective. When we consider the tremendous energy and endurance needed to make his missionary journeys, with the accompanying hunger and shipwrecks (Acts 27:1-41), we can understand why Paul had to maintain self-discipline.

Can we take Paul's example and buffet our bodies? How might we start so we can use our bodies for God's service? Why not do what Becky intended to do before time ran out for her? You could develop your own program or get professional help if you need it.

We do not need to try to look like Barbie. Remember, she's made of plastic. But taking care of our bodies is one aspect of faithfulness with what God has given us, and such discipline can give us the energy to be more faithful in other areas.

While some of us have to work within bodily limitations that we can do nothing about, we can still be faithful with what we have. My friend Noreen was bedridden for over seven years, but even then she did what she could to take care of herself by eating properly. She used her time to call sick people in hospitals and befriend them. She would listen to them talk about their aches, pains, and fears. Then she would share Christ's love and pray with them, leading some to Christ. She took a genuine interest in the people that many of us forget—the hurting, the lonely, the dying, and even the boring. She was faithful within the limits of what she could do, and eventually God expanded her limits so that she could walk again, though not easily. With her capabilities expanded, she expanded her service, earning an advanced degree in counseling to better equip herself to be of help to people.

Faithfulness at its best is working right up to—but not beyond—the limits of our time, energy, and abilities. With all our responsibilities we may feel that "all" we can do in the way of spiritual service is to pray. Prayer doesn't require much physical activity, and yet praying is perhaps the most significant thing we can do. Prayer changes things here on earth and in God's kingdom to come. Imagine moving God's hand, changing things for eternity!

Now let's look at faithful stewardship of our minds. The value of the mind cannot be overestimated because it is through our thinking, not through audible voices or mystical inner impressions, that God guides us toward a significant life. But our culture, and to some extent the church, is losing its ability to think critically. We've become an image-driven society because of television, movies, and computer graphics. Yet Christianity has content and requires thinking. Let's see what it takes to exercise our minds.

DEEPER THINKING THROUGH EXERCISING THE MIND

Paul the apostle was in a cold jail cell facing death when he wrote Timothy these words: "I am already being poured out as a drink offering, and the time of my departure has come" (2 Timothy 4:6). Despite Paul's awareness that he would soon be with the Lord, he asked Timothy to bring not only his cloak (it was cold in the jail, and winter was coming), but also to bring "the books, especially the parchments" (v. 13).

"Books" were papyrus rolls, and "parchments" were expensive sheets of animal skins used for writing. Probably he was referring to copies of the Scriptures and something else besides—we don't know what. What we do know is that rather than sulk about his dreary conditions and mourn his imminent death, Paul was cultivating his mind (as well as taking care of his body).

Author J. Oswald Sanders said of Paul, "He wished to spend his last weeks or months to the highest profit in studying his precious books—a student to the end."[5] Saunders speculates that the books may have been Jewish histories that commented on the Law and the Prophets and perhaps some works of Gentile poets that Paul quoted in his sermons and letters.

Books have always been an important asset to those who cultivate a spiritual mind. William Tyndale, while in jail himself and just prior to his martyrdom, asked for his Hebrew Bible, Hebrew grammar, and Hebrew dictionary. John Wesley stretched his mind, most often while on horseback, by reading the *Imitation of Christ, Holy Living and Dying,* and *The Serious Call.*[6]

I've sometimes wondered whether the lives of people such as Paul, Tyndale, and Wesley would have been any different if they had had television in their day. I doubt that they would have spent as many hours a week watching it as we modern Christians do. For some of us, T.V. can be a "god."

Are you familiar with the Norman Rockwell painting of a man who is putting up a T.V. antenna on an old Victorian home? In the background is a church, and, interestingly, the antenna on the house soars higher in the sky than the steeple. The message is clear that a new god has come into our homes—replacing the old one.

My friend Gail doesn't mind my sharing with you that she and her husband had made T.V. a god for years—they were also in a rut. They would eat dinner in front of the "tube" every night. They planned their schedules around the programs they didn't want to miss. Television controlled their time, actions, and even their thinking.

Fortunately Gail and her husband became convicted, realizing that the television had taken over their lives and that their minds were becoming like Jell-O. Excessive television-viewing kept them from thinking about spiritual things, doing any kind of devotional reading, and faithfully serving God. They decided to do something about it. They limited their viewing to shows they thought could benefit them, such as documentaries. Otherwise, the set was off.

Then, along with getting more involved in the Word of God, they also decided to read books together that would encourage them in their walk with Christ. This not only enhanced their thinking, but it motivated them to become active Christians rather than idle ones.

It's interesting to note that studies on the brain show that when we are watching T.V., the brain is in a state that resembles sleep. By contrast, through reading, we can grow in our spiritual lives, develop our thinking, and "fellowship with great minds."[7] J. Oswald Sanders writes: "If it is true that a man is known by the company he keeps, it is no less true that his character is reflected in the books he reads, for they are the outward expression of his inner hungers and aspirations."[8]

Books are powerful. A few such as Marx's *Das Kapital* and Hitler's *Mein Kampf* have destroyed whole nations and damaged millions of souls. But other books can wonderfully transform lives. Besides, of course, the Bible, I've enjoyed reading a variety of books to help my growth.

Do the books you read stimulate you to further growth? I find that I benefit not only from Christian books but also from other types of books. Reading keeps my mind from getting in a rut, gives me new things to think about, and helps me understand God's workings.

One subject I enjoy reading is history. I love Will and Arial Durant's eleven-volume work, *The Story of Civilization*. And I'll confess to being a Civil War buff. I recently finished a diary titled *Sarah Morgan: The Civil War Diary of a Southern Woman*[9] (I highly recommend it!).

Biographies are wonderful, too! We learn so much from them, especially from Christian biographies that can illustrate good character and the selfless life. And, by showing us how God uses a dedicated person, biographies can inspire us to that same level of commitment.

Reading biographies, history, and other subjects such as science can enhance our understanding of God's world and His workings with people. These books can also introduce us to what people in the past have thought about important issues, which can enable us to dialogue with others and reach them for Christ. For instance, because I had read some of the writings of two skeptics, Bertrand Russell (author of *Why I Am Not a Christian*) and Voltaire, I was able to connect with someone who admired them and held to their ideas. (Reading the works of atheists and skeptics is not recommended for every Christian.) While writing this chapter, I was interrupted by a phone call from a Mormon missionary with whom I was able to talk about the *Book of Mormon* and its problems—only because I've read it. It was exciting—the conversation, I mean.

There are other ways besides reading to stretch our minds. We can listen to music, learn a new skill such as needlepoint, or follow a discussion we are unfamiliar with, such as political commentary. Or we can take a class on something that interests us.

Exposing ourselves to things that are not expressly Christian can help us grow if we see them from a Christian worldview. After reading the diary of a Jewish reporter in Nazi Germany,[10] I was able to understand the Jewish mind-set better. This book, along with studying the prophecies of the Messiah from the Old Testament, has enabled me to share with a few elderly Holocaust victims and with Jewish people in general.

As you can see, so much of what we learn can be used for a spiritual purpose. Even things such as calligraphy, crocheting, or knitting can be used as tools for outreach. But if we use our mind for nothing more than storing knowledge, we haven't used it fully. Our mind isn't just for ourselves, but under God's guidance, we are to use it faithfully for others. Easy? No. However, that goal is more attainable as we cultivate a stubborn faithfulness.

Stubborn Faithfulness

One day I'd had it! I was completely frustrated with a group of women I had been ministering to. Despite my love for them, I couldn't deal with what I call the "administratively challenged." With some of them, deadlines were continually missed, calls went unreturned, and starting something on time was for a few the exception. Though they certainly meant no harm, I was discouraged.

Frustrated, I told the Lord that I was not the one to serve these women. But to my surprise, God didn't seem to be siding with me. Rejecting my feeble explanations and my sense of self-importance (which carry no weight with God), He brought to mind the scriptural admonitions: "Be patient with everyone" (1 Thessalonians 5:14), "It is more blessed to give than to receive," and "Help the weak" (Acts 20:35).

The Lord showed me as I was ready to throw in the towel that the weak I was supposed to help were not just those who were weak physically, emotionally, socially, or even intellectually. I was to help those who were weak in a way that mattered to my situation—the administratively weak. I also learned that my life will one day be judged by the measure of love I demonstrate. I know I wasn't using all the love God had given me for these women.

I shared my frustrated feelings with the group (and got their permission to share this story). I also told them the lessons God was teaching me and that His plan for now was for me to keep on serving them. So how would I stick to it? I would need a stubborn faithfulness.

THE KEY TO STICKING WITH IT

Saints throughout history who have done truly extraordinary things have not just been faithful; they have been stubbornly faithful. They could stick to their tasks through thick and thin.

When Peter and the other apostles stood before the Jewish Sanhedrin, the very group that had such a key role in Jesus' death, the apostles were ordered to stop teaching about Christ. They answered boldly, "We must obey God rather than men" (Acts 5:28-29). When Paul was discouraged with the Corinthians, he never gave up on them; nor did he lose hope for the Galatians, who were dangerously close to spiritual defection (Galatians 1:6).

Missionaries throughout the ages have in a number of cases had to stick to it for decades before ever seeing a conversion. Many pastors have had to stick to it for years before they ever saw fruit. Wives and mothers have had to stick to it in prayer before ever seeing their husbands or children turn to Christ.

So many faithful persons have shown stubborn faithfulness in the face of hardship, apparent lack of success, various frustrations, inconvenience, and loneliness. They took seriously Scripture's charge to be faithful (1 Corinthians 4:2 KJV), not just occasionally or when things went well, but every day *until their last day* (Revelation 2:10).

So what's the secret of developing a stubborn faithfulness? Paul gives us one key to his extraordinary faithfulness—God's strength flowing through his life as a result of Paul's humility. He never pretended to have what it takes, and he frankly told the Corinthians, "Not that we are adequate in ourselves to consider anything as coming from ourselves, but our adequacy is from God" (2 Corinthians 3:5). He saw himself as just a plain clay pot used to hold treasure (2 Corinthians 4:7). So he was actually thankful for trials and setbacks because they constantly reminded him of his weakness and his need for God—and that kept God's power working in his life (12:7-10).

Hebrews 11 reveals the other characteristic of those whose lives have been remarkably faithful. They possessed remarkable faith.

Those in the spiritual "hall of fame" had an intense personal trust in God and could sacrifice earthly pleasures because they knew better things were coming.

In a sense humility and faith are not great character qualities in us. They point away from ourselves and to the character of God. And the greater the task He has for us, the greater the strength He supplies.

God's strength does two great things for us. First, it enhances our talents and abilities; second, it gives us endurance. Let's look at each point.

STRENGTH THAT ENHANCES OUR TALENTS AND ABILITIES

When the Lord first prompted me to write *Choices That Lead to Godliness*, I backed away from the task. Actually I ran from it. Why? I had very little experience in writing and wasn't very good at it. I felt that someone else could do a much better job at writing the book. But the more I prayed about it, the more convicted I became that I should do it.

So I began to get serious about this new calling. I would get up at 2 A.M. when the house was quiet and I could put in lots of writing time before the children got up. My goal was not only to write the book, but also to strive toward competence in my writing. I wrote and rewrote. I edited and reedited. I prayed and prayed.

Soon I found something quite interesting happening. As I tried to be faithful to the calling I felt the Lord had given me, my skills began to sharpen. And the more I worked at it, the better I got. I really thought I understood what Paul meant when he said that his adequacy was from God!

As I look back over those arduous four years of applying myself, I can say without a doubt that had I not received the Lord's strength, there would never have been a first book, let alone a second. His strength truly gives us that stick-to-it attitude. So whatever your calling is, dare to give it your all, for: "The Lord is faithful, and He will strengthen . . . you . . ." (2 Thessalonians 3:3).

THE STRENGTH TO BE FAITHFUL

Paul challenged the Corinthians to "run in such a way that you may win" (1 Corinthians 9:24). Drawing on his readers' knowledge of the

Isthmian games held every two years near Corinth,[11] he reminded his readers that "only one receives the prize" (v. 9:24).

To be in the Isthmian games or any Olympic game, the athletes went through some ten months of rigorous training under the guidance of professionals. After that, they were examined by officials. If they were in good enough shape, they would be chosen to run the race. They were the best, the cream of the crop, the ones capable of enduring to the finish line.

Do you have the sort of faithfulness that can make it to the finish line? Nothing less will do. Run with your whole heart, soul, and mind as if in a race where there is only one winner. Don't just show up at the race and go through the motions; run to win, and the Lord will provide the endurance. If you fall during the race, the Lord will give you the strength to get up again, as He did Peter (John 21:15-17). If you begin to get tired, He will refresh you, as He did Elijah (1 Kings 19:5). Isaiah wrote, "*He gives strength to the weary*, and to him who lacks might He increases power. Though youths grow weary and tired, and vigorous young men stumble badly, *yet those who wait for the LORD* will gain new strength; they will mount up with wings like eagles, they will run and not get tired, they will walk and not become weary" (40:29-31, italics mine).

Commentator J. A. Alexander says that those who are promised strength are the ones who show "their confidence in God's ability and willingness to execute his [*sic*] promises, by patiently awaiting their fulfillment."[12] Whoever has the faith will be given the strength.

Faithfulness Makes Heroes

There is one area in my house I love. It's my long staircase with its large window opening to majestic mountains and forest. But the view isn't the best part; the walls of the staircase are. On my peach-colored walls, I have countless pictures of my "heroes of the faith," along with some profound statement each made printed on the picture. Every day I look at these heroes, read their comments, and get spiritually stimulated as I recall their faithful lives. Many of these heroes reflected a stubborn faithfulness by their very words—the kind of faithfulness for which I am striving. I wish I could share with you the comments of all of these spiritual giants. Here are just two:

Missionary to Native Americans, David Brainerd (1718-1747) said, "I cared not where or how I lived, or what hardships I went through, so that I could but gain souls for Christ."

Sadhu Sundar Singh (1889-1929) said, "The day is fast approaching when you will see the martyrs in their glory, who gave their health, wealth, and life to save souls for Christ. They have done much. What have you done? Oh! May we not blush on that day."[13]

While many of those we regard as heroes of the faith are now in heaven, the age of heroic faithfulness has by no means ended. With us still are believers with shining, godly lives, who have deeply spiritual minds and hearts as well as the God-given ability to stick to it no matter what the difficulties are.

As you live a faithful life, God is molding you into a hero or heroine, a person who prays with faith (Luke 17:5) out of an obedient life (Acts 6:7) that is characterized by faith (Hebrews 10:38). You can become "steadfast, immovable, always abounding in the work of the Lord" (1 Corinthians 15:58). And in living out such faithfulness, our Lord will continue to strengthen you, humble you, and intensify your faith.

Just as the Lord helped Moses who "was faithful in all His house as a servant" (Hebrews 3:5), so will He help you. And although you won't become another Moses, Paul, Abigail, or Priscilla—you will be uniquely you!

If we are faithful to our own unique calling, we will not only have a significant life, but one day soon we shall hear, "Well done, good and faithful servant!" (Matthew 25:21 NIV). Triumphant joy awaits all those who are "the called and chosen and faithful" (Revelation 17:14).

THINKING IT OVER

1. What does faithfulness have to do with the significant life?
2. What do energy and thought have to do with the faithful life?
3. Starting today, how might you buffet your body and exercise your mind?
4. How could you improve at being faithful in the "small things" of life?
5. What does it mean to have a stubborn faithfulness? How do we get it and keep it?

Eight

SACRIFICE—A LIVING ONE

*D*uring the final days of the cold war in 1989, Brian and I were traveling throughout Europe, partly for ministry and partly for pleasure. While we were in England, we visited Wesley's chapel and his adjacent modest home with its study, small bedroom, and cramped prayer room. On the tour of this historic site, we met an elderly British clergyman. He was quite vocal in the group and knew a great deal about the Wesleys and the history of England in general. For that reason, Brian had a question for him. After waiting for the rest of the group to move on, he whispered to the cleric, "Do you know where Karl Marx is buried?"

The cleric (we'll call him Snedley) looked heavenward and replied in slow, reverent tones, "Ahhh . . . there were only two saints that ever lived in this town, Marx and Wesley!"

Brian and I were taken aback. Marx's views and Wesley's seem so diametrically opposed! Marxist philosophy has spawned atheistic tyranny, while in his humble way Wesley tried to connect people to God and help them lead more spiritual lives.

After our initial shock, Brian quietly explained to Cleric Snedley that he was a professor of biblical studies and philosophy and wanted a picture of the gravesite out of historical interest purely for teaching purposes.

Snedley smiled as if he understood a deeper message underlying Brian's straightforward words. With boldness, the cleric gathered the group together and then pointed to Brian and me and proclaimed in a loud, melodramatic tone, "This couple here would like to visit Karl Marx's grave. Can anyone perhaps tell us in which graveyard we can find Mr. Marx?"

At that moment Brian and I felt like digging our own graves to hide in. As we stood before these twenty or so people, no one said a word, but their expressions spoke volumes. Some looked pleased at the thought that we might be committed Marxists. Others looked at us with unutterable disgust, as if we had a part in creating the chaos in the world. It didn't help matters that the cleric clung to us throughout the tour, extolling the virtues of Marx.

After the tour Snedley turned to Brian and me and, with a touch of sentimentalism, said, "I believe I know where my friend Mr. Marx is buried. Let me take you to him." As we walked to the graveyard, he confided to us that he had read every "great" work Marx ever wrote, adding wistfully that there would be far less suffering in the world if everyone embraced Marxism.

After a while the cleric had to stop to rest. While Brian went on to look for the gravesite, I stayed and talked. Wiping the sweat off his brow and cleaning his glasses with a rumpled handkerchief, the frail, elderly man explained that he had given over fifty years of his life to the Marxist cause. He talked about the sacrifices he had made, standing up for what he thought was right, and trying to give up every comfort for the cause.

I broke in and reminded him, "Marxism is now dead."

With a look of disbelief, he shook his head and replied, "Marxism shall never die!"

The cleric's comment reminded me of some Japanese soldiers who were found on a remote island long after World War II, refusing to surrender. Their irrelevant loyalty served only to underscore the defeat of their cause.

After resting a bit, we continued with our walk, arriving at one of London's historic cemeteries. Snedley caught up with Brian while I began to take in all the history that lay silently among those weathered, tilting gravestones.

Walking quite slowly, I came upon the resting place of John Bunyan. I stood there awhile reflecting on his sacrifice for the cause of Christ. In 1660 Bunyan was prosecuted under the Elizabethan Act against Nonconformity. While he was supposed to spend only three months in jail, his term was extended to six years. During that time he wrote six books, such as *Grace Abounding* and *A Defense of the Doctrine of Justification by Faith in Jesus Christ*. Bunyan was released from jail, but rather than conform and enjoy the good life, he continued on with his preaching and writing. That decision predictably got him right back in the cold, stench-filled jail. While serving his second sentence, he wrote his greatest literary work, *The Pilgrim's Progress*.

Leaving Bunyan's grave, I encountered more saints whose sacrificial lives had made a great impact on this world. As I was reflecting over those lives well-lived, our devout Marxist cleric came back to talk further. I decided to ask him what has been for 2,000 years life's most important question, "What do you think of Christ?" (Matthew 22:42).

A bit uncomfortable, he replied cautiously, "Marx says that religion is the opiate of the people."

"Really?" I said. "Then why are you a cleric in a church?"

He smiled and said, "It's a secure living. People are born, and I baptize them. People fall in love, and I marry them. People die, and I eulogize them. Yes, there's always a steady flow of business."

While it's obvious the cleric wasn't a true Christian, it dawned on me that he wasn't even a true Marxist! Marx would never have sanctioned a pseudo-religious life—Marxism in religious clothing.

When I pointed out that Marx would have been disappointed with him, he said, "Think how Christ might be disappointed with Christians. They, too, wear 'religious clothing.' At least I can say I have sacrificed for Marx. Are they sacrificing for Christ? I don't think they are! Look at the Wesley brothers. They gave up much for their beliefs; they gave away themselves because of their beliefs. But today's Christian is too preoccupied with becoming prosperous, living the good life, and being concerned with every comfort. They know so little about sacrifice."

I was pleased that Snedley finally said something about the Wesley brothers, Charles and John. He was right. The Wesleys sacrificed much in their lifetime. Snedley was right about something else. While he sacrificed for a cause now passé, many of us, including myself, aren't always focused on sacrificing for a cause that will outlast all of time. When we do think of sacrifice, what do many of us think of? Naturally, and importantly, we think of Christ giving up His life on Calvary.

Believers and nonbelievers alike agree that Christ died on a rugged cross. But what has it become to many people? To some, it's nothing more than a symbol to be worn around the neck. No one living was at

Calvary to see the suffering, to see the love demonstrated on their behalf. And so Christ's death affects a good many people very little.

I am convinced that some nonbelievers will never be able to truly appreciate the sacrifice of Christ until they see believers living as a daily sacrifice (Romans 12:1). I remember one Costa Rican boy who tearfully accepted Christ after he came to realize what missionaries had given up in order to reach out to him.

I am also learning that by the Lord's design, sacrifice is a blessing not just to others but to us as well. Why? Because sacrifice is very much tied to the significant life. As we sacrifice, we have a purpose, an aim, a mission, just as Christ did on that torturous cross.

To understand sacrifice and the significant impact it can make, let's start at the beginning, looking at the various views of the sacrificial life.

VIEWS OF THE SACRIFICIAL LIFE

Simeon Stylites lived in the fifth century when belief in God was no longer certified by persecution and martyrdom. After thinking long and hard, Stylites came up with the perfect way to sacrifice for God. He would live as a hermit. Such a life wasn't easy. As a recluse he would starve himself, often to the point of death. He would wrap cords around himself so tightly that they pressed to the bone; other times he would wrap his feet in chains.

After a while he resorted to pole-sitting, on a pillar forty cubits high. The platform at the top was so small he was unable to lie or sit down. He could only stand or lean against a post. Stylites did this for thirty-six weary years, exposed to the scorching Middle East sun, the pouring rain, the cold, the howling wind, and the violent storms.

Ironically, as Stylites spent years in what he thought was a demonstration of the sacrificial life, he succeeded only in making himself a spectacle, all the while depending on others to bring him food and care for his needs.[1]

It's unfortunate that Stylites's good intentions didn't do much to help the cause of Christianity. He apparently thought that his tortured lifestyle would earn God's favor. But such a life doesn't impress God; nor is it necessary to try to earn God's favor because His mercy is already ours as a free gift.

Stylites also thought that sacrifice involved keeping himself separate from the world. I know of some Christians who believe this, too. This is a terrible distortion. How can we who call ourselves Christians advance God's kingdom if we separate ourselves from those God desires to save?

In our modern society new ideas have rudely shaken the Christian view of the sacrificial life. Actually, it's more than just a mere shaking; it's an earthquake. To many Christians, sacrifice now means spending more hours at work or moms working outside the home—none of this out of necessity but in order to support a higher standard of living. To others, sacrifice is nothing more than giving up things now so they can put away money to secure a comfortable retirement. Still others believe that sacrifice means giving away money or things but for no higher motive than to receive for themselves something better from God—turning sacrifice into a sort of cosmic Ponzi scheme. I have had more than one conversation with Christians who honestly believe we must have some special "calling" to live sacrificially. "Sacrifice," said one, "is not for every Christian."

Could this sort of thinking be the reason that Rev. Snedley said, "Today's Christian is too preoccupied with becoming prosperous, living the good life, and being concerned with every comfort"? Now, granted, Snedley had sacrificed his life for a futile cause (worse than futile, I would say). When I spoke with him, Marxism was fading, and it seemed no one but Snedley was mourning its passing. But are Christians just as misguided in their views of the sacrificial life?

A theologian by the name of Bengel said over a hundred years ago that "the philosopher forsakes all without following Christ; most Christians follow Christ without forsaking all. . . ."[2] I believe Bengel's words can point to our cleric who did forsake all without following Christ, but I'm afraid that he also speaks to many of us who are following Christ but haven't forsaken all.

FORSAKING ALL

When I was a six-month-old Christian, several other believers and I attended a seminar on the theme "Having a Prosperous Christian Life." I was excited as I listened to the speaker because I wanted to have a solid Christian walk. Unfortunately, as the seminar progressed throughout the day, I was greatly disappointed. I discovered that in the speaker's definition, prosperity did not include spiritual riches.

I heard much that day about how we can become financially prosperous. I learned how to "claim it," as well as how a "lack of faith" could keep me from getting what I want. The speaker excitedly told us that all of us could drive around in Porsches. How could we do that? Whenever we gave our tithe to the church offering, to other ministries, or to someone in need, all we had to do was to write "Porsche" on the bottom of our check. "God," he said, "would honor our request because we gave to Him."

Clearly the seminar promoted wealth as the main ingredient of a prosperous Christian life. Far from forsaking it all, I was being taught how to have it all. After the conference, I asked some of my friends, "What did this seminar have to do with our Christian walk? It seemed more like an investment seminar."

A seasoned Christian replied, "Donna, you can do more for the Lord if you are rich. What kind of impact can we really make when we are poor?"

I replied, "The apostles weren't rich, and they did much for the Lord."

Then another replied, "Donna, in this day and age, when riches are preached, nonbelievers listen and come to Christ."

Could my friends be correct in their assumptions about wealth? I don't think they are. If you were to look at Roman history, you will see that under Nero when people were being horribly persecuted for their faith, the church flourished. When Constantine got into power, he stopped all persecutions by legalizing Christianity in 313.

Now notice the change. Constantine gave back to the Christians their stolen property, and a comfortable relationship developed between the government and the church. That is when Christianity went from being the Roman empire's kicked dog to being its top dog.

Constantine gave privileges to the Christian church that other religions did not enjoy. He gave Christian bishops the authority of judges in their dioceses and exemption from taxation; he allowed those in Christian ministries to take part in the judicial system, to receive donations and the property of the martyrs. As well,

Constantine gave money to needy congregations and built several churches in Constantinople and elsewhere.[3]

With all the earthly benefits of being a Christian, it became trendy to be one. Christianity became associated with wealth, power, and privilege. Many men joined the clergy out of less than spiritual motives.

The church, which was once spiritual in its orientation, began to be compromised. One of the bishops, Cyprian, complained that some Christians were no longer focusing on their holy walk with God, but rather they were "mad about money . . . and denied their faith at the first sign of danger."[4]

The point is that when the Christians lived under persecution, their dedication and willingness to sacrifice made a deep impact on the culture. Those attitudes slowly won over huge numbers of people. But when the persecutions ceased, many Christians focused on this life and its benefits. Those who joined the church were as likely to be converts to a lifestyle of power and privilege as to a relationship with God.

If we draw others to Christianity by wealth and a luxurious lifestyle, how can we know the conversions are genuine? The issue becomes clouded. And I'm afraid we might be a stumbling block if we aren't giving them the whole message of Jesus Christ—which is unavoidably a message of sacrifice.

Patti Roberts will be the first to admit that she, along with former husband televangelist Richard Roberts (son of Oral Roberts), may have been a stumbling block to others. She offered these recollections, with regrets:

> I know a lot of people were blessed and sincerely ministered to by what we sang on TV and by what we said—but the overall picture, I'm afraid, seemed to say, "If you follow our formula, you'll be like us," rather than, "If you do what Jesus says, you'll be like Him." It was certainly more exciting to follow us, because to follow us was to identify with success, with glamour, with a theology that made everything good and clean and well-knit together. To identify with Jesus, however, meant to identify with the Cross.[5]

As in the days of Constantine, it is easy to be a Christian today without having to carry a cross. Not only is there general acceptance of the church, but Christians share the great prosperity that society enjoys.

Wealth certainly isn't wrong, but some Christians have mistakenly taken the promises God gave to Israel and applied them to the church. God promised Israel that their obedience would bring earthly prosperity—land, deliverance from their enemies, and the like. His plan was to reveal Himself by dealing with them as a nation. The church, however, is not a nation but a people within other nations. Unlike Israel, God didn't promise that if Christians obey, they would necessarily have earthly blessings. In fact, Christ warned His followers to expect persecution. The apostles certainly had their share of persecution. They were hungry, thirsty, poorly clothed, roughly treated, and homeless (1 Corinthians 4:11).

Do you think that if Paul lived today he would use the media to build a multimillion dollar empire? Or that he would appear as a glitzy, jeweled, and carefully coiffured televangelist encouraging us to forsake all by mailing him a generous donation?

Jesus summed it up for us when He, as our supreme example, warned, "the foxes have holes and the birds of the air have nests, but the Son of Man has nowhere to lay His head" (Matthew 8:20).

We are sojourners on this earth, not landlords. The proof of our genuineness is the cross we carry, not the jewelry we wear or the car we drive. Every day we must choose between serving two kingdoms—the kingdom of self and the kingdom of God.

Dag Hammarskjöld, a Swedish Christian and the former Secretary General of the U.N., struggled with self like many of us. In his diary two themes preoccupied his thoughts. First, the conviction that no man can do properly what he is called upon to do in this life unless he can learn to forget himself—his ego, his desires, the worldly lusts. Secondly, that in his service, he was to serve God through a life of humility and sacrifice. He contends, "Evil, death, and dearth, sacrifice and love—what does 'I' mean in such a perspective? Reason tells me that I am bound to seek my own good, seek to gratify my desires, win power for myself and admiration from others. And yet I 'know'—know without knowing—that, in such a perspective, nothing could be less important."[6]

Hammarskjöld had learned what I am not yet finished learning, that in the scheme of things what I want isn't really that important. Many Christians would agree with this statement, and yet there is a growing movement in the church to focus more upon ourselves "in a proper way." We must love ourselves, it is claimed. Should we? And, if so, how does self-love relate to the sacrificial life?

SHOULD WE LOVE OURSELVES?

Many Christians believe that to have a proper sense of self, to sacrificially reach out to others, and to be growing spiritually, we first must love ourselves. They argue, "How can we love others if we don't love ourselves?" The idea is often linked to nothing less than part of Christ's summation of the law and prophets: "You shall love your neighbor as yourself" (Matthew 22:39).

Some believe that Christ in this verse is commanding us to love ourselves. Some believe that it means we cannot love others unless we love ourselves. And still others say that we can love others only to the degree that we love ourselves.

Biblical counseling professor Dr. John Street says that Christ is there explaining the whole law and that it hangs on two pegs. That is, we should love God (Matthew 22:37) and love our neighbor (Matthew 22:39). Everything in life, including every problem we face, goes back to these two pegs. How much do we love God? How much do we love other people?

Jesus, therefore, isn't telling us to love ourselves. Rather, He is telling us that we need to learn to love God and others *to the same degree that we love ourselves.*[7] Such love is sacrificial.

Why isn't this truth readily understood? Pastor and writer John R. W. Stott says that it's because "a chorus of many voices is chanting in unison today that I must at all costs love myself."[8]

The idea that we ought to focus on ourselves has certainly been popular throughout history. Going back to the beginning of our country, the Puritans struggled with the "self-love" movement, and by the middle of the seventeenth century they came up with the word *selfish* to describe the person who wasn't making God central in his life. Such people, they said, were putting self at the beginning and end of all their thoughts and their actions.[9]

Paul understood this selfish nature long before the Puritans and warned that the wickedness of the end times would be characterized by people who would be "lovers of self" (2 Timothy 3:2). He also assumed that people are motivated by their own interests. Trying to persuade husbands to care for their wives as they do their own selves, Paul says, "no one ever hated his own flesh, but nourishes and cherishes it" (Ephesians 5:29). Then to try to get Christians in general to care for others, Paul said, "Do not merely look out for your own personal interests, but also for the interests of others" (Philippians 2:4). He goes on to exhort us to follow the example of Jesus, who gave up heaven and its glory to die on a cross for others.

So contrary to popular opinion, Scripture exhorts us to give up our interests in order to serve others. In fact, the primary image of the Christian, and even of Christ Himself, is the servant—someone who pursues the interests of another.

Satan would love for us to focus on our wants, our comforts, and having lots of fun. Truly, a wrong focus is a powerful weapon against us (i.e., Genesis 3:1-7). We forfeit a meaningful life, a significant life, a life God can use.

In order to eliminate any self-serving thoughts, Hammarskjöld wrote a motto for himself. I think it can help us today:

> *The road,*
> *You shall follow it.*
> *The fun,*
> *You shall forget it.*
> *The cup,*
> *You shall empty it.*
> *The pain,*
> *You shall conceal it.*
> *The truth,*
> *You shall be told it.*
> *The end,*
> *You shall endure it.*[10]

I would add one thing to Hammarskjöld's motto: "The interests of Christ, you shall make them yours."

Denying self isn't easy. I know. There have been times when I have failed. It's during those times that I have come to see that worldly self-love and godly self-denial are opposing lifestyles. The two simply cannot coincide.

I have also come to see that when I attempt self-denial while still holding on to selfish tendencies, what results is not genuine sacrifice. It's like the parent who doesn't want to give up any time to spend with her child, so she buys the child some toy. What looks like sacrifice is really only personal convenience; the act was done precisely to avoid sacrifice.

The bottom line is this: The first step toward the sacrificial life is to genuinely forget self. Forget comfort. Forget your wants. Just forget them. You could die tomorrow, and they won't be there for you anyway. So just assume you'll never have it.

Seminary professor Dr. Robert Thomas gives some advice along these same lines. He says that the sacrificial life involves making up our minds to live that way; only then can self-sacrifice work its way out in our actions.[11] We must decisively say, "Yes, I will deny myself."[12]

When we deny ourselves, we have chosen to focus on God's interests alone. What are these interests? Certainly among them would be holiness and purity, as well as a forgiving and generous spirit. Jesus summed it up in terms of loving God and people (Matthew 22:37-40). He gives priority to loving God: "If anyone comes to Me, and does not hate his own father and mother and wife and children and brothers and sisters, yes, and even his own life, he cannot be My disciple" (Luke 14:26).

Wait a minute. I said I would deny myself—but my family members? Must I hate them? Dr. Thomas explains that this passage in the book of Luke is a hyperbole to communicate that our love for Christ, "should be so intense that it makes our love for others look like hatred."[13] Professor Thomas further explains that Christ "certainly did not intend hatred in a nonfigurative sense, because He later ranked love for neighbor as the second greatest commandment (Matthew 22:39) and labeled love for fellow-disciples as a mark of true discipleship" (John 13:34-35).[14]

Of course the kind of love Jesus meant is not a sentimental feeling but a love that acts according to God's interests. Normally there is no conflict between loving God and loving others because to love God is to love others. As the apostle John said, "Whoever loves the Father loves the child born of Him" (1 John 5:1; cf. John 15:9-12). But there may be times when we have to choose between our love for God and love for people dear to us.

Perhaps you have been raised in a non-Christian home and have had to confront the difficult choice between love for your family members and love for your Savior. If so, you understand Christ's warning about loving Him above everyone else. You know that loving Him in a fallen world will create friction, even among family members (Matthew 10:34-36). As Professor Thomas writes, "Whatever the relationship, the duty of keeping all natural affections subordinate to our love for Christ is supreme (see Matthew 8:22; 19:29; Mark 10:29-30)."[15]

That kind of love is a sacrifice, and sacrifice costs. The rich young ruler didn't like the cost of following Christ, so "he was saddened, and he went away grieving" (Mark 10:22). Sad to say, not just nonbelievers but many who call themselves Christians are unwilling to accept the total cost of following Christ. Some are not willing to give up their sin completely. Some are not willing to give up their attachment to the world. Some aren't willing to upset a family member and therefore won't follow Christ completely. But some—perhaps many—are willing to sacrifice as long as it isn't unpleasant. George Eliot wrote about a character named Tito who "was to be depended on to make any sacrifice that was not unpleasant."[16]

Are we ever like Tito? Do we limit our sacrifices only to those things that aren't unpleasant? Do we set limits on our sacrifice when it will take something away from us or our family? Do we sacrifice as long as it doesn't conflict with our social agenda, hobbies, or personal ambitions in life?

I have seen that when I forgo sacrifice because it would hinder my plans, I miss the opportunity to teach my own children about sacrifice. I must show them that the sacrificial life involves giving up something I may want to keep. It means keeping promises. It means thinking of others rather than just myself. It means considering the impact I can make in the life of another. It means not expecting others to sacrifice if I can't do it myself.

Look at Christ. He would never imagine wearing a crown without bearing a cross; nor would He command His followers to carry a cross without doing so Himself. So His expectation that we sacrifice for God and others is based squarely on His own example of dying to self.

DYING TO SELF

The second-century Christian leader Tertullian was once approached by a man who said, "I have come to Christ, but I don't know what to do. I have a job that I don't think is consistent with what Scripture teaches. What can I do? I must live."

To that Tertullian replied, "Must you?"[17]

In our day we focus on enjoying life to the fullest and feeling secure about everything. But the great saints of the past took the view that instead of having to live, they had to die (Galatians 2:20). And they did. They died to worldly desires and pleasures. They died to their own interests and pursuits.

In the nineteenth century Moravians[18] in South Africa became aware of a colony of lepers. Their flesh was rotting away with the disease, and some were missing arms or legs. In order to reach them for Christ, the Moravians chose to live in the leper compound, knowing they would probably develop leprosy themselves—and they did. Two others from the same noble group sold themselves into slavery in the West Indies in order that they might be allowed to preach to the slaves![19]

Saints of the past who were able to die to self needed at some point in their lives to work on their residual selfishness—just as we do. How might they have begun? I believe they started with prayer. Listen as an unknown Confederate soldier explains how God dealt with his residual selfishness:

> *I asked God for strength, that I might achieve,*
> *I was made weak, that I might learn humbly to obey. . . .*
> *I asked for health, that I might do greater things*
> *I was given infirmity, that I might do better things. . . .*
> *I asked for riches, that I might be happy,*

> *I was given poverty, that I might be wise.*
> *I asked for power, that I might have the praise of men,*
> *I was given weakness, that I might feel the need of God.*
> *I asked for all things, that I might enjoy life,*
> *I was given life, that I might enjoy all things. . . .*
> *I got nothing that I asked for—but everything I had hoped for,*
> *almost despite myself, my unspoken prayers were answered.*
> *I am among all men most richly blessed.*[20]

Truly, prayer is the beginning of helping us die to self. Along with prayer, here are a few practical steps to try for the next few days. On the first day, deny yourself something. In its place do something that will benefit someone else. Maybe you are hooked on a certain television show. For just one day, say no to yourself on that and spend some extra time with your children or call a friend and encourage her. Or do whatever else comes to your mind.

The next day, deny yourself something different. For example, get up a little early and pray for people you know.

The third day do something that you don't necessarily feel like doing but that would be a sacrificial investment in your own life. Exercise or start that diet or spend some time memorizing a verse that means a lot to you. Sharpening yourself in a way that requires self-discipline is a form of sacrifice. And, as I mentioned in the last chapter, it can put you on a higher level of effectiveness.

Have any thoughts for the following day?

Giving up little things and doing some small sacrificial thing in their place may not seem like much, but a lot of little things over time can add up to an effective life. An attitude of selflessness empowers us toward greater and greater challenges. It gives us momentum to creatively develop and use our potential to the fullest.

I experienced a little of that when I was asked to start teaching a Bible study to elderly women at a retirement home. I first had to count the cost. It would involve my time, and I didn't have a lot of it to spare (when we don't have much time to spare, we must discern how to use it wisely).

As I prayed about the opportunity to serve, God put strongly on my heart a desire to serve those elderly women. And so I did, *albeit reluctantly*. But I found that soon after I began, I started thinking about the elderly in other retirement homes. Then came a genuine zeal (and apparently more time), because I ended up teaching at three different retirement homes in three different cities every Saturday.

So how did I get from being reluctant to teach in one retirement home to wanting to serve in several? I had to die to myself—which means—I had to pray, asking the Lord for help. I prayed one prayer then, as I do now, "Lord, give me a large heart!"

WHAT A LARGE HEART ENTAILS

Many of us think that a large heart involves doing something major, such as going off to some foreign land as a missionary or committing our lives to some other type of ministry that takes so much of ourselves. While these are tremendous sacrifices, let's not forget that so, too, are those small daily sacrifices. Actually the little sacrifices are at times harder than the big ones because the little ones require a constant giving up of our desires. And besides, little sacrifices don't feed our pride because, after all, no one notices them. No one but God.

Each day I see how God is answering my prayer, enlarging my heart and also testing it. For instance, when I am reading a book, cleaning the house, or sitting at the computer, and the children come in from play asking me to take them on a walk, go to the park, or to tell them a story, what does sacrifice ask me to do? It tells me to go on that walk, go to the park, or tell a story. The book, the house, the computer will still be there for me later.

When I am at church and I see someone that seems uncomfortable and out of place, sacrifice is telling me, "Forget about talking to your friends for the moment; go and reach out to that person."

Looking at my large living room, sacrifice is asking me, "What sacrifice can you make?" I can use it, not just for my family but for others too, such as for a Bible study. That would be a greater way to reveal God's love.

When I have an opportunity to speak up for the defenseless or to share Christ, what is sacrifice telling me to do? It's telling me, "Forget what others may think of me; don't mind the cruel words of others."

Sacrifice also reminds me that I made a commitment—that is, to take the bad along with the good in following Christ (cf. Matthew 5:11-12).

When I am up at night and the children are down in bed, sometimes sacrifice is calling my name again. It's saying to go to bed early so that I can get up before the children to pray, be in the Word, and discover areas of further spiritual growth. When we sacrifice time, extra sleep, and other desires in order to build ourselves up spiritually, it benefits us as much as others. We and they can't help but be blessed by a life that's close to Jesus. In the process, we are offering up "spiritual sacrifices acceptable to God through Jesus Christ" (1 Peter 2:5).

Do you hear sacrifice calling your name? Is it telling you to spend more time with the children? To be more loving toward your husband? To be in prayer and the Word more? To share your material wealth or your precious time? To give others the benefit of your wisdom or knowledge? To give a helping hand or a kind word? To use your talents and skills purely for the privilege of blessing others rather than for material gain?

You can be assured by what God thinks of sacrifices that come from a big heart: "Do not neglect doing good and sharing, for with such sacrifices God is pleased" (Hebrews 13:16). Imagine God being pleased with you. That one thought alone should motivate you. And not only is God pleased, but because of His love for you, He tailor-makes sacrifices specifically for you, to help you grow.

TAILOR-MADE SACRIFICES

I believe that sometimes God allows special opportunities for sacrifice to come our way as a means of helping us work on specific weaknesses. For example, Jacob was a schemer, relying on his own cleverness and trickery to get ahead rather than on hard work and God's blessing (Genesis 27). God had to work on Jacob, letting him labor for years on his father-in-law's terms. Jacob had to submit, work, and rely on God rather than on his own stratagems. After a few years he learned to give God the credit for his prosperity and to recognize the role of hard work (Genesis 31:6-7).

The person who doesn't use time or other things wisely may find herself tested with just the perfect sacrifice to help her grow in the deficient area. Likewise with the woman who can't control her spending. She may soon find that with debts to pay, she can no longer buy the things she wants and even has trouble covering her needs. I once heard a woman say that after she got out of debt, all she wanted to do was use her money to help others rather than give it to a credit card company. Truly, this woman learned how to sacrifice the hard way.

In most cases, our willingness to sacrifice in any area helps us to conquer in other unrelated areas. The person who sacrifices time, for example, will soon find it easier to sacrifice money. The person who goes out of the way to offer encouragement may find that she has less trouble with her temper.

We have to see these sacrifices that come our way as God-ordained. If He knew everything before the foundation of the world, He knows what has to come our way to help us grow.

When we offer Him our sacrifices, we associate with His willingness to sacrifice for His creatures, to be a part of lessening the tide of human sorrow, adding to another's happiness. God's supreme way of doing this was the way of the cross.

THE WAY OF THE CROSS

The cross has come to be recognized the world over as a symbol of Christianity. It is used in art and jewelry, and it decorates even the church buildings of people who don't understand its significance. But those who do understand it respond to God the way the apostle Thomas did, who with awe and adoration said, "My Lord and my God!" (John 20:28).

Elisabeth Elliot is one woman who understands all too well the true meaning of the cross. She was the wife of missionary Jim Elliot who, along with four other missionaries, was martyred in 1956 by the Auca Indians, a stone-age tribe deep in the jungles of Ecuador.

After the tragedy Elisabeth continued to serve the very Indians who had murdered her husband until the Lord later called her and her daughter back to the States. Years later Elisabeth would marry again. Then she had to watch her second husband, Addison Leitch, die a painful death. Today Elisabeth is again remarried—to Lars Gren. Some years ago I was blessed with the opportunity of having a lengthy interview with Elisabeth on several topics, including sacrifice and the cross. Here are some of her thoughts:

> When Jesus spoke of discipleship, He said, "If you want to be My disciple, you must give up your right to yourself, take up your cross, and follow Me." Giving up your right to yourself is by far the most rigorous of Jesus' commands—that you turn over all the rights with none left.

> Picking up the cross is a matter of saying yes to God no matter what happens. It's accepting the events and conditions of every day. Pick up your cross daily and say yes to Him, and then following is a matter of obedience, one step at a time.

> When I speak of being a follower of the Crucified, it is the way He is taking us . . . the way of the cross. We need not be surprised when we're asked to die. Paul said, "I die daily, death worketh in me, but life in you." He said that this death is "at work in me in order that the life of Jesus may be manifest in my mortal flesh." The whole pathway of the Crucified means learning to die to oneself.

> "Crucified with Christ, nevertheless, I live, yet not I, but Christ lives in me." Here is the paradox of life coming out of death, gain coming out of loss, joy coming out of sorrow, and light coming out of darkness.

> There is no such thing as sacrifice when you consider what we are being offered in exchange. Jesus said, "If you suffer with Me, you will also reign with Me." He was crowned because He suffered. Many women are suffering—that is one way to appeal to them—not the way the popular television evangelism is doing it by offering them health, wealth, and prosperity. That is a false gospel. But [we can show] them that Christianity is the only religion in the world that deals directly with suffering in a transforming way.

> I know from experience that He does give beauty for ashes, the oil of joy for mourning, the garment of praise for the spirit of

heaviness. It takes the willingness to be a corn of wheat that falls into the ground and dies. It doesn't fall into the ground and die in order to be dead. It falls into the ground and dies in order to be fulfilled, to bring forth much fruit. Jesus said, "If you lose your life for My sake, you'll find your true self."

I'm continually asking women, "What kind of difference does Jesus Christ make in your life?" It's all very well to talk about going to heaven and being saved, but what I want to know is, what difference does Christianity make to you if you get a telephone call saying that your son has been killed or your husband has cancer? If you live in a house you don't like, does Christ promise you a better house? What difference does Jesus make to you in your *present situation*? Right now I'm taking care of my four grandchildren and feeling very inadequate about it. What can I expect that my Christian faith is going to do in this situation?

What do you mean when you call yourself a Christian? What are you doing? What have you done that warrants calling yourself a Christian? If it doesn't make any difference here and now, why bother?[21]

WHAT SACRIFICE BOILS DOWN TO

As Elisabeth Elliot shows us, sacrifice is not an option; it is part of obedience and the genuine Christian life. Without obedience, what evidence is there of change in our lives? And without change, where's the evidence of true repentance—that we have turned from self to follow a Messiah with a cross?

While our worth isn't based on obedience, obedience strengthens our spiritual life and empowers us to impact the lives of others. You see, as we follow Christ's example of selflessness, then to the positional significance of who we are in Christ, we add the practical significance of who we are in the outworking of His plan. So obedience is a privilege!

Consider: When we obey, we look to the example of Christ who "did not please Himself" (Romans 15:3).

When we obey, we prove the sincerity of our love and devotion to Christ. God always puts a premium on our deeds. John wrote,

"Let us not love with word or with tongue, but in deed and truth" (1 John 3:18).

As we obey, we change. We move further from what we were in our unbelieving, unregenerate days. Look at the apostles. First they obeyed by following Christ physically—leaving their nets, their families, their occupations. Then as they grew spiritually, they learned to give up their old ways, habits, thoughts, and, for many, their remaining possessions. But they gained so much more than they gave up.

OUR GAIN

We gain many things when we live sacrificially. Some of those gains we might not even think about—such as character. And character is something that can never be taken away against our will, even in our world where so much is fragile. Character is our soul's garment. Those who sacrifice here on earth are forever enriched because they have ennobled their character. And they are eligible to receive another reward, which is joy.

Joy goes hand in hand with sacrifice when the sacrifice results in something we genuinely care about. It was that way for Christ who "for the joy set before Him endured the cross, despising the shame, and has sat down at the right hand of the throne of God" (Hebrews 12:2). Certainly there were times when it seemed almost unbearable, such as the day Christ prayed, "Father, if You are willing, remove this cup from Me; yet not My will, but Yours be done" (Luke 22:42).

Paul knew that same joy in sacrificing for people he loved. He told the Thessalonians, "For what thanks can we render to God for you in return for all the joy with which we rejoice before our God on your account" (1 Thessalonians 3:9). He called the Philippians his "joy and crown" (Philippians 4:1).

Joy isn't inconsistent with sorrow. The apostle Paul was "sorrowful, yet always rejoicing, poor yet making many rich; as having nothing yet possessing all things" (2 Corinthians 6:10). For Paul, as for Christ, sufferings were more than worth it because he cared so much about the goal—the good of other people. Their joy was wrapped up in God's will, no matter what sacrifice had to be made.

Joy, then, is both the result of sacrifice and a way of persevering in order to make the sacrifice. As we focus on the reward, the sacrifice fades into perspective. Paul said, "For momentary, light affliction is producing for us an eternal weight of glory far beyond all comparison" (2 Corinthians 4:17). When Paul said these words, he was being run out of town, lied about constantly, beaten, left for dead, shipwrecked, jailed, and so on. But joy and sacrifice go hand in hand. No wonder Nehemiah told his stressed-out, remorseful people, "Do not be grieved, for the joy of the LORD is your strength" (Nehemiah 8:10).

Do we have this joy that is wrapped up in God's will, no matter what the cost? While it may seem that our sacrifices are quite poor and feeble compared to those of Christ, Paul, and others, we can be encouraged. When we have a right heart, even the smallest sacrifice is valued by God. Jesus said that whoever gives one of His children even so much as "a cup of cold water to drink, truly I say to you, he shall not lose his reward" (Matthew 10:42).

In conclusion, let me take you back to that centuries-old cemetery I mentioned at the beginning of the chapter. As I continued to look among those weathered gravestones, I found a sacrificial saint whose life was wrapped up in Jesus. His name was Joseph Hart, and in life he was a pastor. He died in 1783 at the age of fifty-six. His own words were engraved on his tombstone: "Though I am a stranger to others and a wonder to myself, yet I know Him (Christ) or rather am known of Him. 'Where sin abounded, grace did much more abound. O bring no price; God's grace is free, to Paul, to Magdalene, to me.'"

Mr. Hart says it all. God's grace is free. No amount of sacrifice could come close to what Christ has done for us. And because God spared sinners such as Paul, Mary Magdalene, Joseph Hart, and me, I am prompted to give my all. How about you?

Now you may be wondering if we ever found Marx's tomb. Yes, but it wasn't easy! After searching, we realized that Marx was not buried at that particular cemetery. So after a little research and a bus ride across town, we arrived at the high gates of another cemetery. The place was deserted, but we explored through some weeds and tilting headstones until Brian found not just a simple marker, but an imposing monument to Marx standing like some holy shrine. For me, the bust of Marx on its marble column was a sad sight really. There it stood like some sinister opening to the gates of hell.

When Marx was an adolescent, no one would have guessed how his life would turn out. While his adult years were spent undermining belief in God, as a youth he wrote: "The fruit of our union with Christ is our willingness to sacrifice ourselves for our fellow man. And the joy which the Epicureans in their superficial philosophy sought in vain . . . is a joy known only to the innocent heart united with Christ and through Christ to God. . . . Who would not bear suffering gladly, knowing that by his abiding in Christ, by his works, God himself is glorified."[22]

How meaningless words are when we do not back them up with our lives! May we take our Christian walk seriously and sacrificially so that one day our lives will mark the entrance to the gates of heaven and to the presence of the one who is worthy of any sacrifice.

THINKING IT OVER

1. How did the church change as the Roman Empire changed? What parallels do you see today?
2. During what times were the kingdom of self and the kingdom of God manifested in the life of Peter? (See Mark 8:31-33; Luke 22:54-62; John 21:15-19.)
3. What would our spiritual adversary prefer us to focus on?
4. What forms the bridge between the two contrasting kingdoms? How do you walk across that bridge in your own life?
5. How might God tailor our sacrifices to our needs, and why?
6. As we make sacrifices, what is our greatest reward?

Nine

SALT—THAT FLAVORS A
TASTELESS SOCIETY

*W*hen Ken Burns's documentary *The Civil War* aired on public television, it was the most watched program in television history. Why? I believe it was because to this day the United States still carries the scars from that destructive and brutal period—the country's bloodiest war.

Have you ever wondered why England never had a civil war over slavery? That country led the world in slave trafficking, transporting 38,000 terrified and dehumanized individuals to America.[1] A major reason they avoided war is that they had what the United States never had—William Wilberforce (1759-1833).

Wilberforce was from a well-to-do family, but personal tragedy marred his youth. When William was nine, his father died, and he was sent to live with his uncle. Things must not have gone well, because at the age of twelve he was sent back home. Wilberforce neglected his studies at school, and he didn't improve when he went to Cambridge in 1776. He inherited a lot of money, which further sapped his motivation to accomplish anything.[2]

Despite his disinterest in education (which he later regretted), his great oratorical skills won him a seat in Parliament in 1780. His general lack of direction changed in 1784 when he became a Christian. After his conversion, he considered leaving politics and entering the pastorate. But his friend John Newton persuaded him to stay, to "serve the cause of Christianity in Parliament."[3] As you may recall, Newton, once a notorious slave trader, came to Christ and became a pastor and hymn writer, composing such songs as "Amazing Grace."

Wilberforce followed Newton's counsel and went about being salt and light in Parliament, starting with a bill he wrote to end the evils of slave trading. However, the bill was defeated. Undaunted, Wilberforce tried again in 1798, 1802, 1804, and 1805; but his efforts repeatedly failed.[4]

All the while Wilberforce was becoming increasingly unpopular with British merchants because slave trading brought in lots of revenue. But Wilberforce refused to listen to the merchants. He risked political suicide by his untiring efforts to end the slave trade. Finally in 1807 his bill to abolish the atrocity passed.

Wilberforce and the Christians who supported him knew that this victory could be just the beginning. Pressing on, they campaigned for the emancipation of slaves in all territories under British rule.[5] After forty years of fighting slavery, they saw victory. On August 28, 1833, one month after Wilberforce's death, slavery was abolished on all British soil.[6] England honored the greatness of his life and effort by burying Wilberforce in the famed Westminster Abbey.[7]

It is possible that the efforts of that obedient Christian spared Britain and the Commonwealth countries from a bloody civil war. Thousands of slaves were freed, and thousands more avoided being transported by British ships. Furthermore, England was spared the deep wounds that have left America scarred for well over a century. While the United States had Abraham Lincoln, Wilberforce is unique in that he labored for an unpopular cause for forty years.

It is hard to imagine how history would have been different without Wilberforce. Imagine, too, how history would have been different if Martin Luther had decided *not* to nail his thesis on the Wittenberg church door. What if Raphael had never shown his paintings to anyone? What if Handel had let his *Messiah* lie forgotten in some cabinet?

What if D. L. Moody, Charles Spurgeon, Billy Sunday, or Billy Graham had ignored their calling? What if Susannah Wesley had neglected to raise her children well? What if Catherine Booth had ignored her idea to start the Salvation Army? What if the ten Boom family had refused to open their door to Jews during the Nazi occupation? Or what if C. S. Lewis, Elisabeth Elliot, Edith and Francis Schaeffer, and other writers had never bothered to write down their thoughts? What a loss to the world and to the kingdom of God!

What comes home to me is that not one of us has a right to keep our gifts to ourselves. You and I have something quite significant to give—our influence. Influence is not ours to keep; it belongs to the human race. We see this in the life of Christ. In three short years, His influence would affect the entire world for all time.

Influence is like a fragrance. When a potpourri candle slowly melts, its scent doesn't stay in one place but fills the entire house. In essence that's what influence does. It cannot be contained.

THE POWER OF INFLUENCE

Look in the pages of Scripture, and you will find examples of people influencing others—Ruth encouraging her mother-in-law by her loyalty (book of Ruth). Watch Deborah inspire a nation with her faith (Judges 4—5). Notice Huldah spiritually motivate a king so he in turn could turn an apostate nation back to God (2 Chronicles 34:22-33; 34:1-21; 35:1-19). Observe the zealous Samaritan woman lead others to belief in Christ (John 4:39). See spiritual nurturing by Lois and Eunice as they build up Timothy in the faith (2 Timothy 1:5; 3:14-17). See Mary Magdalene encourage the grieving apostles with good news (John 20:18).

That's just a taste of what influence is. Can we dare to think that we ourselves might have as much impact as those women of Scripture, or is that some impossible ambition? That all depends. It's been said that while most people *hope* to influence others, truly effective people *resolve* to influence them. In other words, the wise woman does not merely *hope* that she will have an influence and then expect that it will happen by accident. No. She decides *that* she is going to have an influence and then gives some thought to *how* it will happen. So whether we have a great influence depends somewhat on us.

RESOLVE TO INFLUENCE

It was a day the apostles would never forget, a day when they were still nursing the wounds received as they fled Christ's side to let Him suffer and die alone. It was also a day when some of the apostles were still doubtful about Christ (Matthew 28:17).

In this setting fraught with human emotions, the resurrected Christ met with His disciples in Galilee to give them a command and a challenge that would consume the remainder of their lives. He told them, "Go therefore and make disciples of all the nations" (Matthew

28:19). From that day on they were to influence all the nations, winning people to Christ and bringing them to maturity.

It's quite apparent that the apostles aggressively took up Christ's challenge. Otherwise the Gospel wouldn't have made it to the second century, let alone to the twenty-first. We are to have the same vision they had. The truth they proclaimed we are to proclaim. The hope they shared we are to share. The Christ-life they lived we are to live. How did the disciples accomplish such a feat? By embracing Christ's formula, to strive to be the salt of the earth and the light of the world (Matthew 5:13-14).

We are to be the salt that preserves and puts flavor into a tasteless society, that stings the open wounds of a sinful generation, that awakens the awareness of thirst that can be satisfied only by the living water of Christ. We are to be the light that illuminates darkened pathways, answering life's perplexing questions about meaning, purpose, and destiny—the light that shines in a very dim world.[8]

BEING SALT

Salt has been used for ages to prevent spoilage in food, and the Christian salts society in the same way. Practically no one would doubt that we live in a society that tolerates the erosion of godly principles. It seems that as long as individuals can enjoy their personal freedom and prosperity, they care little about what happens around them.

With so much of our moral foundation eroded, tolerance and neutrality have been turned into virtues—and the only virtues people agree on. Remember the old days when moral convictions were something to be honored rather than rejected as intolerant?

Imagine what society would be like if people in the past had not held firm moral convictions. Imagine if, for example, slavery had been tolerated indefinitely. The secular philosopher Dante had it right when he said, "The hottest places in hell are reserved for those who in a period of moral crisis maintain their neutrality."[9]

Are we as Christians maintaining neutrality where God takes a stand and expects us, as His representatives, to do the same? Of course, the true Christian would never end up in hell, but might we lose some of our reward because we are failing to be salt? If we aren't doing anything about an issue that God cares deeply about, then we may have to face the possibility that we are part of the problem. As the old saying goes, "Evil triumphs when good men do nothing."

The people who have made a significant difference in this world were not those who remained neutral. They were what Christ expected them to be—salty. I desire to be a very salty Christian. How about you? If that's your desire, let's look at some ways to accomplish that goal.

SALTINESS THROUGH PRAYER

It seems that the more things affect us personally, the easier it is to pray about them. It's easy to pray about our health, our job, our relationships. It's easy to pray for people who are close to us—that they may either be receptive to the Gospel or grow strong in the Lord, and for our church that it may flourish spiritually. As Christians we hear a great deal about being salt in this way (and it's right that we do). But rather than talk more about this, I would prefer to focus on some other ways we can be salt, such as interceding for things that don't benefit us directly.

I am learning that a significant prayer life doesn't just deal with things that affect me directly, but includes things that affect our whole society. Scripture says that we have an opportunity—and a responsibility—to pray for our nation's leaders. When was the last time you heard someone pray for them? I will never forget the day when President Clinton was sworn into office and Rev. Billy Graham prayed for him. A woman gave me a call to talk about the event and asked, "How could Rev. Graham pray for that man?"

I think quite a few Christians miss out here because it's easy to think that anything even remotely related to politics is somehow unspiritual. But Paul says to pray for "kings and all who are in authority" (1 Timothy 2:1-2). Who would that include today? At the very least it would be those in national politics, members of the Supreme Court, people who control education, and the like. Paul doesn't say to pray so that your country can be rich and powerful, but "so that we may lead a tranquil and quiet life in all godliness and dignity" (1

Timothy 2:2). Godliness grows best when people in authority act wisely and morally.

If you find it difficult to pray for some of our leaders, imagine what Paul must have felt when he wrote this command. He was under the cruel leadership of Nero, who was the ruler under whom half the city of Rome burned in A.D. 64. Because the public thought Nero to be insane, they suspected that he had set the fire himself. So what did he do to counter the rumor? Tacitus, a man who lived at the time, tells us that "Nero blamed the Christians" and that "before killing the Christians, Nero used them to amuse the people. Some were dressed in furs, to be killed by dogs. Others were crucified. Still others were set on fire early in the night, so that they might illumine it. Nero opened his own gardens for these shows, and in the circus he himself became a spectacle, for he mingled with the people dressed as a charioteer."[10]

It's not clear if this cruelty had already started when Paul said to pray for leaders. However, people knew what kind of man Nero was. And Paul still says "pray for them."

So how might we pray?

1. Pray for their salvation, that they come to see their personal sinfulness and their need for Jesus Christ.

2. Pray that they might have God's wisdom rather than relying on worldly wisdom.

3. Pray that they do what is right despite political pressures.

4. Pray that they have the best interests of the country at heart rather than what's best for their own political careers.

5. Pray that in their conduct they will be good examples to the fathers, mothers, sons, and daughters of this nation.

6. Pray that they will realize their accountability before almighty God for the decisions they make.[11]

7. Pray especially for our brothers and sisters in Christ who represent Him in political office. They make a very real sacrifice—something few people are equipped to do. Why? Often the righteous are smeared with false accusations and misrepresentations. You've seen it. So often if the opponents of the righteous can't win by argument, they will try to discredit their opponent. If that doesn't stick, they will misrepresent the person's views as somehow dangerous to society. This isn't anything new. Though public life was different in ancient Israel,

the same kinds of attacks were made on the righteous people who served publicly. Amos, for instance, had rebuked the nation because of its social evils. Amaziah, the priest of Bethel, may have been jealous that people were listening to Amos rather than to him, so he sent word to the king of Israel saying, "Amos has conspired against you in the midst of the house of Israel; the land is unable to endure all his words" (Amos 7:10).

8. Pray that God's will be done on earth as it is in heaven (Matthew 6:10).

In our praying, let's be encouraged. For a few thousands years now, God has turned the hearts of many men and women. This is no difficult matter for God, for "the king's heart is like channels of water in the hand of the LORD; he turns it wherever he wishes" (Proverbs 21:1).

SALTINESS THROUGH OUR VOTE

The book of Judges tells the sad story of Abimelech, one of the sons of Gideon (the leader who had rescued Israel from a vast army with so few men). Abimelech wanted to rule the people of Shechem. To secure that rule, he successfully destroyed the competition by killing seventy of his brothers (Judges 9:56). Then he had himself crowned.

Jotham, the one brother who escaped the bloodshed, warned the people about Abimelech by telling a parable about trees who sought a ruler. They asked the olive tree to rule, but it declined. They asked the fig tree, and it declined. They were turned down by a vine also. Then rather than seek someone who was righteous and available, the trees stooped to be ruled by a mere bramble (Judges 9:8-15). As history shows, the bramble was Abimelech.

God held the people of Shechem accountable for selecting and supporting such an evil man. Scripture says that "God returned all the wickedness of the men of Shechem on their heads, and the curse of Jotham . . . came upon them" (Judges 9:57). God holds people responsible for the leaders they choose. Just imagine how much better things would have turned out had the people of Shechem picked a righteous leader.

There are some who believe that we as Christians shouldn't be involved in politics in any form—not even to vote. What do you think?

It is not as simple as saying that the New Testament doesn't command it, because, of course, there was no opportunity to vote then. Good citizens were expected to simply do what they were told. Modern democracies, however, do not function unless people are informed and involved, at least enough to vote.

Consider what happened in Germany. On March 13, 1932, the German people had the opportunity to vote for the president of their choice. Eighteen million voted to reelect President Hindenburg; eleven million voted for Hitler, and four million for Thaelmann. Hindenburg's votes came to 49.6 percent of the total. Since no candidate had the necessary 51 percent, the election had to be held again[12] one year later. History was forever changed by a few votes.

During that waiting period Jewish reporter Bella Fromm (whose own life would soon be in danger) wrote from inside Germany, "Every day brings many casualties, wounded and dead, in 'political clashes.' . . . There is little question, of course, as to how the voting will turn out. Goebbels's collaborator, Dr. Brauweiler, is known to be an expert in correcting 'defective' ballots."[13]

As we all know, Hitler did win the presidency on that second vote, most likely through fraud.[14] If everyone had used the freedom to vote the first time around, millions of allied servicemen might never have died in the war, and millions might not have died in concentration camps.

Recently the Christian Coalition released their survey results showing that only one in five evangelicals is even registered to vote. This might seem surprising, but after watching a recent television documentary on voting, I think I understand the attitudes of many who aren't registered. The documentary began in a Christian college with a choir practice where the students were passionately singing, "I love You, Lord."

When the song was over, an interviewer asked these students if they were going to go out and vote. With the exception of one, all replied no. The reasons each gave were pretty much the same, summed up by the lead singer: "There's nothing in it for me." This comment reminded me of a quote in the Jewish book the Mishnah (the first part of the Talmud): "If I am not for myself, who will be for me? And if I am only for myself, what am I?" (Aboth 1:14).

Christians with the attitude of the students in the documentary fail to see how voting can be a way of loving one's neighbor (Matthew 19:19). Possibly you can't think of any issue that might stir you to vote, but how might your five minutes at the voting booth help someone else? Think of your friend who is home-schooling her children. Your vote could make it possible for her to continue raising her children the way she believes is best. What about the public school children on your street? There always seem to be public education issues that require wisdom at the ballot box. Are any pro-life candidates running for office? If so, how might your vote reach out to the many unborn babies at risk?

For myself, it seems a little hypocritical if I try to tell people about a God who cares about them while I don't care enough to spend a few minutes to vote on things that matter to them. It also seems hypocritical for me to say that I am against things such as pornography, abortion, crime, corruption in government, and so on, but then not bother to take even a few minutes every couple of years to do something about it.

Showing that we care is one way of building credibility for sharing the Gospel. We can show that we care when we vote to get the best men and women in government and onto the judicial bench. Voting can show that we are interested in righting wrongs, doing justice, serving mankind (cf. Micah 6:8), and generally preventing society from deteriorating further.

THE DECLINE OF A CIVILIZATION

Historian Will Durant said that one of the essential causes of Rome's decline "lay in her people."[15] Or, as another historian put it, the decline was due "to a changed attitude of [*sic*] men's minds."[16]

We certainly don't need to belabor the atrocities of Hitler, but very few realize that Germany's decline was partly due to the changed attitudes of the professing church. In 1932 the German Christian Church wrote "The Platform of the German Christians," which forsook biblical principles to endorse Hitler's program for racial "purity." Here are some statements drawn from their ten points:

> 7. Therefore racial mixing is to be opposed. On the basis of its experience, the German foreign missions have for a long time

called to the German nation: "Keep yourself racially pure," and tells us that faith in Christ doesn't disturb race but rather deepens and sanctifies it.

8. We know something of Christian duty and love toward the helpless, but we demand also the protection of the nation from the incapable and inferior.

9. In the mission to the Jews we see a grave danger to our national character. It is the entryway for foreign blood into our national body . . . as long as the Jews have the rights of citizenship and thereby there exists the danger of racial deterioration and bastardization. . . . Marriage between Germans and Jews is especially to be forbidden.[17]

How horrid! It's hard to imagine that there could have been any true Christians in that church. At first one wonders if any groups spoke up, especially in light of the experiences of people such as Kay Bonner Nee, a witness to the Holocaust. She said: "This unbelievable experience changed my values, my attitude, my whole life. I had not been politically active or even aware before the war, but I became so afterwards. And whenever I feel that one person cannot do much, or that what I'm doing is not important or not having any effect, I remember the Germans saying, 'No, we are not responsible,' and our answer, 'Yes, you are. You allowed it to happen.'"[18] As Nee points out, we do have a voice, and we can do something; we cannot stand by and allow evil to be done. But unfortunately a lot of us do allow it.

So where were the true believers in Germany? Were any of them speaking up (questions our posterity will ask in regard to abortion!)? Now in all fairness, I believe that many Germans were silent because by the time they figured out what was going on, it would have been very dangerous to try to stop it. Fortunately, despite real risks, a number of Christians did speak up. The German Evangelical Church, though not "political" by any means, realized the importance of taking a stand when such evil was occurring in their society. They not only protested Hitler's agenda but also the German Christian Church's platform, and wrote The Barmen Declaration in May 1934.[19]

There were also individual German believers who considered it better to live a salty life than let their lives lose their flavor (Matthew 5:13). So committed were they that they risked their lives to denounce the horrors of the Nazi program. Read sometime about German theologian Dietrich Bonhoeffer who challenged other Christians to confront the evils of their society. Also read Bonhoeffer's book *Letters & Papers from Prison* or *The Cost of Discipleship*, which he finished writing as the Nazis closed down a seminary he headed and then arrested twenty-seven students.[20] *The Cost of Discipleship* has greatly influenced the lives of Christians throughout the world.

As we know, things eventually got better in Germany, but not without a cleansing of the church within. In 1945 the German Evangelical Council of Churches got together and wrote the "Stuttgart Declaration of Guilt." The declaration recognized the "great community of suffering, but also in a solidarity of guilt. . . . we accuse ourselves that we didn't witness more courageously, pray more faithfully, believe more joyously, love more ardently."[21]

Must we confess our failures like the Evangelical Christians in Germany? Are we silent on issues that need to be addressed? We may be guilty as former Senate Chaplain Richard Halverson charges: "Evangelicals seem to have been more influenced by the world than they have influenced the world."[22]

But, some may ask, how can we be a real influence when things are so bad? King David might have thought the same thing. During a time when wickedness was rampant, he questioned, "If the foundations are destroyed, what can the righteous do?" (Psalm 11:3).

I believe that the righteous can do what the evangelical Christians in Germany did. We can confess that we haven't prayed more faithfully, believed more joyously, loved more ardently. And some of us may need to confess our lack of courage. Proverbs tells us, "Open your mouth for the mute, for the rights of all the unfortunate. Open your mouth, judge righteously, and defend the rights of the afflicted and needy" (Proverbs 31:8-9). Might this be a call for us to actively demonstrate compassion?

WHAT'S BECOME OF CHRISTIAN COMPASSION?

Prior to the early decades of the twentieth century, evangelical Christianity generally held that practical compassion should go along with preaching the Gospel. In that spirit, many Christian groups, such as the Christian and Missionary Alliance and the Salvation Army, did vigorous work among the poor. Others started rescue missions, relief programs, homes for fallen women, and outreach programs for immigrants and the downtrodden. Historian George Marsden said of the period that "preaching the gospel was always their central aim, but social and evangelistic work went hand in hand."[23]

By the 1890s something new was happening. Some liberal religious groups began doing social work with little or no evangelism, promoting what came to be called a "social gospel."[24] Conservative evangelicals were upset about the new trend because works of compassion were replacing—rather than complementing—evangelism.

Men such as Evangelist D. L. Moody (1837-1899) were very upset that the Gospel was being left out of social outreach. Furthermore he saw the world as a "wrecked vessel," implying that one should just concentrate on saving souls and refrain from social work *unless* it was for the purpose of preaching conversion and repentance.[25]

Moody's colleague, Baptist minister Cortland Myers of Brooklyn, said that the church "is not a benevolent institution nor a social institution, but an institution for one purpose—winning lost souls to Christ and being instrumental in redeeming the world." Nevertheless, continued Myers, the "practical side of Christianity" is *essential* even if secondary. So, unlike Moody, Pastor Myers believed that preaching without practical charity would be empty.[26]

From the same era, James M. Gray, later President of Moody Bible Institute, summed up in a simple way the Christian's duty to his neighbor: "I shall feed him if he is hungry, clothe him if naked, visit him if sick, and especially seek to win his soul if lost."[27] For Gray, the Gospel and practical compassion went hand in hand. Even Moody did not reject the connection between the two.

In the early decades of the 1900s, there was an outright battle between the conservatives and the liberals, and the social gospel became a target. According to Marsden, it was then that Evangelicals shunned works of compassion because they were associated with liberal theology.[28]

Over the years the evangelical church has reacted so strongly against the social gospel that now when people come to it for help, they are likely to receive little more than a list of government programs they can turn to. (As one pastor replied when asked if the church could help a member who was a destitute mother of five, "What does she think we are, a charity?") The result has been that in less than a century, the church has gone from believing that good works validate the preaching of the Gospel to the view that good works compromise it and sap resources.

Somehow we as believers need to strike a balance among good deeds, acts of kindness, our personal growth, family life, and evangelism and discipleship (Matthew 28:19-20). As believers in the living God, we have no less than the Compassionate One living within us to give us, not worldly compassion, but His heavenly compassion for hurting people. Are we using the compassion God has given us?

THE GREATEST EVIDENCE
OF SALTINESS: COMPASSION

God has always desired that His compassion be shown to the world through His children. For that reason, he wrote compassion right into the laws of Israel. The poor were allowed to gather up all the olives that didn't fall off the tree (Deuteronomy 24:20; Isaiah 17:6) and to collect the excess of grain at the corners of a field (Leviticus 23:22). The poor could also walk behind the reapers and pick up anything left behind. In this way Ruth collected a basket of barley (Ruth 2:7, 17), enough to feed herself and her mother-in-law Naomi for about five days.[29] Every seventh year the entire harvest had to be left for the poor (Exodus 23:10-11).

In His life Jesus amplified the importance of compassion. Go with Him to a wedding and see the compassion He had for the bride and groom who ran out of wine (John 2:1-11). Walk the dusty roads with Him and see an array of poor, helpless, sick, disabled, and miserable people all become special objects of His care. Sit by His side as He takes time to talk about a Samaritan traveler who had compassion for a dying man (Luke 10:30-37) and a father who had compassion for his runaway son (Luke 15:20-24). See Judas, who grasps neither the depth of his own corruption nor the sadness of his doom, be treated kindly by the Messiah he betrayed (Matthew 26:50). Finally let your heart be moved as the Compassionate One dies for the sin and misery of the world (John 3:16).

Christ also tells a story about the neglect of compassion. The portrait is of a man not named in Scripture but sometimes referred to as Dives (Latin for "rich man"),[30] who sits at his dinner table dressed in purple. He is the picture of splendor, living luxuriously every day! But there is someone else in the story. A beggar named Lazarus lies at Dives's gate. The poor man's body is covered with ugly, painful, and possibly bloody sores that the dogs lick. Lazarus isn't as concerned about his sores as he is about food. He is starving and longing to be fed—even if just with the crumbs that fall from the rich man's plate (Luke 16:19-21).

But Lazarus's suffering moves neither the heart nor conscience of Dives. What could have hardened him so? I'll suggest a few things. First, he did not put himself in Lazarus's position, asking himself, "If I were deprived like that, how would I want someone to help me?" Secondly, he never developed sensitivity. He never made the attempt to talk to Lazarus, listen to him, or try to understand how he got the sores or why he had no home.

Possibly Dives had seen this type of misery so often that he had become numb to it. Because of a lack of sensitivity, he allowed Lazarus's most basic need of bread and water to go unmet.

Dives lost the opportunity to make a difference. Are we also losing opportunities to make a difference to the people who come our way? In such an affluent society, we will rarely meet a person going hungry, but people with real pain and struggles do cross our paths. How might we be sensitive to the evil and the suffering around us? For myself, the answer lies in developing a more compassionate heart that I may use my salt more effectively.

DEVELOPING GREATER COMPASSION

I have come up with nine questions that have helped me in my journey toward greater compassion. I hope they can be of help to you, too.

1. *Am I moved with sympathy when I see or hear about suffering?* When I was a diet clerk at a local hospital, my shift started at 5 A.M. five days a week. As soon as I got into the office, the phone would ring. I knew

who it was, and I didn't want to talk with her. Her name was Karla, a patient at the hospital. She was severely ill. Having ignored her diabetic diet for many years, she was paying a heavy price. She first came in with gangrene on her right foot. That foot had to be amputated. When she left the hospital, she still ignored her diet. Eventually, she was a regular customer, coming in and out of the hospital for more amputations because of spreading gangrene. She also went blind.

Now why wouldn't I have compassion on this woman? Because it seemed to me that she wouldn't give me a chance. Every morning Karla would call for a change in her diet. And each morning I would have to explain why her requests couldn't be granted, but nevertheless I would promise to talk to a dietician. And then the usual curses would spew from her mouth like waste from a ruptured sewer.

One morning everything was going to change (except the diet). Karla called asking for a large glass of grape juice. I told her, "Your diet allows you to have only a quarter cup."

Again the curse words, and then she said, "Why can't anyone give me this. You know I'm dying!"

Those words hit me. Karla was right—she was dying. Yet because of my irritation at her, I soon lost sight of that very tragic fact. I had spent a lot of time arguing with Karla about her physical condition, and I completely ignored her spiritual condition. She needed to know the Great Physician.

I came to see through that incident how easily we can each be hardened and uncompassionate. Compassion requires that we open our eyes to the needs of others and then respond. Scripture shows that Christ felt compassion when He saw the condition of the multitude. They were "distressed," "dispirited," "like sheep without a shepherd" (Matthew 9:36).

Compassion is a Christlike quality that "weeps with those who weep" (Romans 12:15). It's powerful. It's not just a passive thing, a feeling; it motivates us to significant action. Compassion sent David Brainerd to the Native Americans, Hudson Taylor to China, Amy Carmichael to India, Adoniram Judson to Burma, Helen Roseveare to the Congo; and it led Corrie ten Boom to open her door to Jewish fugitives. It was compassion for the perishing that brought Jesus Christ to earth and then on to the cross.

While we cannot calm every human cry (certainly there are millions entitled to our attention), the question we must ask is: Will we ignore the cries we personally hear? We won't if we are sensitive enough to listen and caring enough to respond. And if we do these things, though no one else may never know, we can make a significant difference in the lives of the hurting, the grieving, the lost, or the dying.

2. *Do I have a divine perspective, seeing evil as God sees it?* It's difficult for us to imagine how God sees evil. To get an idea, I think of abortion because it is perhaps the most serious of our society's evils. Do I see the taking of a helpless unborn life the way God does?

Interestingly, inscribed in the corridors of the great hall of the Library of Congress are these words: "There is but one temple in the universe, and that is the body of man."[31] Our government exalts the human body while also considering unborn humans to be worth less than whales, eagles, and the like. I recently heard someone advocate using human tissue for experiments on the grounds that "we wouldn't have to use laboratory animals."[32] In the town I live in, even a weed has more protection than an unborn child. If I want to pull weeds, the "rules" are that I must get permission, since some weeds are endangered!

Christian philosopher Francis Schaeffer pointed out that if we allow people to determine who can come into this world, then we will allow them to determine who will go out. Euthanasia is the next logical step.

In this confused day, we need to take a stand where God does. Pastor John MacArthur says, "We need to speak against abortion and any other moral evil every time we have an opportunity."[33] Tolerance of the wrong things is the same as accepting evil. God says, "Hate evil, you who love the LORD" (Psalm 97:10). Opposing evil is a loving and compassionate thing to do.

3. *Do I have love for those who are blatantly evil?* Usually those involved in evil do not want to change. We can test the waters with such people, but if they are not the slightest bit responsive, continuing our efforts will only provoke opposition. It may be better to stay off the subject of what they are doing and concentrate on sharing the love of God with them. *Souls are not saved by scolding.* They must be drawn to Christ, not driven away from Him.

Often I must remind myself of Christ's words. He said, "Love your enemies" (Matthew 5:44). Let us do that ever so gently. Have compassion on their lost souls and try to meet some of their needs. Show them that you genuinely care about them. This act of love may be what they need in order to see their wrong and their need for Christ.

4. *Does my compassion move me to pray?* The Compassionate One was a man of prayer. We don't know all that He prayed, but we can assume that He prayed for the lost sheep of the house of Israel (Matthew 15:24). He prayed for the inflexible people (Luke 14:1-6), the inflated people (Luke 14:7-11), the indifferent people (Luke 14:15-24), and the indulgent people (Luke 14:25-35). So concerned was He for His enemies that He prayed for them, too (Luke 23:34). He even prayed for all who would come to believe in Him, which includes you and me (John 17:20). If Christ, who was God incarnate, was a man of prayer, how can we not be?

5. *Do I have accurate information about the issues that concern me?* If you want to resist evil and be compassionate, if you want to be salt, then it helps to know something about the issues. Do you know what is happening in the abortion industry or the facts regarding any social issue about which you feel strongly?[34] After researching, we have to ask ourselves: What is the best way to use the information? Each of us must ask God what her part should be.

If you want to be salt to your community, consider learning about local issues. There are, for example, issues in your schools. There might be problems with vice. I never thought much about these things until one day I heard that our neighboring community was about to change drastically. A group of Christians and some in the community became concerned about a casino that was going to be built. It was only a mile away from a high school, and a lot of freeway traffic stopped near there.

The Christians gathered information by talking to a deputy sheriff in our church who could tell them about the problems that come with casinos—loan sharking, organized crime, prostitution, robbery, and drug dealing. The Christian group decided to try to block the project and were soon joined by other concerned people. They took up the issue with our state congressman, city and county officials, zoning department, and the like. In the end nothing worked, and the place opened for business.

Shortly afterward I was driving by and noticed that next door to the casino an old pizza place was being painted purple and pink. Whatever was happening, I knew it couldn't be good. My suspicions were confirmed when I drove by a couple of weeks later and saw the new sign blazing in neon lights: "Girls, Girls, Girls." Standing outside was a sleazy-looking woman in a very short, low-cut, tight dress, inviting men into the "lounge" to engage in forms of lewd conduct, including prostitution. Not long after that I heard that the huge truck stop across the street had joined the act and began featuring a topless show. Our area had suddenly become a cesspool of vice.

Christians did some thinking about what their response should be. They asked themselves: What are the dangers of having these influences in the community? How will this affect everyone, including the children? And, most importantly, what does God say about this? Again He tells us to "hate evil" (Psalm 97:10). To hate is to loathe and abhor something. Therefore, how can we idly sit by? Answering these questions automatically answered another question: Should we try to do something about it? That was now obvious. So the next question was, What can we do? Be salt!

All of us prayed daily that God would shut down the ungodly places. Some wrote letters to the newspaper. The sheriff in the church we attended at the time set up an official meeting with the owner of the truck stop and warned him about what happens to businesses that bring in vice. The ugly picture included the likelihood of lawsuits from the kind of patrons that are attracted, legal liability, what it is like to deal with organized crime, and so on. It scared him enough to shut down the topless act.

Others picketed the main stripping place across the street. You might be thinking that praying and writing letters of protest is fine, but picketing? Isn't that a bit radical? Yes, in a way. I admit I struggled a bit when I first saw the picket line. I think many Christians did. Many of us think that any involvement with issues beyond our personal lives— such as social and political issues—always takes away from evangelism and the mission of the church. But in this case picketing provided opportunities to minister and evangelize in ways that otherwise would never have happened.

The picketers had a twofold agenda. First, they thought that their presence in front of the strip joint would let the owners and prospective patrons know they were unwelcome in the community. The picketers stayed well within the law and were polite. Secondly, they realized they would be mixing with others in the community who have the same traditional values and a strong sense of right and wrong but might not be Christians. So they used this opportunity to share with these nonbelievers, which led to some hearts opening to the Gospel.

Because of the prayer, outcry from citizens, and contacts with local government, law enforcement quietly made the situation a high priority. Within a few months we heard on the news that the owner of "Girls, Girls, Girls" had been arrested on multiple charges in an undercover sting. So now "Girls, Girls, Girls" is closed, closed, closed (and the owner is in jail, jail, jail). The truck stop is back to selling nothing more harmful than coffee, donuts, and gas; and the casino is now a quaint little restaurant that local church people love to patronize.

The best part of the story is that our area, which was becoming a magnet for vice, is once again a family town where our teenagers can grow up without being exposed to neon-lighted vice. The change is a great reminder to the Christians who know what happened and who drive by of what salt combined with compassion can do to the corruption in this world. It truly makes a significant difference.

Although it all turned out well, there were some wonderful God-fearing individuals in the community who opposed taking any measures to combat evil. A few of them have reasoned with me that we are living in the end times, and Scripture tells us that life around us is supposed to get worse. Therefore we are supposed to let everything simply "be." "This is Satan's turf," they told me.

To those who agree that the end times are near and believe it a waste to put our energies into a society that is degenerating, may I share some thoughts? What if the end isn't for quite a few years, perhaps even a hundred? This world is rightfully God's. Do we have to let it go to "pot" in the meantime? Besides, did He say that those of us living in the end times don't need to be salty since He's coming back soon? God doesn't ignore evil. Should we?

Harriet Beecher Stowe (1811-1896) answered this question. Her novel *Uncle Tom's Cabin*, in which she portrayed the evils of slavery, had an enormous impact on society. She said:

> There are cases where not to speak is a strong form of assertion—not to condemn is to approve—When a great moral question is made a test question before the public mind—or a great evil is threatening to spread in a community—and any body of men professing eminently to be the representative men of Christianity, decline publicly and clearly to express any opinion about it, this want of assertion is immediately received by the powers of evil as the strongest affirmation.[35]

6. *Am I demonstrating pure motives?* (Matthew 6:1-3). When Jesus healed the deaf man, He gave orders to him and the spectators not to tell anyone (Mark 7:36). Jesus did not seek the praise of men but the glory of God. I must ask myself: Do I seek God's glory or my own? If my motives are to receive praises from others, then my compassion may not really be genuine. Though perhaps no one else knows it, God, who looks at my heart, will know. *Real concern for people and a desire for them to know God is a pure motive.*

7. *Is my relationship with the Lord vibrant?* If I ignore God by neglecting prayer and His Word, my salt can easily begin to lose its flavor, and my compassion can be compromised with worldly values. To really make an impact in my society, I must give God first place in my life. As the old saying goes, "It isn't what you know; it's who you know." Why ignore the one who gives me the power and strength to be effective?

> *In Thy strong hand I lay me down,*
> *So shall the work be done;*
> *For who can work so wondrously*
> *As the Almighty One?*[36]

8. *Am I more concerned about the lost than about fighting for a cause?* Have you ever read *Oliver Twist* by Charles Dickens? In the story there is a Christian woman by the name of Rose Maylie who wants to help a

young girl consumed with a life of sin. Rose pleads with Nancy to hear her words and to turn to God.

Nancy replies, "You are the first that ever blessed me with such words as these, and if I had heard them years ago, they might have turned me from a life of sin and sorrow; but it is too late, it is too late!"

"It is never too late," said Rose.[37]

Rose is right. It is never too late for even the most sinful of God's creatures. Compassion looks not at what the lost person has done in the past, but at what she can become through Christ.

Because compassion never gives up, it very often sees results. As Nancy revealed: "If there was more like you, there would be fewer like me,—there would—there would!"[38] Thus if we in compassion would aggressively reach out to the lost, the result would be profound. We would see more come to Christ and grow in grace. The goal of being salt then is to glorify God and reach others with His love so that they might know Him.

9. *Am I willing to accept the worst that comes with following Christ rather than the best of following the world?* When we follow Christ, when we speak of Christ, when we act like Christ, when we have the same convictions as Christ, there will be people who won't like it. At times our bold walk in Christ will lead to consequences.

I remember that once on a very busy boulevard I encountered an elderly Jehovah's Witness who offered me a *Watchtower* magazine. Rather than take the magazine, I thought I would give her the Word of God. She became so upset with what I had to say that she began viciously hitting me over the head and back with her stack of magazines. The spectacle was a real traffic-stopper. Another time a wrathful rabbi yelled at me on a college campus (in front of many students), and an enraged UCLA student cursed at me and spat food in my face. The parents of a college student I led to Christ forbade her to speak with me. More recently a Jewish parent I had known for years furiously said I had been "worse than a child molester" after I merely answered questions his inquisitive teenage daughter had asked about Christ.

Like the early Christians, I have a particular sense of privilege (Acts 5:41), but the issue here is not what I've experienced (it's been pretty mild compared to what Paul encountered in 2 Corinthians 11:23-27). The real issue is twofold. First, I must forgive those who oppose my biblical views. In most cases they really don't understand what they are doing (Luke 23:34). Secondly, I must be prepared to face wrongful behavior.

As Christians, we all must be prepared to accept inconvenience, rejection, ugly words, the harsh disagreement of others, and opposition when we share the Gospel or when we try to make a difference. Esther was prepared for trouble when she was asked to help the Jews (Esther 4:6). And in looking at Peter's life, we could say that he had plenty of hard knocks in his preparation. His advice to us is, "Do not fear their intimidation, and do not be troubled" (1 Peter 3:14).

If we feel intimidated, we can follow Peter and John's example after they were commanded by authorities to stop speaking about Christ. They said that they had to keep doing what God wanted regardless of the consequences (Acts 4:18-20). Then upon release from jail, they immediately found comfort from other brothers and sisters in Christ (Acts 4:23). After sharing what had happened to them, Peter and John sought prayer from the brethren regarding their situation.

The Christians did not pray that the persecution would be stopped. They prayed, "Grant that Your bond-servants may speak Your word with all confidence" (Acts 4:29). They acknowledged God's sovereign plan "to do whatever Your hand and Your purpose predestined to occur" (Acts 4:28).

These early Christians show me that I am not to focus on what others may do to me, but rather on God's plan behind what happens. He can use the worst things to accomplish the best of things. For instance, the persecution of the early Christians recorded in the book of Acts resulted in the spreading of the Word of God to new areas. The imprisonment of Paul resulted in a jailer coming to Christ and the writing of many of Paul's epistles. The crucifixion of Jesus resulted in eternal life for us.

Is someone giving you a hard time because of your Christian witness? Has anyone yelled at you? Is someone ignoring you or saying mean things about you? The difficulty you experience now and the love you continue to show may one day lead your persecutor to Christ.

So in spite of it all, "Rejoice and be glad, for your reward in heaven is great" (Matthew 5:12). Imagine—through our being salt here on earth, we not only make a significant difference, which would be reward enough, but there's another reward—*a great one awaiting us in heaven*. Isn't that just like the Lord? It seems that He never really takes from us—only gives.

What might I give back to Him? Along with my salt, which His strength provides, how about my light, which He also provides? It's guaranteed that regardless of what we give to Him, He'll give back more—such as a greater life of significance. Let's see how the light God entrusts to us will allow you and me to be more effective than we are now.

THINKING IT OVER

1. As you strive to make a significant impact, what lessons can you learn from William Wilberforce's life?
2. Should Christians ever try to communicate the heart and mind of God to people regarding issues of the day? Should Christians ever be involved in political or social issues? What should be our attitude if we are?
3. How does compassion help in living out a "salty" life?
4. If you had lived in Nazi Germany, what kind of Christian do you think you would have been? Would you have spoken up? Do you think you would have helped the Jews? Is there anything today that you consider to be sin on a mass scale? Should you do anything in response to such issues? What place does voting have in these matters?
5. What are the possible risks and rewards of being salt in a sinful world?
6. What leaders will you pray for on a regular basis?

Ten

LIGHT—THAT ILLUMINATES DARKENED PATHWAYS

As a college student I moved around a lot (always looking for cheaper rent). Also I worked a variety of jobs, sometimes two at a time, just to get through school. One place I lived was the student town of Isla Vista. It gained a worldwide reputation during the 1960s when a bunch of hippies burned down the local bank.

Living in Isla Vista in the late seventies was a quirky adventure, especially working in the general store. There I met many of the original bank-burning hippies who came in every morning for their bottle of wine before going to the park to relive their glory days. Then there were the university students who would chat with me as I rang up their case of macaroni and cheese or a quick-fix candy bar.

The streets were always filled with students; life always seemed merry. But once it got dark, you didn't see a soul out because Isla Vista didn't have enough streetlights.

One night after work, I did what I always did—I walked home. The way was dark, but all I had were two short streets and then one long one. No problem. I could walk home blindfolded. On this particular night as I walked, a hint of light from across the street revealed to me that a shadow was following me—and it wasn't mine. I decided to walk a bit faster. The shadow walked faster. I decided to run—run like the wind. So did the shadow.

As I was coming up on my apartment, I sprinted so fast that it confused whoever was chasing me. I went to the side door of my apartment, and he must have thought I went in through the front door. He opened a front door, but it wasn't mine; it was my neighbor's.

While I was frantically calling the police, I could hear my neighbor screaming. Because I didn't know the Lord, I didn't think to pray while the assailant took a knife to my neighbor's throat, forced her roommates to sit on the couch, and then raped her.

When the rapist fled the apartment, he took off on my ten-speed bicycle. A few days later the police caught the man and returned my bike. I was told by the officer who arrested him that he was an escapee from Washington State Penitentiary.

I have reflected many times on that event, and what I always come back to is that the thing that saved me was light. However dim, it was light. Because I wasn't a Christian, when I recounted the story to the police, my parents, and my friends, I said that it was luck that had provided me that light and luck that had spared my neighbor's life that terrible night.

As you might imagine, I moved out of Isla Vista and into my parents' house for a while. But before long I was out on my own again, graduating from one school, transferring to another, moving from one apartment to another. One apartment I'll never forget. On the second floor, it had a huge streetlight right outside my bedroom window. That light rudely glared all night right into my room.

The streetlight didn't bother me though. I had since become a Christian and made a little game of thinking of all the biblical metaphors for light and how they applied to my life. One of my favorites, most appropriately, was, "Awake, sleeper, and arise from the dead, and Christ will shine on you" (Ephesians 5:14).

The streetlight constantly reminded me that it wasn't luck that had provided the light to illuminate my darkened pathway back in Isla Vista that terrifying night, but God. More important, He provides me the light necessary for my path throughout my life and into eternity.

God shines prominently in His Son Jesus Christ and in His Word through its warnings, commands, and promises. But His light also shines through His people. Jesus told His followers, "You are the light of the world" (Matthew 5:14). Does your light help illuminate the darkened pathway of another?

HOW BRIGHT IS YOUR LIGHT?

One biblical proverb uses light to contrast two very different kinds of people. One verse encourages me: "The path of the righteous is like the light of dawn, that shines brighter and brighter until the full day"

(Proverbs 4:18). The next verse is tragic: "The way of the wicked is like darkness; they do not know over what they stumble" (Proverbs 4:19).

Here a human drama unfolds. One person's way is lighted, not just dimly but brighter and brighter, as he or she stays to one path—the path of righteousness. The other person's path is dark because of unrighteousness. The righteous can see the road ahead; the unrighteous can't see even what's in front and stumble. What a contrast!

"The path of the righteous" consists of all that is good, including truth, purity, joy, peace, love. If we are weak in these areas, then our light is dim. The dimmer it is, the less it will guide anyone to the Lord. So growing in righteousness means growing brighter as a light in darkness. For myself, I want a light that radiates brighter and brighter each day. How about you? Together let's grow in truth, purity, joy, peace, and love—all of which radiate from our flame.

A FLAME THAT GROWS

Candace was a real "brain." She went to the finest of schools and eventually became a lawyer in a prestigious law firm. A few years later she accepted Christ. She wanted to learn all she could about the Lord. So she quit her job and enrolled in a Bible college, soaking everything up. She took tough courses, such as Greek and Hebrew, and naturally excelled. Within a few years Candace could quote Scripture verses, outline books of the Bible, and explain theological terms.

As I personally got to know her, I admired her determination, but I noticed something missing. She didn't seem to be growing spiritually from all that exposure to learning, not from her hours of intense study in the Word nor from being around godly people.

Eventually Candace stopped going to church, married a nonbeliever, and went back to being a lawyer. Now she has nothing to do with Christians. I was saddened to see that she had once seemed to respond to truth and learned it but never really grew in it. Whatever significant impact she could have had on the lives of others, at this point in her life it's all lost.

While Candace is an extreme case, I believe there are many of us who could lose the opportunity to have a significant impact. Why?

Because while we are growing in truth in most areas, there might be one area (or possibly more) where we aren't growing at all.

Look at the rich ruler. He explained to Christ that since his youth he had kept the law. He was sincere, he was genuine. Despite his earnest desire to please God, Jesus said, "One thing you still lack." That word came as unwelcome truth to the ruler's ears (Luke 18:22). The ruler allowed truth to penetrate his soul, but the one thing he had a problem with was holding on to his worldly goods. Candace lacked one thing—truth penetrating her soul.

Certainly most of us have embraced truth that penetrates our souls—but is there "one thing" that is coming between us and God, keeping us from growing further in truth?

The most decisive thing we can do to communicate truth is to open areas of our heart that we have kept closed off. We have to let the light of God's Word shine into dark places, those things we want to ignore, to forget.

I described earlier how I struggled with impatience toward the administratively weak. The one truth, that as a Christian I must "be patient with everyone" (1 Thessalonians 5:14), was something I needed to grow in. If I had continued to be impatient with those precious women, how could I have had a significant impact on their lives?

Any area we need to grow in, especially one in which we are blocking out God's voice, is that "one thing" that threatens our impact—our significance in the outworking of God's plan. Laziness, lack of sensitivity, lack of discernment, covetousness, and jealousy are just a few examples of such hindrances. Look at the apostles. When Christ explained to them that He would be delivered into the hands of men but that He would also be raised up (Matthew 17:22-23), they let sorrow and hopelessness guide them rather than an understanding of the truth that they repeatedly heard from Jesus.

Sometimes we can repeatedly hear something from Scripture and yet never let it penetrate our souls. It conflicts with things we hold more dear, whether our own ideas, our own way of doing things, our own habits. So we shut out the light and lose an opportunity to radiate it.

The first step to having a greater impact for God is to honestly seek after the truth regarding ourselves. The seeker is a person of prayer who knows that the deepest spiritual truths are not discoverable by speculation or unaided introspection; they are revealed in communion with God and His Word.

Secondly, and just as important, once we see some area that needs work, we need to get right on it and stay on it. That means repenting (deciding we've been wrong and that we want to change) and setting up some practical steps for change. It's tempting to allow ourselves to think we'll get around to working on it later. But if it's something we've been ignoring, or even something we have never realized we're doing, it's crucial that we don't put it off.

OPENING UP TO GOD'S LIGHT

Having a vague desire to change rarely does much. Usually we know where we want to end up. It's just that we haven't figured out practical steps to get there. Here are some steps I've found helpful.

1. *Write down one to three things that you want to change and then pick the most important one.* For example, let's say Nancy feels convicted in three areas: a) Her lack of time in God's Word; b) Her light depression; c) Her tendency to overspend the family budget. She decides that her time in God's Word must be the priority (and in her devotions she will try to work on her depression).

2. *Find a verse(s) from Scripture that will motivate you to make the necessary change.* Nancy found Psalm 119:97-105, which promises that those who love the Word will have more wisdom than their adversaries, more insight than their teachers, and more understanding than the aged. Two verses were especially helpful: God's Word is "sweeter than honey" (v. 103); "Your word is a lamp to my feet and a light to my path" (v. 105).

3. *Look at a person in Scripture who would be a good role model for you and explain why.* Nancy decides that her role model is King David, who wrote Psalm 119. This psalm is the longest chapter in the Bible, and it's all about David's deep love for the Word. He treasures the Word (119:11), clings to it (119:109), rejoices in it (119:14), delights in it (119:16), meditates on it (119:15), and, above all, obeys it (119:55-56).

4. *Think of a person today who is a good example of what you are trying to become.* Nancy chooses her husband as an example. She can learn from him by observing more closely his own time with God and by imitating those things that make him the godly man he is.

5. *Find the resources that will help you.* Nancy has found that some basic Bible study tools will help her. She begins with *Strong's Exhaustive Concordance of the Bible*, a Bible dictionary (or encyclopedia) such as Nelson's *New Illustrated Bible Dictionary*, and an atlas (because her Bible didn't provide one). She could add the *Evangelical Dictionary of Biblical Theology*.[1]

6. *Put in order the steps you will take to accomplish your goal.* This Monday Nancy will go to the bookstore and buy the resources she needs. Tuesday she will get up half an hour earlier and get familiar with her concordance by looking up passages that would help her deal with her sense of hopelessness. So to start with, she simply looks up the word *hope* and writes down all the pertinent Scripture verses. She then reads them thoughtfully in her Bible.

Wednesday Nancy will get up half an hour earlier and get familiar with Nelson's *New Illustrated Bible Dictionary* by looking up the word *hope*. This will enable her to better understand the meaning of the word in the Bible verses she found in her concordance. She knows that in ordinary speech, hope is an expectation that what we desire may possibly come about or that events may turn out for the best.[2]

By contrast, according to the Bible dictionary, hope is a "confident expectancy."[3] She will find that the Christian's hope comes from God (Romans 15:13). She will find that as a Christian she can live a hopeful life because of God's calling (Ephesians 1:18; 4:4), His grace (2 Thessalonians 2:16), His Word (Romans 15:4), and His Gospel (Colossians 1:23). She also discovers that through God's hope given to her, she can look forward confidently to salvation (1 Thessalonians 5:8), righteousness (Galatians 5:5), eternal life (Titus 1:2; 3:7), the glory of God (Romans 5:2; Colossians 1:27), the appearing of Christ (Titus 2:13), and the resurrection from the dead (Acts 23:6; 26:6-8).

Thursday Nancy will get up one-half hour earlier and get familiar with her Bible atlas. The Bible atlas will help Nancy understand where events in the Bible took place and give her an understanding of the difficulty of the journeys biblical characters took.

Friday Nancy will get up one hour earlier. She will make a concerted effort to come to God's Word alert and prayerful so she can begin her systematic study of Scripture. In other words, she will begin a regular and orderly study of the Bible.

Saturday Nancy will continue what she began on Friday. As she becomes consistent in her Bible study, her devotional life will be built up, and in the process she will be finding ways to deal with her depression. She will come to better understand the meaning of hope and related behavior such as reliance, faith, and trust. As she studies the Word more thoroughly, she will begin to see a change in her relationship with the Lord and with others and in how she thinks about herself.

Sunday Nancy will take all she has learned and meditated on that week and bring it with her in her heart to church. She will look for opportunities to share what she has learned with her friends.

7. *Decide what criteria you will use to determine whether you are making definite progress or have reached your goal.* Nancy will consider herself successful if she can, first of all, get up earlier and spend consistent time in the Word for more than one month. Secondly, she will consider it progress if she can use her tools to get more out of her study. Third, she will see if she is growing in other areas as a result of her new habits.

8. *Decide when each week to assess your progress.* Nancy has chosen to evaluate how she has done during the week every Saturday and think about how she can do better the next week.

9. *Who should benefit from this change in your life?* Nancy knows that not only will she benefit personally, but everyone around her, Christians and nonbelievers alike, will be affected by her changed life.

10. *Finally pick a second priority (if you have one). Mark on the calendar when you will begin to work on it; then do the same with a third priority.* Nancy could write, "Got second priority accomplished while working on first priority; will continue working on depression each day until the end of March." Under the first week in April she will write: "Third priority: Grow in being a better manager of money."

Taking these ten steps is one way of making solid progress toward change. Now it's time to consider some ways to increase our brightness to beacon strength.

A FLAME THAT ILLUMINATES PURITY

A few years ago while I was watching the news (what a waste that can be!), a reporter spoke about an unusual parade in Mexico that advertised, "One last day to indulge before Lent!" In this parade were floats featuring half-naked women belly dancing in celebration of their last day of "fun."[4] The following day Lent began, the season before Easter during which those in some traditions deny themselves something in order to purify their lives.

Before I dedicated my life to Christ, I, too, would give something up for Lent, but when that season ended, so did my purer life. Since coming to Christ, I've stopped making purity a seasonal thing and have come to see that it must be a daily pursuit. God watches over us in the interest of purity and expects us to have a high understanding of it, to live it, and to grow continually in it.

Desire for purity is what makes us willing to find those dark corners of our heart and yield them to God. Once those areas are brought under His Lordship, we continue to probe for other areas in which to grow.

Everything about God is pure. His eyes are "too pure to approve evil" (Habakkuk 1:13). His words "are pure words; as silver tried in a furnace on the earth, refined seven times" (Psalm 12:6). His commandments are pure (Psalm 19:8).

We are to be the same. So does that mean we will become completely sinless in this life? Impossible! Now not all Christians would agree with me on this statement. One woman recently shared with me that she firmly believes we can experience a "second work of grace" by which we become sinless in this life. She confirmed to me that she is now without sin. I certainly wish I could say the same—but I can't, and I honestly don't believe any of us can be absolutely without sin. Why? Because John says, "If we say that we have no sin, we are deceiving ourselves" (1 John 1:8; cf. James 3:2). So purification must go on throughout this life. It's like continually cutting something in half; there's always half left, however small the remainder is! For our lives to burn as an ever-purer flame, it takes prayer (Psalm 50:1-2, 10) and a focus on God's love while developing His loathing of sin.

One thing that has helped me through the years is to live in the presence of Christ. By that I mean to be aware always that He is with me. This focus helps me tremendously to live a purer life. For instance, one time I noticed an advertisement for a television movie that sounded quite interesting. Curious, I decided to watch the movie. But shortly after it began, I became increasingly aware that this was not a good film and that it would not be pleasing to God. I tried to ignore the conviction, telling myself, "The movie will get better. I'll give it a few more minutes."

As the minutes went by, I became increasingly uncomfortable and felt I was grieving the Holy Spirit (Ephesians 4:30). I could sense God's presence in my life dimming. Turning off the television, I asked for His forgiveness.

Incidents like that should stiffen our resolve to be pure—and to do something about it. I changed after that. I decided that I will turn off something as soon as it looks bad rather than wait, hoping it will get better.

We can all take advantage of the Lord's presence by daily focusing on what He must be thinking about our words, our actions, our thoughts, and what we expose ourselves to. Countless individuals have been guided to Christ because of a person who radiated a pure life. What an impact we can make in the life of another as we grow not only in purity but also in joy.

A FLAME THAT DANCES

Theologian William Barclay once said, "A gloomy Christian is a contradiction in terms, and nothing in all religious history has done Christianity more harm than its connection with black clothes and long faces."[5]

Preacher Charles Spurgeon also decried the long faces many Christians wear. He said, "If you want to talk about Heaven, let your face light up with heavenly glory. But when you talk about Hell, your everyday face will do."

Have you ever known a gloomy Christian, one who can never seem to smile? One who never shares the wonderful things God is doing in her life? It's miserable being around gloom, because such a woeful person always has a dark cloud floating overhead. It's downright depressing! What must the non-Christian think? Would you listen to a gloomy person who claimed to have good news?

I maintain that even the gloomiest Christians with the deepest frown lines have occasion for joy. First, they have been given all the grounds for being joyful—forgiveness, God's love, His continual presence, and a place in heaven. Secondly, they have received the very life of the Holy Spirit who has come to dwell in them. His divine nature is joyful—and it is this joy that dwells in us.

So then why the gloom in some people? I think there are two main reasons. It's possible they may not be genuine Christians. They may be attending church as a way to experience "religion," but they do not yet have a relationship with Christ. A true believer is connected to God by His saving grace, and thus has the Holy Spirit as the source of joy.

My second theory about the gloom in some Christians is that, while they are true believers, their joy has been choked out. This can happen because of sin, lack of faith, or long-term grief from a major loss.

From what I've seen, sin is by far the most common cause. Any one of us can from time to time be guilty of sin, and it's a miserable way to exist. Moreover, sins develop from other sins. A number of things can result. First, we have anxiety. We worry a lot, we are troubled, we feel tremendous guilt. As Isaiah says of those who are in sin: "There is no peace . . ." (Isaiah 57:20).

We can also develop fear of chastisement, which is typical of those who sin. "The wicked flee when no one is pursuing, but the righteous are bold as a lion" (Proverbs 28:1). A sign of God's chastisement for Israel's sin was that "the sound of a driven leaf will chase them . . ." (Leviticus 26:36).

Also discontentment can get a foothold because sin can't satisfy us. Solomon, who had everything, learned: "He who loves money will not be satisfied with money, nor he who loves abundance with its income" (Ecclesiastes 5:10). When we are discontented, we can develop a critical spirit. The people of Israel in the wilderness complained and criticized constantly.

To cover our sin, we can develop an outer show of righteousness. The Pharisees of Jesus' day were long on rules and on self-righteousness but very short on true righteousness.

Sin always prevents the release of God's joy, and thus His strength. By contrast, growth in joy comes through wholehearted obedience. Obeying God makes our joy full (John 16:24) and complete (1 John 1:4). It's been said, "Joy is not the absence of pain but the presence of God." Joy was evident in Jesus. And when the disciples came to see the resurrected Christ, they, too, had joy.

To the degree people have joy, they are content in trouble, hopeful in sorrow, cheerful in depressing circumstances, and positive in spite of tribulation. Joy frees people to look away from themselves to a holy God for their "progress and joy in the faith" (Philippians 1:25).

Are we always rejoicing in the Lord (Romans 15:13; Philippians 4:4)? If so, our growth in joy will encourage believers who have fallen into gloom and bring light to the nonbeliever who knows of nothing other than darkness.

A FLAME STEADY IN THE WIND

Today you can find historians who believe Napoleon was a hero who struggled to give unity and law to Europe. But other historians believe he was an egomaniac who shed the blood of French soldiers and ravaged Europe in order to feed an insatiable will to power.[6] Which is it? Perhaps only God knows, but whatever the case, it did seem that in 1815 the people loved Napoleon, as the piece below suggests:

> *What news? Ma foi!*
> *The tiger has broken out of his den.*
> *The monster was three days at sea.*
> *The wretch has landed at Fre'jus.*
> *The Brigand has arrived at Antibes.*
> *The Invader has reached Grenoble.*
> *The General has entered Lyons.*
> *Napoleon slept last night at Fontainebleau. . . .* [7]

To the French people back in the nineteenth century, it mattered little what trouble was around them. As long as Napoleon was in their midst, they had a sense of peace. As history unfolded, it would turn out that their peace was based on mere wishful thinking.

Those of us who have given our lives to Jesus Christ have true peace—greater than anyone could have from trusting Napoleon. But many believers forget about the peace they have access to because they are frazzled about many things. The consequence? A dim light.

Growing in peace involves relying on God's peace when in trouble. Imagine how bright our light can be in a very dark world when our trust is in God. We can shine steadily, like a flame sheltered from the wind.

The psalmist had his times of trouble, but because he trusted God, he could say, "I will not be afraid of ten thousands of people who have set themselves against me round about" (Psalm 3:6). And he could say, "God is our refuge and strength, *a very present help in trouble*. Therefore we will not fear, though the earth should change and though the mountains slip into the heart of the sea; though its waters roar and foam, though the mountains quake at its swelling pride" (Psalm 46:1-3, italics mine). Neither the threat of a massed army nor of the earth falling apart could shake him.

What peace we can have in our hearts, knowing that the very power that runs the universe is on our side and that He comforts us (2 Corinthians 1:3). Would you like that kind of peace in your life?

Peace That Keeps the Flame Going

If we want to grow in peace, we must trust God. Trust that He is in control of all events. Trust that He will see us through every trouble, pain, loss, and all confusion. Trust that He is ever near. Trust that He is working, though in His way and His time.

Without trust there can be no peace. And without peace, we can have little impact on a world so desperately seeking it. Peace grows when we focus on the works of the Lord (Psalm 46:8), on what He is doing, rather than on our trouble. When the Philistines were after the Israelites, David sought God's help and had peace in knowing the Lord would intervene (1 Chronicles 14:8-17).

Growing in peace also involves heeding God's counsel. And what does He tell us? He says: "Cease striving and know that I am God" (Psalm 46:10). Theologian Charles Ryrie says that to cease striving means to "cease from warlike activities and acknowledge God's supremacy."[8]

Do we ever strive? Are we in constant struggle, ever embroiled in some conflict? Do our emotions churn? Do we ever fight our battles by ourselves rather than come under the Lord's headship?

I believe we often lack peace because we haven't gained victory over ourselves. We can be our own worst enemy when we constantly dwell on our problems, our trials, our worries, and thus keep focused upon ourselves rather than upon God. He can take care of us and the things that concern us. He declares, "I have made, and I will bear; even I will carry, and will deliver you" (Isaiah 46:4 KJV). Such confidence in God gives us a peace that surpasses all understanding (Philippians 4:7). Unbelievers are puzzled and attracted by the divine peace that emanates through the growing Christian.

Just today I received news that a Buddhist monk (aren't monks known for their supposed peace?) in Burma approached a Christian missionary saying, "I notice you have so much peace. Why is that?" The missionary told him that Jesus Christ gave him peace. He then told the monk about the Prince of Peace. The monk is no longer a monk, but he's now a brother in Christ. How beautiful this peace is!

Here's a challenge. As you grow in peace, make a concerted effort to display it regardless of your situation. See if someone approaches you with questions about God's peace.

A Flame That Warms

Years ago in my hospital days, I worked with a Jewish woman named Ruthie, a victim of the Holocaust. Her entire family—her brothers, sisters, her mother, her father, her aunts, uncles, and cousins—were taken by the Nazis. The day the Nazis raided her house, Ruthie alone escaped, going out the back door and running, running, running for miles. She hid in a stranger's barn under a haystack. The owners eventually found her and allowed her to stay there, bringing her food each day.

After many months Germany was overrun by American soldiers. They searched every corner for Jewish people that were hiding. And on one momentous day, the soldiers came to the barn and found Ruthie. At first she couldn't believe they were not Nazis, and she was terrified. When the soldiers finally convinced her by pointing to their uniforms and speaking with English accents, she burst into tears of relief. But she still clung irrationally to the haystack that had concealed her for so long. They ended up pulling her away from the place.

Ruthie eventually married one of her liberators—a man whose language she could not yet speak and became a citizen of the United States. Years later in 1978, we would meet and become not only coworkers but friends.

Ruthie's story is a moving one. Her experiences left her with permanent emotional scars. I remember one day at work she asked me, "Why would God have allowed this atrocity, the Holocaust?" Because I was a nonbeliever at the time, I had no answer. All I could do was put my arms around her each time she broke into tears.

Now, as a Christian, I have gone back to Ruthie's question and thought about it a lot. Though we could ponder God's great purpose for it all, I would like to refocus the question to one that no one ever seems to ask: How is it that love could be found anywhere in the rumble of World War II? How do we account for the good in the face of so much evil?

For instance, what empowered Corrie ten Boom after the war to forgive the very man who was her jailer in the concentration camp, who had watched her in the shower room? In a word—love. Love overcame her deep bitterness. But real love doesn't stand alone. It is connected to forgiveness. You see, such love wasn't easy for Corrie. She said, "I struggled to raise my hand. I could not. I felt nothing, not the slightest spark of warmth or charity. And so again I breathed a silent prayer. 'Jesus, I cannot forgive him. Give me Your forgiveness.'" As Corrie shook the man's hand, she said, "My heart sprang a love for this stranger that almost overwhelmed me."[9]

If you're having a difficult time loving someone who has hurt you, could it be that you haven't forgiven the person? We all know that forgiveness isn't easy. While the atrocities of World War II happened long ago, there are still cruel people in this world. We may not suffer evil of historic proportions, but we often have to deal with people who are gossipy, insensitive, demanding, and simply hard to get along with. It's hard to give God's love to such people.

Since love requires forgiveness, we can look to Matthew 18, which shows us how to expand our capacity to forgive. Jesus told a parable of a slave who owed a king an incalculable amount of money, implying that he had embezzled it. After the servant begged for mercy, the king forgave him the entire debt. But then the slave was merciless with someone who owed him only about three months' wages. When the king heard about it, he was enraged and punished the slave. The man who had been forgiven so much should have forgiven the one who owed him, declared the king (Matthew 18:23-35).

Jesus's message is clear: We forgive others by remembering how much we have been forgiven by God. Not only that, but we are not to put limits on the number of times we forgive. When Peter asked if we should forgive as much as seven times, Jesus answered, "up to seventy times seven" (Matthew 18:22). In other words, we should strive to be like God, whose forgiveness is both limitless and endless. If God has forgiven us of everything, how could we withhold forgiveness from others?

Like Corrie ten Boom, when the moment arises, we can take God's love and pray, "Lord, you know I have a difficult time loving this person on my own, but I know that Your Spirit can help me love this person right now."

It is God's love that forgives, and He uses us as the vessel to show His love. God's love is not a natural love that we automatically have. It is supernatural. Furthermore, the love we have did not originate with us but with Him. We love because God loved us first (1 John 4:19). Such a love isn't human. It's the same love that Christ gave us (John 15:12), a love that is possible because of our love for God (1 John 4:7-8).

Because love goes beyond forgiveness, there must be reconciliation. " . . . God, who reconciled us to Himself through Christ and gave us the ministry of reconciliation" (2 Corinthians 5:18). Just as God has reconciled us to Himself in Christ, so we need to begin anew with those we forgive. Rather than be captive to bitterness, we are set free through reconciliation.

As happened with Corrie ten Boom, I believe the Lord puts situations in our lives to teach us what love is really all about. Love doesn't mean we have to like everyone, but it does mean we must give divine love—a love of the Spirit, a love that forgives, a love that goes even beyond forgiveness to reconciliation.

If loving through forgiveness and reconciliation is at this moment difficult for you, keep in mind the words of John Calvin: "If we wish to adhere to the true law of love, our eyes must chiefly be directed not to man . . . but to God."[10] Since living without loving is only existing (Matthew 22:37-39), with whom might you share God's love today?

As we grow in love and in truth, purity, joy, and peace, we give "light to all who are in the house" (Matthew 5:15). And by all in that house, we are being watched.

A FLAME OTHERS SEE

On his voyage to Massachusetts in 1630, John Winthrop, the governor of Massachusetts Bay Colony, wrote a discourse titled, "A Modell [*sic*] of Christian Charity." In that discourse he said, " . . . we must consider that we shall be as a City upon a hill. The eyes of all people are upon us. Soe [*sic*] that if we shall deal falsely with our God . . . and so cause him to withdraw his present help from us, we shall be made a story and a byword throughout the world."[11]

It's a fact. You are being watched, especially by nonbelievers. Your words are weighed. Your deeds are scrutinized. Your choices in life are judged. Nonbelievers evaluate us not on biblical grounds, but on the basis of whether or not they think we are genuine. This can be a good thing if indeed we are living godly lives.

Being light before the watching world isn't always easy. It wasn't in Winthrop's situation; nor will it likely be in ours. And in the time span between Winthrop's and ours, things haven't changed, despite advancing technology. For most of us there are difficulties—financial, emotional, spiritual, or physical. We may experience the death of a loved one, be in constant pain, or have a life-threatening illness. While it is much easier for us to say, "God is good," when things are going well, the essence of Winthrop's message is, "Are you able to proclaim God's goodness when your world is falling apart?"

The answer is yes if we allow ourselves to continue to be influenced by God's Word, focusing on growing in truth, purity, joy, peace, and love. And if we do, our light will continue to grow. We can be confident of that. Forget the notion that God's light shines only from the "super spiritual" person or the deep Christian thinker. Isn't it true that a small pond can reflect the sunlight as brightly as a wide lake?

Our business in this life isn't to concern ourselves with how effectively our light is penetrating, but rather seeing to it that we have done our job by lighting our lantern and setting it out.

SETTING OUT OUR LANTERN

Centuries ago in England lanterns were hung in some of the church steeples at night. They were also hung in front of homes. When the lantern was missing or had gone out, the night watchman would cry,

"Hang out your light," or "Light your lantern." The lighted lanterns helped to guide those walking at night through London's fog and darkness.[12]

You've heard the words of Jesus many times now, but they are worth repeating, "You are the light of the world." Lights are made for dark places. In which dark place is God calling you to hang out your light so that others "may see your good works, and glorify your Father who is in heaven" (Matthew 5:16)?

The way to answer that question is to discern your burdens, desires, convictions, and gifts. After evaluating these, go to God in prayer and start seeking His direction. Then look for opportunities.

IS YOUR LIGHT ON AT HOME?

All of us, whether we live in an apartment, a condominium, or a house with a white picket fence, would like our home to be a haven of rest. And because home is our place to escape from the commotion of the world, it's easy to forget that we should be opening our home up to others, not just to entertain but to serve.

Writer Karen Burton Mains points out, "Entertaining says, 'I want to impress you with my beautiful home, my clever decorating, my gourmet cooking.' Hospitality, however, seeks to minister. It says, 'This home is not mine. It is truly a gift from my Master. I am His servant, and I use it as He desires.' Hospitality does not try to impress but to serve."[13]

Along with our family, whom else can we serve in our home with God's love? Do you know of anyone who is struggling? You may want to invite that person over for a day or two and offer encouragement. Give your friend food for the soul and the stomach, a soothing bath for worn nerves, with Christian music playing in the background. And don't forget light-hearted moments of fun and laughter. From personal experience, I have seen this as a great outreach to those who don't know Christ, and it's helped some Christians regain their spiritual vitality. Is your home large enough for a weekly Bible study? Along with Christians you know, invite some neighbors!

The key is to pray, asking God to use you and your home for His purposes. It's guaranteed that He will bring people your way. Just in the past year we have had the opportunity to help several strangers who have come to our front door asking for help. One woman pounded on our door late one night and said, "I'm sorry for disturbing you, but I saw that your light was on, and I need help." I was glad that our front porch light drew her to our home. I just hope that in the future, it'll be the light in our lives that will draw her as well.

Is the light in your life on so that others will be drawn to your home?

LIGHTING UP OUR NEIGHBORHOOD

Living in any neighborhood can be a blessing or a curse, depending on the neighbors you have. There are plenty of people who choose to move away because they cannot handle their neighbors.

While we have no control over what our neighbors do, we do have control over ourselves. If our neighbors are receptive toward us, we have one of the best ministry opportunities to reach people for Christ. We can begin by having them over for dinner, making cookies for them over the holidays, listening to their troubles, or watering their plants when they go on vacation.

We can start a children's Bible club in our backyard or take children to Vacation Bible School (especially those who aren't Christians).

We can invite neighborhood women to a Bible study or to the women's group at our church.

When a family moves into our neighborhood, we can help move the boxes into the home or make a hot meal to welcome them.

BRINGING LIGHT TO THE MODERN WIDOW

Life was hard in ancient times, which left a lot of widows and orphans. The church saw the need to care for these people. Today we do not have nearly as many persons in that category, but we have another group that is needy. Unfortunately, many in the church don't recognize the need.

I call this group the "modern-day widows." Women become members of this group because of a husband's abandonment. In many cases, the woman's children live with her (except perhaps every other weekend); yet she has very little or no financial support from her ex-husband. As well, there is a stigma to being a divorcée in the church, which never existed for widows in ancient times. That stigma prevents many of them from getting the assistance they so desperately need.

I wonder what Paul would say to the church today about our "modern-day widows" and fatherless children? The Bible is clear about reaching needy families in ancient times: "Pure and undefiled religion in the sight of our God and Father is this: to visit orphans and widows in their distress" (James 1:27). Might God want us to have a part in helping "the widow's heart to sing for joy?" (cf Job 29:11-16).

We can:

Offer financial support and/or food.

Extend a helping hand with the children, offer our friendship, and provide practical things such as clothes.

Assist with errands.

Start a food pantry at church or volunteer at an existing one.

Have our husbands come alongside the "widow's" children, who perhaps rarely see their father (who might not be a good role model), and be like a second dad.

If her children are visiting their dad for the holidays, she will be alone—unless we welcome her as part of our family.

OFFERING LIGHT TO THE FORGOTTEN PEOPLE

God is very concerned about forgotten people. He says to us, "If you give yourself to the hungry and satisfy the desire of the afflicted, then your light will rise in darkness" (Isaiah 58:10). Have you ever thought what it might take to satisfy the desire of the afflicted? I believe, humanly speaking, there is one thing—the human touch. It helps heal many hearts. What a difference we can make as we do any of the following:

• Befriend such people, invite them into our home, share a meal.

• Help them to get to a proper facility. If they are on drugs, we can introduce them to an organization such as Teen Challenge (a nonprofit ministry). If they are homeless, we can take them to a rescue mission. If they are spiritually lost, we can take them with us to church.

• We can reach out to the forgotten elderly people by making

them a part of our family. Have your children adopt one or
two as "grandparents."

• Visit the elderly in rest homes and retirement homes. If you
feel led, start a Bible study there.

• We can reach out to the grieving using the obituaries. The
news article will give a short account of the person's life and
the name of the mortuary that handled the funeral. Send a letter to the family in care of the mortuary. Express your sorrow
for their loss and tell them how much God loves them. Invite
them to call you if they ever need a listening ear; perhaps you
will get an opportunity to invite them to your church.

It's important to remember that the "forgotten people," especially
the elderly, have all seen hard times. Most have seen war (many served
in a war); they have experienced the death of loved ones; many currently feel rejected because their own children rarely visit them.

Reaching out to forgotten people can ease some of the hurt and
pain they feel, as we give them the greatest touch of all—God's love
working through us.

LETTING YOUR LIGHT SHINE IN A CPC

If you would like to be involved in the pro-life movement, you might
consider being light through your local Crisis Pregnancy Center.
They could use volunteers to:

• Speak to the youth in high schools (they will train you).
• Assist in a Walk for Life campaign.
• Counsel and befriend frightened young women with prob-
lem pregnancies (you will be trained).
• Provide maternity clothes and baby clothes or financial
support.

SHINING IN THE PUBLIC SCHOOLS

We can be light in the public school system by joining the PTA where
we can have a voice. Years ago in a public school district, the Rainbow
Curriculum (promoting an "alternative lifestyle") was going to be

implemented. A Christian woman joined the school PTA so that she could speak against this curriculum. She got other parents to rally together in opposition to the material that was about to be taught to their children. Because they spoke up, the children of this school district were never exposed to such things as Heather "having two mommies."

If we don't feel led to be in the PTA, we can volunteer to teach a class such as art or a foreign language (or whatever our expertise), be a playground aid, or run for the school board.

SHINING IN PRISONS

I get letters from time to time from women in prison. If there is a lonelier place on earth, I wouldn't know where to find it. These women feel rejected by society, receive little compassion from workers inside the jail, and rarely get letters to comfort them. If you can't minister outside your home, you can lift the spirits of an inmate just by writing a letter. Chuck Colson's organization Prison Fellowship has a pen-pal ministry. If you would like to reach out to a woman prisoner, write: The Pen-Pal Program, Prison Fellowship Ministries, P. O. Box 17500, Washington, DC, 20041-0500. You may be the catalyst for someone to come to Christ or grow stronger in the Lord through your encouragement and words of wisdom.

Some other options might be to visit women in a correctional facility with a group in your church or help start a prison Bible study. You might support your "hubby" in holding a Bible study in a men's facility (if he feels led to do it).

LIGHT TO THE DYING

Let's keep in our prayers the young and the old who will soon be passing from this earth in pain, in sorrow, and in their sins. That person whose days are quickly evaporating could be a neighbor, a relative, one of our children's classmates, or someone we barely know. May the Lord give us the opportunity to be light to just one of these lost souls. And possibly, because of us, they too can look forward to the place where "there shall no longer be any night . . . because the Lord God shall illumine them;" for "its lamp is the Lamb" (Revelation 22:5; 21:23).

A FINAL THOUGHT

There are so many significant opportunities available. Who knows of the divine plan God has in store as we consider our abilities and then follow His leading? But we may not immediately see all the opportunities in front of us or even the results of our labor. What we need is patience, which includes confidence in the wisdom of God's timing. So as we now turn to develop that patience, let us remember that God can shine His light through us whatever our limits. Nineteenth-century author and preacher Edward Everett Hale said it best: "I am only one, but I am one. I cannot do everything, but I can do something. What I can do, I should do and, with the help of God, I will do!"[14] And what a significant life we can have in doing it!

> Lord, remind us that Your call is not just to the treasured time of worship or to those peaceful moments of prayer, but because of the resurrection it is to move with courage into the encounters and arenas of life where many have not heard the Gospel's call. Help us to speak when it is not easy, to act when it is safer to just go along with wrong. Help us to know that in the day of Jesus Christ, His Kingdom will come; and let us, O God, be bound by a love amazing and divine, and then go out and embrace a weary and despairing world and lift that world to You." Amen.
>
> KENNETH WORKING

THINKING IT OVER

1. In what ways specifically can you grow further in truth, purity, joy, peace, and love?
2. If you could pick one area in which you would like to grow during the next month, what would it be? Work on it through the ten steps for change.
3. Can we love without forgiving or forgive without loving? Explain your answer.
4. In what outreach effort does your light currently shine? What further opportunity for ministry would you like?

Eleven

PATIENCE—IN GOD'S TIMING

*P*atience has always been a hard virtue for me to master. I love action; I hate to wait. I want answers—now. I want to get things done—now. I want God to use me—now. But I've been learning that now isn't always best.

There is much wisdom in waiting for God to put me in a place of significance rather than striving for it. In the spirit of Ecclesiastes, everything has its time (Ecclesiastes 3:1-8). I can rest in the fact that though I weep today, I shall laugh tomorrow. If I must be silent now, I may have opportunity to speak later. If I struggle now, the time to relax will return. If I feel hindered in my service to God, even this will pass.

But if you're like me, during these times of waiting for things to pass, you can't help feeling as if you're going nowhere. Usually when I experience these feelings, it's because I am either being impatient, or I am unaware of what God may be doing in my life. When our frustration is with ministry, we simply may be working outside our area of giftedness.

As a young man, Moses tried to live in a significant way, but he failed because he was out of step with God. His desires fit neither God's timing nor His ways. Fleeing Egypt must have been an utterly crushing experience for Moses. He had been willing to give up the power and splendor of the palace for a chance to deliver his lowly people from bondage, having boldly defended a fellow Jew being beaten by an Egyptian. But it had all come to nothing.

Gradually he grew accustomed to the anonymous solitude of sheep herding, his occupation for the forty years that followed. By the time God was ready to fulfill Moses' long-forgotten desire to deliver his people—one of the most significant roles in history—he wasn't emotionally ready or even interested.

Like Moses, we too can get out of step with what God may be trying to do through us when we are impatient with His ways, His will, His timing.

TRUSTING GOD'S WAYS

In 1829 Robert and Mary Moffat were missionaries to the Bechuana tribe of South Africa. For ten years they had not even a ray of encouragement that their efforts were effective. Even the mission board questioned their calling since they had not led a single person to Christ. But the devoted couple felt sure that eventually they would see fruit, and they were able to convince the board to allow them to stay. And so they did, for two more years—still without one convert.

Then a friend in England wrote Mrs. Moffat that she wanted to send a gift and asked for a suggestion. In her reply Mrs. Moffat simply said, "Send us a Communion set; I'm sure we will need one soon."

God honored the Moffats' patience. The Holy Spirit began to work in people's hearts, and a short time later six people accepted the Savior. Soon a small group had united to form a church, and on the very day before their first Lord's Supper was to be observed, the Communion set arrived. Imagine the Moffats' joy that morning!

Do you long for such joy? Do you want to have such a sense of purpose? Do you desire, like young Moses, to make a difference? You can. And one way is to "rest in the LORD and wait patiently for Him" (Psalm 37:7). How simple and yet how difficult this seems!

Some of the difficulty we have in waiting patiently for the Lord may have to do with our motivation. We can become selfish, even if it is ministry we're impatiently striving for. Remember Simon the magician? He had come to an outward profession of faith (Acts 8:13) and was constantly amazed at the signs and great miracles occurring through the apostle Philip. Seeing that others were receiving the Holy Spirit at the hands of the apostles (Acts 8:18), Simon offered Peter money saying, "Give this authority to me as well" (Acts 8:18-19).

Peter urged Simon to repent. Simon replied in effect, "Pray for me that I may escape punishment" (8:24). It is evident that Simon was still thinking in terms of magical powers instead of repentance and the power of the Holy Spirit.[1] Rather than wait patiently to see how God would gift him and where he would fit into God's plan, Simon merely coveted spiritual power.

In our fast-paced, quick-fix society, we've grown accustomed to having everything now and doing everything now. We want everything to come to us as easily as possible. We want the Holy Spirit to "do something" and to do it according to our timetable so that our lives will have significance.

Young Henrietta Mears (who would later influence thousands through her Christian education curriculum) wondered how God would use her. She especially struggled with the question of whether she could ever live up to what her mother had been and had done. Henrietta said:

> I prayed that if God had anything for me to do that He would supply the power. I read my Bible for every reference to the Holy Spirit and His power. The greatest realization came to me when I saw that there was nothing I had to do to receive His power but to submit to Christ, to allow Him to control me. I had been trying to do everything myself; now I let Christ take me completely. I said to Christ that if He wanted anything from me that He would have to do it Himself. My life was changed from that moment on.[2]

What an encouragement Henrietta's words are. Unlike Simon the magician, she reached the point of submitting to God's plan, allowing the Holy Spirit to work in whatever way He chose. No longer was she impatient to accomplish what she thought was significant. Because patience won out, God's will won out. And because God's will won out, she had a significant impact for the kingdom of God.

Those of us who desire to make a significant impact (I think that's most of us) must focus upon one main motive.

THE MOTIVE THAT SUSTAINS US

Hudson Taylor questioned several young volunteers for the mission field to determine their qualifications for this difficult calling. "And why do you wish to go as a foreign missionary?" he asked one.

"I want to go because Christ has commanded us to go into all the world and preach the Gospel to every creature," was the reply.

Another said, "I want to go because millions are perishing without Christ, not having even heard of the one name whereby the lost may be saved."

Others gave various answers. Then Hudson Taylor said, "All of these motives, however good, will fail you in times of testings, trials, tribulations, and possibly death. There is but *one motive* which will sustain you in trial and testing, namely, 'For the *love of Christ* constraineth us' (2 Corinthians 5:14 KJV, italics mine)."[3]

Hudson Taylor knew the importance of motives. We all live and breathe by our motives. Good, bad, or mixed—motives are what drive us and, to some extent, define us. Taylor wanted the missionaries' motive to be the love of Christ, and that alone.

Is our motive to love and serve God and others? If not, we ourselves will likely become the focus of our efforts.

People who have led highly significant lives throughout history were not wrapped up in themselves or their own interests. Instead their lives were wrapped up in a cause bigger than themselves. Like Paul the apostle, they recognized that Christ *"died for all, so that they who live might no longer live for themselves"* (2 Corinthians 5:14, italics mine).

Living for ourselves—which can take the form of wanting to be somebody significant—reveals a heart that really doesn't belong to God. The key to keeping self out of the picture is to allow the love of Christ to control us.

And so our real goal, paradoxically, *is not* to become a significant person. Such ambition is somewhat selfish. Significance is best obtained when it is a by-product rather than a goal. Our higher goal, one that can be pursued directly, is to have a heart that completely belongs to God—loving Him with our whole heart, soul, and mind (Deuteronomy 6:5-6). Then, and only then, will we have a significant life—not as the aim of our efforts but as the result of our pure love for God. And in our pursuit of pure love for God, the significant life is one that patiently waits for God's perfect will.

LIVING OUT GOD'S WILL

In Jeremiah's day many of the Israelites were ignoring the will of God and not considering His good pleasure. They were impatient with His plans and thought they knew what was best for their lives. Because they "did not listen to His voice" (Jeremiah 40:3), they sinned in ways that brought calamity upon themselves. In that calamity—conquest by their enemies—they were dragged off to Babylon. The Lord told the people through Jeremiah that their captivity would last seventy years, no more and no less (Jeremiah 29:10). Yet they still were impatient and refused to believe God and wait for His will. They listened to false prophets (Jeremiah 29:8-9, 24-32) who told them what they wanted to hear, that they would be back in their homeland very soon (cf. 28:10-11, in "two years").

Calamity can come to the Christian who runs away from, or who knowingly runs ahead of, the Master's plan. If a believer gives only lip service to that plan, the person's life will truly be wasted. This Christian lives *by selfish* impulses, whims, and dreams rather than the leading of the Spirit.

How blessed are the Christians whose spiritual focus aligns with God's will. Because the Lord knows all things, they can trust Him with all the unknowns in their lives—current and future circumstances, difficulties and trials, and the opportunities that will come.

In Scripture waiting for God's will means much more than merely letting the clock run until something happens. One Bible dictionary sums up what Scripture means by "wait": "To remain in readiness or expectation"; it suggests "the anxious, yet confident, expectation by God's people that the Lord will intervene on their behalf." The conclusion is that "waiting, therefore, is the working out of hope."[4]

Patiently waiting for God requires faith in Him, faith that He is good and that He is not failing us now, nor will He ever—no matter how things may appear. That precious package of attitudes keeps us from straying off the straight and narrow path. It enables us to stay in His will and over time to do the significant things He has planned for us to accomplish.

Patiently waiting for God takes not only faith but endurance.

When James wrote to Jewish people experiencing trials, he reminded them of Job: "You have heard of the *endurance* of Job" (James 5:11 KJV, italics mine; "patience"). The woman who wants to fulfill God's plan for her life will need to persevere through the dry spells as she keeps focused on serving others. Eventually, possibly years later, she'll see the fruit of her efforts. Paul uses an illustration from farming to prove this point. He says, "Let us not lose heart in doing good, for in due time we will reap if we do not grow weary" (Galatians 6:9).

I know just enough about farming to see that it is a great illustration of working for God's kingdom. It takes work to sow, and sometimes it's not only inconvenient; it's nothing short of miserable. Farmers in Israel didn't plow until the winter rains. By then the mud and water were enough to deter the sluggard (Proverbs 20:4). After sowing, it takes patience (and faith) until the crop sprouts. And when the crop comes—there is joy.

Patience is tied up with joy. But joy always comes at a price. This is true whether it is the joy of a new mother at childbirth, of a farmer at harvest, or of a soldier in victory. It costs the travailing woman great pain, the farmer months of backbreaking labor, the soldier hard training and great risk.[5] Unlike the patient farmer, anyone who wants quick results will never last long enough to harvest anything. And, of course, anyone who harvests too early will only waste all the effort. That person will be depressed rather than joyful.

If you want to have joy, if you desire to have a life of significance, you must pay the price of waiting, enduring, and praying. Also you may have to work through defeat, discouragement, despair, or a lack of understanding of what God wants. Joy does not require that we understand.

WHEN WE DON'T UNDERSTAND GOD'S WILL

Have you ever been confused by God's will, unsure of why He is working a certain way? Many of us have, and so were the Israelites during the time of Jeremiah. When he prophesied to his rebellious people being taken away to Babylon, he warned them not to flee to Egypt. They were afraid of the conquering king of Babylon; however, God promised He would protect them while they were captives and that he would bring them back to Israel in due time (Jeremiah 42:11-12). Quite naturally, to them Egypt seemed safer. At that point they did not need to understand how or why they would be safer as prisoners in Babylon. They were simply to obey.

It should not matter to us if we don't understand what God is doing. The issue is obedience, not understanding. We don't need to know, for example, why we are at the bottom of the totem pole at work or why we are still single or why we are still childless or why we seem to have less money to use for God's work than the ungodly have for carrying on their sinful lifestyle. Nor do we need to question why our giftedness is nowhere near the level of our zeal to serve. None of this really matters. What does matter is that we patiently endure, following in God's will, trusting that God's plan for our lives is the very best a loving and omnipotent God can give.

If only the Israelites had considered this! Many of them eventually disobeyed God and fled to Egypt. God asked, "Why are you doing great harm to yourselves . . . ?" (Jeremiah 44:7). It was their final act of distrust and rebellion.

When we do not trustingly wait for God and follow His leading, we harm ourselves. We lose the blessings of service and the chance to have a significant role—our role, the one tailored just for us—in the unfolding of God's wonderful plan. As well, we lose sight of what God may be doing in our lives as He fits us into His perfect timing.

PATIENCE IN GOD'S TIMING

The Moffats waited more than twelve years before they ever saw their first convert. Why couldn't God have given them a convert in their first year? Certainly this would have speeded up His program. And why, for that matter, did God's prophecies in the Old Testament take so long to be fulfilled? Micah's prophecy that the Lord would be born in Bethlehem (Micah 5:2) and Isaiah's prophecies about the suffering Messiah (Isaiah 53) were not fulfilled for hundreds of years.

Sometimes God's timetable seems arbitrary and full of unnecessary delays. When Jeremiah asked God whether it was okay for the Israelites to migrate to Egypt, the Lord didn't respond to Him for ten days (Jeremiah 42:1-7). And when the wine ran out at a wedding reception, Mary asked for Jesus to help. Yet He didn't respond immediately (John 2:4). Nor did He come immediately when His friend Lazarus was sick. He waited until Lazarus was dead and buried (John 11:6-11, 38).

Remember Hannah? She was burdened with sorrow because of seeing women around her raising children while she was still childless. So she began to pray that the Lord would remember her and give her a son (1 Samuel 1:11). And God answered. But how many years do you think Hannah had been praying for a son before God answered? We don't know, but it had to be several years because her husband married another woman so he could have children. Obviously Hannah was miserable because of the second wife (1 Samuel 1:6-7), but she was even more miserable about not having any children, weeping bitterly before the Lord (1 Samuel 1:10).

The point is that God took his time with Hannah. And in the process she became more submissive to God's ways while she patiently waited. Because of her longing, Hannah promised the Lord that if she were given a son, she would dedicate him to lifelong Levitical service (1 Samuel 1:11). Had Hannah gotten pregnant shortly after being married, her promise to dedicate her son to God might never have been made.

Behind God's timing is a divine plan. Hannah waited a long time, and she suffered emotionally during the wait. But the waiting benefited all of Israel. How so? God blessed her with a child that would one day be Israel's last judge and first prophet. Samuel became a powerful spokesman for God, reforming Israel's idolatrous worship. I am sure that Hannah would say in retrospect that the wait was well worth it.

So many things in God's plan require the right timing, and not often do we understand the details. For example, Paul was a zealous Pharisee until well into his adult life. Looking back, he realized that the timing of his coming to Christ was all in God's plan (Galatians 1:15-16). When the resurrected Jesus met His followers, they were anxious to know if God was now going to restore the kingdom to Israel. Jesus replied simply, "It is not for you to know times or epochs which the Father has fixed by His own authority" (Acts 1:7).

Is there something you are waiting upon God for? A more significant role in His divine plan? Are you completely confused as to why God allows you to go through such waiting?

I believe that God tests our patience, not because He takes sadistic delight in doing so, but because He is working things out for our spiritual good. He is building up trust in our longing hearts, showing us evidence of His love, His favor, and His goodness. He is purifying our faith, showing us where sin may still reign, disciplining us where needed, making us more spiritually fit before He fulfills His plan through us.

SPIRITUAL FITNESS

Gen. Lew Wallace was a man who wanted something tremendous out of life. He was a dreamer and a romantic. He thirsted for fame, fortune, and, most of all, for glory. He was impatient. He thought his chance for glory would come when Congress declared war on Mexico in 1846. But it wasn't to be. He and his men saw little action. They suffered more from disease than from the fighting.

When the Civil War came in 1861, Wallace thought this might be his chance for recognition. And he did receive some fame when he attained the rank of major general—the youngest man to do so. He attained more when he saved the nation's capitol from a Confederate sneak attack. But his glory was diminished on the day in which he mistakenly marched 6,500 men in the wrong direction at Shiloh, one of the bloodiest battles of the war.

After the war Wallace took up writing. Though not a religious man, he began to write a novel woven around the story his mother had told him as a child, one about a baby in a manger and three wise men. His novel ended during the infancy of Christ. When the first draft of his manuscript was completed, he put it in a drawer and forgot all about it.

One day on a train to Indianapolis, Wallace met the famed agnostic Col. Robert G. Ingersoll. In their conversation, Wallace asked Ingersoll if he believed in God, the devil, an afterlife, heaven, or hell. Ingersoll not only responded in the negative but argued his convictions with Wallace for over two hours. The cynic's arguments shook

Wallace out of his religious indifference and challenged him to prove to himself that Jesus was the Son of God.

Wallace not only researched the claims of Christ, but he took the long-forgotten manuscript out of the drawer. Having originally ended with the three wise men, Wallace now continued the story to include the life and the crucifixion of Christ. And so in March 1880, years after he had first started the novel, it was finished. The book was titled *Ben-Hur.*

Wallace had said that it was through writing his expansion of *Ben-Hur* that he came to accept the claims of Christ and committed his life to Him shortly thereafter.[6] For the first time in Wallace's life, he was no longer seeking personal glory. He wanted God to be glorified in all he did. Apparently God had to take Wallace through certain experiences in his life before it would be possible for him to write *Ben-Hur*. Had Wallace never committed himself to Christ, there wouldn't be a *Ben-Hur*. The manuscript would have stayed in the drawer, and its impact for the kingdom of God would have been lost.

Doesn't it seem that an important part of God's activity in our lives is to make us spiritually fit through our waiting? Notice that Wallace didn't have much to say until he came to see the truth and relinquished his desire for self-glory. Possibly God's most important blessings await our willingness to relinquish something or to grow into some godly attitude. *In that sense a significant life is founded upon willingness, plus time, plus growth.* But there is one more thing—contentment. It's the soil in which patience can grow.

BEING CONTENT

Paul the apostle, who lived a major portion of his Christian life in jail, knew the value of being content. He said that godliness is a means of great gain, *when accompanied by contentment* (1 Timothy 6:6).

Godliness involves being other-centered, Christ-centered, and praise-centered. But our godliness is greater gain when we have contentment. In a sense, when we are godly, we are doing something for others. But when we are content, we do something for ourselves. We grant ourselves an inner rest independent of circumstances, a rest that cannot fade or diminish and cannot be disappointed. We disconnect our happiness and our sense of peace from the turmoil around us, from our social and economic status, from our appearance and long-ings, and from our mental, social, and spiritual abilities.

Contentment is neither complacency nor apathy, which would accept things in ourselves and our world that we should work to change. Though contentment brings inner rest, it also works, gets involved, and strives for God's will. And in doing so, contentment brings peace because it is not focused upon personal gain, even in the quasi-spiritual form of wanting God to do something in our lives to give them more meaning and significance.

Contentment doesn't come to any of us easily because we naturally focus on personal gain. Paul said, "I have *learned* to be content" (Philippians 4:11, emphasis added). The verb "learned" (*emathon*) in the original Greek points to what we have gleaned from our experiences and trials.[7] In other words, we don't just absorb information, but we should be growing from all we have been through, and our lives should show the results. What we learn should become part of who we are, bringing the formation of new habits and attitudes. So we should be making it a habit to be content; it should be our basic attitude.

My father-in-law had to learn contentment in a very difficult way. When he was a teenager growing up in London, the Nazis were bombing the country day in and day out. While teenagers in America were playing ball, he was just trying to stay alive, often hiding in a stifling bomb shelter. More than once during that dark time, he remembers people gathering among the rubble of their city, not to express despair at the destruction all around, but in unison they would all sing:

> *O God, our help in ages past, our hope for years to come,*
> *Our shelter from the stormy blast, and our eternal home!*
>
> *Under the shadow of Thy throne still may we dwell secure;*
> *Sufficient is Thine arm alone, and our defense is sure.*
>
> *Before the hills in order stood, or earth received her frame,*
> *From everlasting Thou art God, to endless years the same.*
>
> *A thousand ages in Thy sight are like an evening gone;*
> *Short as the watch that ends the night, before the rising sun.*

> *O God, our help in ages past, our hope for years to come,*
> *Be Thou our guide while life shall last, and our eternal home!*[8]

Keeping an upward focus helped the citizens of London through that difficult time, and it let them rest in the knowledge that God was with them and in control. I am sure the Christians learned through the bombings that the most important thing in life was not preserving themselves but knowing God.

What have your experiences, your trials, and the passing of time taught you? Have they, as yet, led you to a point where you can say you are truly content with whatever God does in your life? If you can, then you are well on the way to having the kind of faith-inspired endurance that patiently waits for God to unfold His plan and then follows it until it bears much fruit.

In summary, how might our patience advance God's glory? Let's consider. Isn't God glorified in greater magnificence because of Hannah's waiting that produced her heart-felt song of praise (1 Samuel 2:1-10) and gave Israel an extraordinary prophet to challenge and guide the nation?

Isn't God more impressively revealed through the resurrection of a dead Lazarus rather than the healing of a sick Lazarus?

Doesn't the glory of God reveal itself more profoundly when He allows us to struggle so that He might lift us up (1 Samuel 2:8) and make us walk securely (Habakkuk 3:19)?

We have a very dramatic God who seeks the highest revelation of Himself in all things. Understanding that makes the timing of His will a little more comprehensible. And as we have the patience to fulfill His will, we can't help but glorify Him. But we can never know the full mind of God, so we will never understand all the reasons behind His will for us (Deuteronomy 29:29). All we need to do is rest in the truth that "it is God who is at work in you, both to will and to work for His good pleasure" (Philippians 2:13).

May we keep ourselves useful to God by abiding in His will, striving toward His good pleasure, holding on to our confidence that, though we see nothing now, our "vision is yet for the appointed time" (Habakkuk 2:3).

THINKING IT OVER

1. When young Moses strove to have a significant life, he failed. Why?
2. What does God's timing have to do with the significant life?
3. When Hannah was discouraged, what did she do? What was the result of her waiting?
4. What might God be trying to teach you during this time of waiting?
5. Why is contentment so important during our time of waiting?
6. In reflecting over past events of your life, do you see a time when God worked things out slowly—for which now you are thankful? Explain.

Epilogue

WHAT IF YOU HAD NEVER BEEN BORN?

*L*et's go back to the nineteenth century and enter a state asylum that was something like a dungeon. There people were locked up in cages with very little light. Among those forgotten people worked an elderly woman who was nearing retirement. Little was known of her. Were we to isolate her life from the pages of history, it might appear to amount to nothing. And yet the woman couldn't hope to be fairly judged by her own generation, nor could she fairly judge her own life. She may have thought of it as inconsequential and incomplete. She never gained fame in her day, nor was she viewed as "important" by those who worked with her.

Eventually the shadow of death came upon this fragile woman, and she was buried without much of a eulogy. Little did those who knew her best realize how important she had become to one young girl. The girl was known only as "Little Annie."

Like many of those in the asylum, Annie and her brother Jimmy were considered beyond hope. Abandoned by their father (their mother had died), the two were put in a room in the asylum where dead bodies were stored until someone found time to dig the graves. Their only toys were the rats that ran freely on the floor. In that miserable, lonely world Annie's brother died virtually unnoticed.

Annie would have spent her entire life in that horrible place had it not been for the elderly woman who believed she was not beyond hope. Rather than treat her like an animal, the woman spent all of her remaining days caring for Annie, giving her love and acceptance. Such kindness allowed the girl to flourish, and eventually she was judged fit to be released. At the age of fourteen she left, never to return.

Years later another young girl would need help. Her name was Helen. In infancy she had become completely blind and deaf and was therefore mute. Though she was raised by loving parents, she, too, would have remained cut off from the world were it not for "Little

Annie." Annie Sullivan became Helen's teacher and pulled Helen out of her isolated world.

Eventually the lives of millions of people, all with their own unique problems and sense of isolation, would be helped and inspired by the woman known as Helen Keller.[1] Helen was able to help others only because she was helped by Annie. Annie could help Helen only because she had been helped by the seemingly insignificant elderly woman. What if that elderly woman had never been born? The ripple effect of comfort and inspiration certainly would never have reached the world.

So allow me to ask about your life: Will it make a difference that you have been born? Not sure? Well then, let's see what would happen if we tore your life from the pages of history.

Suppose, like George Bailey in the movie *It's a Wonderful Life*, you did not exist. No one would know you. Some people, possibly you, assume that the gap you would leave in history's book would present no great loss to mankind. The human race would still greet the sunrise in the morning and watch the sun go down at night. They would eat, drink, and be merry. It is hard to imagine that one less life would really make that much difference.

Yet, like George Bailey, you might be surprised at just how much would be different. Without you, the past and future would have a piece missing, like one piece lost from a jigsaw puzzle. Let's understand this better by first looking at the past, then the present, and then the future.

THE PAST

I'll never forget the time when my grandfather, who was born at the end of the Victorian age (1895), said to me, "I shook the hand that shook the hand of Abraham Lincoln."

I immediately grabbed my grandfather's hand and began shaking it, saying, "I shook the hand that shook the hand that shook the hand of Abraham Lincoln!"

Though that was only a handshake, I felt distantly connected to America's great president. That handshake in a small way showed me how we are linked to events of the past.

Some people believe that our place in history is no more intricate than one person in the past kicking a rock to a particular place. Then years later we come along and trip over it, setting some other event in motion.[2] But history is so much deeper and more meaningful than this.

God has created each life with a specific purpose, and if we allow Him to fulfill it through us, He will continue to use us long after we are gone. Since the beginning, events have been connected in an endless chain, one thing influencing another, going on in unbroken succession until the Lord's return. You and I are a part of this chain, along with the people of the past and those yet to come.

Look at King Solomon's life. His father, King David, desired more than anything to build a house of worship. It would be his way of serving God and giving to the Israelites a permanent altar on which they could give to God their offerings.

Yet David's cherished dreams and desires were not to be fulfilled. The Lord stopped him by saying, "You have shed much blood and have waged great wars; you shall not build a house to My name." God then told David that he would be given a son who would build that house of worship instead (1 Chronicles 22:8-9). Although David wouldn't be the builder, he had a part in fulfilling his dream in that he was the one to amass the building supplies (1 Chronicles 22:1-5). Solomon used these materials to build the actual temple (1 Chronicles 22:11-19).

The same kind of partnering takes place in the principle of "sowing and reaping" (John 4:36-38). Though the partners in this case may never meet this side of eternity, it is their joint effort that brings a person into God's kingdom.

I became very aware of this connection years ago when I shared my faith a number of times with an elderly woman named Francine. In due time she accepted Christ. But my sharing wasn't the first time she had heard the message of salvation. She remembers hearing the gospel message as a young woman many times from a radio preacher. She didn't respond when she was in her twenties, but many decades later in her eighties she came to Christ.

In a sense I was a partner across the better part of a century with a preacher I will never meet in this life. Though I'm sure he is long gone, his efforts in the early twentieth century are still bearing fruit. See how the chain links, reaching back to the past and forward to the future? While my own efforts depend on those who went before me, my ministry also reaches into the future. So like the preacher, I'm sure my life will affect people long after I am gone—and so will yours. Our significance can reach much further than any of us realize. What would happen to the chain if our lives fail to form the links that connect past and future?

THE MISSING LINK

When we fail to fulfill the role God planned for us, we in effect fail to forge our link in the chain. What would history be like, or for that matter what would our lives be like, had the people of the Bible not fulfilled their place in God's plan? They each had their part in Israel's history, in forming the content of Scripture, in preparing for the Messiah, and in passing God's message to the next generation. Had King David not done his part, for example, he would never have strengthened Israel nor prepared the way for Solomon nor written so many of the psalms (1 Chronicles 23:5; Amos 6:5). And without David's life there would be no Solomon to raise Israel to a golden age, to gather proverbs, and to write Ecclesiastes. Think of John the Baptist's ministry, spiritually preparing many in Israel for the Messiah. Without his heralding, Christ's message would not have fallen on so many responsive hearts.

While it is true that each person's place in God's plan is crucial, it is also true that God in His wisdom and power can accomplish His will in spite of our failures. But He wants to bless us by using us; and while He can get things done without us, He may also allow history to be a little impoverished if we do not do our part. In a sense our ability to do our part can be enriched by strengthening our links with the past, with those who have gone before us.

STRENGTHENING OUR CONNECTION
WITH THE PAST

There have been times when I have wondered what it would be like to have lived in some past century. I'm sure I'm not the only one. And while I consider so many elements of each century interesting,

I would like to revisit certain centuries just because of the people who lived in them.

For instance, I would love (like most Christians) to go back to the first century and sit at the feet of Jesus and follow Him on the dusty roads of Palestine. But if I couldn't go that far back in time, I would love to go to the sixteenth century and listen to Puritan preacher Thomas Manton, or to the seventeenth century to learn from scholar and preacher Stephen Charnock, or to the nineteenth century to listen to the sermons of Charles Spurgeon. These men drew from deep spiritual wells.

Fortunately though I have not missed that much. I can still be at the foot of Christ by learning from His Word. And I can still learn from Manton, Charnock, and others through their writings. Manton's complete works are still available in twenty-two volumes. Charnock's monumental work, *The Existence and Attributes of God*, is still in print, all 1,150 pages of it. And Spurgeon's sermons have been collected in multivolume sets. I have been affected deeply by the lives and thoughts of such great Christians of the past.

Our generation is heir to the riches of the past, and we have the opportunity—and responsibility—to enrich that spiritual legacy and pass it on to those who will come after us. So our significance is ultimately to contribute a part of the vast heritage of this age. Eventually we and our generation will be gone, and memories of us will fade. But our legacy will live on even when our names are forgotten.

THE FUTURE

King David, though he sinned miserably, also served God mightily. He made a tremendous impact in his day with music, poetry, exhortation, and theology. In his old age he realized the need to make some decisions. He wasn't going to be around much longer. He knew that if the causes he had worked and fought for were to be secure, he would have to make provision for the future. So he chose his son Solomon as king (1 Chronicles 23:1). By giving Solomon his main possession—the throne—David's influence would continue on in the Lord's work.

Following David's example, we should strive to keep alive the causes we have worked for. While the legacy of our words and our example are built over years, what becomes of any earthly possessions we have accumulated is determined at a single point in time.

Leaving Our Property

Our property can continue to be used for God way into the future. Many Christians have used their assets to build churches, hospitals, and schools and to establish missions abroad. No matter how little is left, our assets can be of some service, making an impact after we are gone.

What implements this part of our legacy is simply a will, the legal document that tells the state what we want done.[3] And, like any other area of stewardship, making a will should be approached with thoughtfulness and prayer in order to ensure that we glorify God as much as possible with the possessions He has entrusted to us.

There's more we can do to be sure our legacy reaches forward into the future. After David gave the throne to Solomon, he then gave "his last words" (1 Chronicles 23:27).

Leaving Our Last Words

Since I have no idea whether I shall live as long as David or die as soon as tomorrow, my thoughts and words are continually written down in bound record books for Michelle and Johnathan. I have already completed several such books for them (having started their first book when they were a few days old). I will give them the books when they are older (the longer I live, the more books they will receive).

In the books I share not only the funny and adorable things they have said and done, but, more important, my thoughts about everything from world events to my faith in the Lord and my hopes and desires for them spiritually. If I live long enough, I desire to do the same thing for any grandchildren that may come along. It is my hope that by sharing my love for them, my love for the Lord, and the importance of living solely for Him, I will be imparting to them my mind and spirit. I shall live on in their lives and in their children's lives long after my physical presence is gone.

If you don't have children, you can leave the same sort of legacy to other family members, such as nieces or nephews, or to the children of close friends. In so doing you will hold a special place in their hearts and possibly in the hearts of their descendants, speaking from heaven about God and His accomplishments.

You may think, *I'm not a writer*, or *I just can't find the time to write or type things down*, or, *What if I don't feel I have anything to share? Can I still pass on a spiritual legacy?* Absolutely! You and I can leave a heritage to the extent that we live a life worth following. We also influence the future by praying for the spiritual welfare of generations yet to be born. In a broad sense we influence the future whenever we use our spiritual gifts, touch someone's life by caring, or take time to disciple someone younger in the faith. What an honor to have such an influence!

Of course between the past and the future is the ever-present now. What should we be especially alert to?

CREATED FOR SUCH A TIME AS THIS

One of the most amazing examples of seizing opportunity is found in the book of Esther. Esther had just gotten the alarming news from her cousin Mordecai that all Jews were to be annihilated (Esther 3:12-13). Esther desperately wanted to bring the matter up with the king, but she knew she would be risking her life to approach him without his invitation (Esther 4:11).

While hesitating, Mordecai told her point-blank that she was at risk regardless of whether or not she approached the king (Esther 4:13). He then made a profound statement that still speaks to us: "And who knows whether you have not attained royalty for such a time as this?" (Esther 4:14). Those strengthening words motivated Esther, and her actions spared the Jews (but not Haman, who had hatched the plot against the Jews).

Just like Esther, our place and time in history are no accident. God has appointed us to be a part of His plan. And in that outworking, God is no mere spectator. He was more than an observer when He used Moses (Exodus 4:15). He was more than an eyewitness when He prevented the Magi from returning to Herod (Matthew 2:12). He was more than a bystander when the apostles were chosen (Luke 6:12-13). He was more than a witness when Peter miraculously got out of jail (Acts 12:7-8). He was more than an onlooker when you were formed

(Psalm 139:13). And He is more than a passerby as you live your life (Psalm 139:1-3).

Consider: Why have you been born in this day and age? You could have been born during the time of Christ, the early history of this country, or sometime in the Victorian age. But you weren't. Could it be that you were born "for such a time as this?"

Ponder: Why did God keep you single? Or why did He have you marry? Why did He give you the children you have? Or why did He keep you childless? Why are you living in this nation? Why are you serving in the church? Or why are you working in the secular arena? Again, could it be for a special purpose, for such a time as this?

Think: In God's plan He has caused all events to come about so that you could be used in a highly significant way. Why did He give you certain abilities, gifts, and burdens? Because you were born for such a time as this.

As we consider, ponder, and think, there is one thing we must be aware of: Opportunities in life are fleeting. Esther wasn't given much notice before playing her significant part. She had to act quickly. What if she had not? Well, we would have a different story in the book of Esther. Its theme would be "what might have been."

WHAT MIGHT HAVE BEEN

John Greenleaf Whittier wrote over a century ago, "For all sad words of tongue or pen, the saddest are these: 'It might have been!'"[4] Have you ever mused over the paths you could have taken in life and wondered about what might have been? I've thought about that at times. But, too, I have wondered whether God looks back and sees what ought to have been.

I wonder how God might have worked in and through me had I responded differently to opportunities I passed up. I wonder what divine intervention I would have been able to see, what fruit would have come from my life had I chosen to take some particular opportunity.

I've realized as well, in all my pondering, that it's the opportunities that, by God's grace, I have seized that make my life worth looking back on. And myriads of bygone saints were able to look back upon their lives with contentment simply because they took advantage of opportunities that came their way.

So how can we avoid regret over lost opportunities? There are many ways. One is by just keeping prayerfully alert, asking God to show us how we might minister to others. Another way is by having what Esther had—a Mordecai.

LOOKING FOR A MORDECAI

We all need a Mordecai in our life, one who has an eye for opportunities we might otherwise miss. Queen Esther needed Mordecai to open her eyes to the impact she could have. A Mordecai can help us see how we might use our giftedness, talents, or resources.

My husband, Brian, is my Mordecai. I would never have started writing had he not been able to see an ability that was at that time completely undiscovered and undeveloped. He believed it was there and that God wanted to use it. As I mentioned in an earlier chapter, I was hesitant about writing, but Brian was persistent, telling me that God had given me things to say as well as the gift to write it for such a time as this. Since those early days, Brian has in many other ways continued to be my Mordecai.

Do you have parents, friends, or someone such as a pastor who might be a Mordecai, helping you see opportunities? If so, keep in contact with the person and talk about how much you desire to make a significant difference in "such a time as this." Ask the person to help you see opportunities to benefit others. We saw something of the variety of those opportunities in the chapters on being salt and light. Are you challenged to take advantage of them? What opportunities can you think of that will benefit your family, friends, nonbelievers, and believers alike? Who knows? Like Esther, your opportunities may allow you to affect an entire nation! Hard to believe?

In this book my desire has been to encourage you, showing you your worth, value, and how very significant you are in God's eyes. I have also wanted to show you how you can make the most of your life—by having a significant impact. I hope I have done that. But maybe I haven't. Are you this moment questioning your purpose in this world?

QUESTIONING OUR PURPOSE

One day ninety-two-year-old Jane said to me, "Nothing dramatic has ever really occurred in my life, and at this point nothing ever will. I lived, and now I am going to die. What could have been my purpose in being born?" Jane thought her life had been pointless because after ninety-two years, she expected there would be more visible accomplishments.

Maybe we, too, think our life should show something quite dramatic, something of substance, some clear evidence of purpose. Sometimes it can seem that all we have done in life, and all that we probably will do, is pretty insignificant.

Looking at Jane and knowing her only casually, I saw plenty of usefulness. She had known the Lord, been a wife, raised two children, and had been a friend to many people. But sometimes we just can't see the practical significance of our own lives. Sometimes only God knows our true significance.

There is a true story of a man who didn't think his life would count for much. He lived as a bit of a loner, against the pleas of his family and friends. At odds with them and society, he lived as a drifter on the streets of London. His rootless existence was partly the cause of his being turned down for service in the British army during World War II.

Bitterly disappointed at not being able to serve in the war, his feelings of dejection and failure deepened. He was one of the many people on this earth who thought their lives would never count for anything. Eventually his lifestyle and the foggy dampness of England got the best of him, and he died of pneumonia.

It so happened that at the time of the loner's death, the British military was hatching a brilliant and daring plan to fool Hitler's military machine. The Allies were about to stage a massive landing on Sicily, and the Germans were bound to expect it and be ready. So the British reasoned: Why not trick the Germans into thinking that the Allied ships would be somewhere else and cause them to move their men and equipment away from the real landing site?

And so, after much strategizing, the British decided to plant phony plans of two other invasion sites on a corpse and let it wash ashore in Spain where German spies were sure to get hold of them.

But they faced a few obstacles. First, where would they get a corpse? Secondly, how would they fake the drowning of the corpse? In a real drowning the lungs have water in them. Any other corpse would not—unless the person had died of pneumonia.

When it was learned that a homeless drifter had just died of pneumonia, the parents of the man were contacted by the military. They gave permission to use their son's body on the condition that his identity would never be revealed.[5] So he was given a new identity as a Major Martin and set adrift just off the coast of Spain. He became known as "the man who never was."

The ruse worked, and even Hitler himself was fooled. Huge numbers of German forces were diverted from Sicily, saving thousands of Allied lives in what became a relatively easy landing. So the man who grieved that he could not help in the war effort ended up playing a major role. He was buried with military honors, and he rests under Spain's sunny skies.[6]

It shouldn't surprise us, even as Christians, if our lives sometimes seem insignificant despite our best efforts. Look at Christ. The moment He died, the apostles must have thought of Him as something of a failure. He was supposed to be their Messiah, and there He was in the grave. They may well have wondered, *What was the purpose of Christ's life? Wasn't He supposed to save us?* At that time they didn't fully grasp God's plan nor how Christ's life was going to be continued and completed.

From our limited perspective, one passing life can seem so insignificant. We question the timing of a young person dying apparently all too soon. We wonder why anyone who seems to have great potential would have an untimely end. We look at an elderly person and wonder what impact those many years have made here on earth. We may even wonder whether our own purpose will be fulfilled by the time of our death.

Our comfort is this: Though our life is but a vapor, it is not lived in vain. We are living out our purpose if we have committed our lives to Christ, if we pursue His kingdom and righteousness, if we live in obedience to His will, are devoted to His glory, and if we are concerned about the eternal well-being of the lost. Such a life has an excellence that true wisdom does not despise.

Just think: Through a chain of events connecting the past, the present, and the future, you are a part of history—not just ordinary history, but *His-story*. It is a story that is part of God's great plan, one that reveals the likeness of Jesus. A story that recognizes that the smallest act done for Christ is not lost. A story that portrays the child of God as spiritual royalty. That royalty extends a hand to the world and the soul to God—producing a ripple effect felt not only in this age and in generations to come but also forever.

Neither you nor I could ask for more significance than the value we have because of who we are in Christ. And, as we continue to cultivate our renewed heart, we will become ever more significant in God's eternally unfolding plan.

I say with all sincerity that the world would have missed out on so much had you never been born. So too would have heaven.

THINKING IT OVER

1. In what ways do our lives connect the past and the future?
2. What can you do to ensure that your influence continues beyond your earthly life?
3. Why is it important to have a Mordecai in your life? Is there a Mordecai in your life now? If not, whom might you ask to fill that role?
4. How can we avoid missing out on God's blessings?
5. Read Deuteronomy 29:29. How might the full significance of your life be unknown to you at present?
6. With all that was discussed in this book, what area(s) do you need to work on most?

$\mathcal{N}otes$

CHAPTER 1
IF ONLY I COULD CHANGE WHO I AM!

1. Adapted from John Allen Paulos, *I Think, Therefore I Laugh* (New York: Columbia University Press; reprint, New York: Vintage Books, 1990), 139.

2. Elisabeth Elliot, *A Chance to Die* (Old Tappan, N.J.: Fleming H. Revell Co., 1987), 24.

3. *Old World History and Geography: In Christian Perspective* (Pensacola, Fla.: Pensacola Christian College, 1981, 1991), 219.

4. Elliot, *Chance to Die*, 260.

5. H. D. M. Spence and Joseph S. Exell, eds., *The Pulpit Commentary, Ezra, Nehemiah, Esther, Job* (Grand Rapids: Wm. B. Eerdmans Publishing Co., 1950), "Job," 5.

6. *The Oxford Dictionary of Quotations* (New York: Oxford University Press, 1979), 145. Taken from the poem "Ninth Philosopher's Song."

7. Charles Sykes, *A Nation of Victims* (New York: St. Martin's Press, 1992), 133.

8. P. J. O'Rourke, *A Parliament of Whores* (New York: Atlantic Monthly Press, 1991), 72; quoted in ibid., 133.

9. Sykes, *Nation of Victims*, 133.

10. *Larry King Live*, (CNN, August 1999).

11. *Encyclopaedia Britannica*, vol. 16 (Chicago: William Benton, Publisher, 1956), 959.

12. When Paul wrote to the Galatians, he referred to some problem that could have tempted them to despise him (Galatians 4:14). That would fit malaria, which he could have gotten in parts of Asia Minor. He seems to have had trouble with his eyes as well (Galatians 6:11). When Paul stood before the Sanhedrin, the high priest Ananias commanded those who stood by Paul to "strike him on the mouth."

    Paul responded, "'God will strike you, you whitewashed wall!'"

    Those who stood by Paul said with a gasp, "'Do you revile God's high priest?'"

    Paul replied, "'I did not know, brethren, that he was the high priest; for it is written, "You shall not speak evil of a ruler of your people"'" (Acts 23:1-5 NKJV).

    Paul may have had poor eyesight if he didn't recognize the high priest who would have been wearing special religious garb.

13. Adapted from Charles Merrill Smith, *How to Become a Bishop Without Being Religious* (Garden City, N.Y.: Doubleday & Co., 1965), 24.

CHAPTER 2
HOW CAN I COMPETE WITH MRS. PROVERBS?

1. David Wallechinsky and Irving Wallace, *The People's Almanac #2* (New York: Bantam Books, 1978), 695.

2. *Appleton's Cyclopaedia of American Biography,* vol. 6 (New York: D. Appleton & Co., 1889), 504.

3. William Shakespeare, *The Tragedy of Julius Caesar,* act 3, scene 2, lines 124-126.

4. L. E. Maxwell, *Crowded to Christ* (Grand Rapids: Wm. B. Eerdmans Publishing Co., 1952), 20.

5. D. H. Field, "Buy, Sell, Market," *The New International Dictionary of New Testament Theology,* ed. Colin Brown (Grand Rapids: Zondervan, 1975), 1:268. At the time of writing, Professor Field taught at Oak College in London.

6. Romans 1:1; Philippians 1:1; 2 Timothy 2:24; Titus 1:1. Cited by Gary T. Meadors, "Slave, Slavery," *Evangelical Dictionary of Biblical Theology,* ed. Walter A. Elwell (Grand Rapids: Baker, 1996), 3:741.

CHAPTER 3
THE "100 MOST IMPORTANT WOMEN" . . .
THEN THERE'S ME

1. *Ladies' Home Journal: 100 Most Important Women of the 20th Century* (Meridith Corporation, 1999).

2. George Grant, *Grand Illusions: The Legacy of Planned Parenthood* (Brentwood, Tenn.: Wolgemuth & Hyatt, Publishers, 1988), 49. He cites an unpublished master's thesis by Albert Gringer, titled "The Sanger Corpus: A Study in Militancy" (Lakeland Christian College, 1974), Appendix, IV, 473-502.

3. Grant, *Grand Illusions,* 50.

4. Ibid.

5. Ibid.

6. Ibid.

7. Ibid., 56.

8. Ibid.

9. Ibid., 57.

10. Margaret Sanger, *The Pivot of Civilization* (New York: Brentano's, 1922), 264.

CHAPTER 4
GETTING RID OF FEELINGS OF UNWORTHINESS

1. Ruth A. Tucker, *From Jerusalem to Irian Jaya* (Grand Rapids: Zondervan, 1983), 430.
2. Ibid., 431.
3. Ibid.
4. Ibid.
5. Ibid., 431-432.
6. Ibid., 432. Also quoted by James and Marti Hefley, *By Their Blood: Christian Martyrs of the 20th Century* (Milford, Mich.: Mott Media, 1979), 46.
7. Robert H. Schuller, *Self-Esteem: The New Reformation* (New York: Jove Books, 1982), 61.
8. Charles Caldwell Ryrie, *The Ryrie Study Bible* (Chicago: Moody Press, 1978), 540.
9. James E. Rosscup, *Abiding in Christ* (Grand Rapids: Zondervan, 1973), 137, 138.
10. Ibid., 138.
11. Ibid.
12. Ibid., adapted.
13. Ibid.
14. Joni Eareckson Tada, *Joni* (Minneapolis, Minn.: World Wide Publications, 1976), 190.
15. Adapted from Rosscup, *Abiding in Christ*, 139.
16. Frank N. Magill and Ian P. McGreal, eds., *Christian Spirituality* (New York: HarperCollins, 1988), 375.

CHAPTER 5
THE THIRD BEATITUDE, HEAVENLY BEAUTY

1. Lucius Beebe, "Pandemonium at Promontory," in *American Heritage*, Vol. 9, No. 2 (New York: American Heritage Publishing Co., 1958), 20-23.
2. Ibid., 23.
3. C. F. Keil and F. Delitzsch, *Commentary on the Old Testament in Ten Volumes,* Vol. 1, *The Pentateuch,* translated from the German by James Martin (Grand Rapids: William B. Eerdmans Publishing Co., 1991), 131.
4. R. Winterbotham, *Numbers,* in H. D. M. Spence and Joseph S. Exell, ed., *The Pulpit Commentary: Leviticus, Numbers,* Vol. 2 (Peabody, Mass: Hendrickson Publishers), 253.
5. Curtis Vaughan and Thomas D. Lea, *1, 2 Peter, Jude* (Grand Rapids: Lamplighter Books, 1988), 126.

6. Colin Brown, *Dictionary of New Testament Theology* (Grand Rapids: Zondervan, 1976), 2:262.

7. William Temple, *Christ in His Church*, quoted in *The Book of Wisdom* (Sisters, Ore.: Multnomah Publishers, 1997), 343.

8. Adapted from John Bunyan, *The Pilgrim's Progress* (Westwood, N.J.: Barbour and Co., n.d.), 282.

CHAPTER 6
TRUE DIGNITY, OUR BIRTHRIGHT

1. Slaves called their mates "husbands," but marriage among slaves during this time was illegal. *American Heritage*, Vol. 44, No. 6 (Chicago: Chicago Historical Society, October 1993), 72.

2. Radford Ruether and Rosemary Skinner Keller, eds., *Women & Religion in America* (Cambridge, Mass., San Francisco: Harper & Row, 1983), 2:236. Also William W. Hening, *Statutes at Large: Laws of Virginia I* (New York: Barton, 1832), 552. The point of reference is the 1640 Sweet case in which the white man (Sweet) was found guilty of getting a black servant pregnant. She was whipped, and he was sentenced to public penance. The case is cited by Ruether and Keller.

3. Ruether and Keller, ibid., 259. Taken from a sermon on the death of Sarah Johnson (1845), preached at St. James First African Methodist Episcopal Church. From the Historical Society of Pennsylvania.

4. John Calvin, *Institutes of the Christian Religion*, ed. John T. McNeill, trans. Ford Lewis Battles, 1.15.4 (Philadelphia, Penn.: Westminster, 1960), 1:189.

5. Anthony A. Hoekema, *Created in God's Image* (Grand Rapids: Wm. B. Eerdmans Publishing Co., 1986), 72.

6. H. D. M. Spence and Joseph S. Exell, *The Pulpit Commentary, Psalms* (Peabody, Mass.: Hendrickson Publishers), 278.

7. *The O'Reilly Report*, The Fox News Channel, April 2, 2000.

8. Bernard of Clairvaux, "In Dedicatione Ecclesiae," Sermon V (MPL 183.531-534); tr. *St. Bernard's Sermons for the Seasons*, II, 419-426; quoted in Calvin, *Institutes*, ed. McNeill, 3.2.25, 1:572.

9. William Shakespeare, *The Life of Henry the Fifth*, Act 5, Scene 2, lines 155-160.

10. John MacArthur, Jr., *Security in the Spirit: Study Notes, Romans 8* (Panorama City, Calif.: Word of Grace Communications, 1985), 171.

11. Stephen M. Smith, "Hope, Theology of," *Evangelical Dictionary of Theology*, ed. Walter A. Elwell (Grand Rapids: Baker Book House, 1984), 532.

12. Ibid., 532-533.

13. John Bunyan, *The Pilgrim's Progress* (Westwood, N.J.: Barbour and Co.), 7.

CHAPTER 7

FAITHFULNESS—IN THE MANY FACETS OF LIFE

1. R. C. H. Lenski, *The Interpretation of the Epistles of St. Peter, St. John and St. Jude* (Minneapolis, Minn.: Augsburg, 1966), 948. According to Lenski, this would equal $560 if it means a mina of Hebrew gold, $32 if Hebrew silver is meant, and $17 if Greek silver is meant. He thinks it most likely means Hebrew gold.

2. Ibid., 955-958.

3. Ibid., 958.

4. Charles Caldwell Ryrie, *The Ryrie Study Bible* (Chicago: Moody Press, 1976, 1978), 86.

5. J. Oswald Sanders, *Spiritual Leadership*, rev. ed. (Chicago: Moody Press, 1980), 147.

6. Ibid., 148, 149.

7. Ibid., 152.

8. Ibid.

9. *Sarah Morgan: The Civil War Diary of a Southern Woman* (New York: Simon & Schuster, Touchstone, 1992; Athens, Ga.: University of Georgia Press, 1991).

10. Bella Fromm, *Blood & Banquets* (London: Geoffrey Bles, 1943; New York: Carol Publishing Group, 1990).

11. Ryrie, *Ryrie Study Bible,* 1739.

12. Joseph Addison Alexander, *Commentary on the Prophecies of Isaiah*, rev. ed. (1875; reprint, Grand Rapids: Zondervan, 1978), 116.

13. This display was easy to make. I got the pictures from the calendars supplied each year by donating any amount to the Institute of Evangelism, Billy Graham Center, Wheaton College, Wheaton, IL 60187-5593. Each month features a portrait of a great person in church history along with a quotation. I cover each picture with clear plastic and staple the edges. Then I set a tack in the top center. I make a frame by covering the stapled borders and tack with Victorian lace. It's ready to put on the wall.

I have no idea how long the Institute will be able to continue providing these wonderful calendars (perhaps if there's interest, they will continue). I never thought that I or my family would be so spiritually motivated by them. I am indebted to the Institute of Evangelism at Wheaton College.

CHAPTER 8

SACRIFICE—A LIVING ONE

1. F. L. Cross and E. A. Livingston, eds., "Stylite," *The Oxford Dictionary of the Christian Church* (Oxford, England: Oxford University Press, 1983), 1317.

2. H. D. Spence and Joseph S. Exell, eds., *The Pulpit Commentary: Matthew* (Peabody, Mass.: Hendrickson Publishers), 270.

3. Will Durant, *Caesar and Christ*, Vol. 3, *The Story of Civilization* (New York: Simon & Schuster, 1972), 656-657.

4. Ibid., 657.

5. Patti Roberts, with Sherry Andrews, *Ashes to Gold* (Waco, Texas: Word Books, 1983), 110-111; quoted in Hank Hanegraaf, *Christianity in Crisis* (Eugene, Ore.: Harvest House Publishers, 1993), 192.

6. Dag Hammarskjöld, *Markings*, trans. Leif Sjoberg and W. H. Auden (New York: Alfred A. Knopf, 1970), 83.

7. John Street, "The Peril of a Narcissistic Christianity," chapel message, The Master's College, Santa Clarita, Calif., October 22, 1999.

8. "Must I Really Love Myself?" *Christianity Today*, May 5, 1978, 34; quoted in Paul Brownback, *The Danger of Self-Love: Reexamining a Popular Myth* (Chicago: Moody Press, 1982), 13.

9. Spence and Exell, *Pulpit Commentary: 1 & 2 Thessalonians, 1 & 2 Timothy, Titus, Philemon, Hebrews, James*, Second Epistle to Timothy, 51.

10. Ibid., 201

11. Robert Thomas, *Christian Self-Concept: A Death-Life Paradox* (Christian Focus Publishers, Scotland, forthcoming), n.p., chapter titled "What the Self-Concept Means in Valuing One's Own Earthly Possessions" in the section "Faith, Discipleship, and Self-Concept."

12. Ibid.

13. Ibid., chapter titled "What the Self-Concept Means to Family Ties" in the section "Choosing a Side in the Feud (Matthew 10:37)." I would like to thank Dr. Thomas for allowing me access to a prepublication draft of his work.

14. Ibid.

15. Ibid.

16. Herbert V. Prochnow, *1400 Ideas for Speakers & Toastmasters* (Grand Rapids: Baker Book House, 1964), 69.

17. John MacArthur, *The MacArthur New Testament Commentary: Matthew 1-7* (Chicago: Moody Press, 1985), 223.

18. The Moravians followed the teachings of Reformation leader John Hus.

19. Charles H. Spurgeon, *Lectures to My Students* (1875-94; reprint, Grand Rapids: Baker, 1981), 3rd ser., 49.

20. Prayer written by an unknown Confederate soldier. From Walter B. Knight, *Knight's Treasury of 2,000 Illustrations* (Grand Rapids: Wm. B. Eerdmans Publishing Co., 1963), 270.

21. Taped interview with Elisabeth Elliot, June 1987. My gratitude to her for her insightful comments. Since that time she has been blessed with more grandchildren.

22. Quoted in Hans Küng, *Does God Exist? An Answer for Today* (Garden City, N.Y.: Doubleday, 1980), 219. Here Marx gave token allegiance to Christianity in an essay titled, "The Union of Believers with Christ according to John 15:1-14, showing its basis and essence, its absolute necessity and its effects." Küng notes that the assignment was to write on a "social theme from a religious standpoint" and that Marx wrote in the "spirit of an idealistic humanism."

CHAPTER 9

SALT—THAT FLAVORS A TASTELESS SOCIETY

1. Will and Ariel Durant, *The Age of Napoleon,* Vol. 11 of *The Story of Civilization* (New York: Simon & Schuster, 1975), 367, 368. While British vessels transported 38,000 slaves to America, French ships transported 20,000, Portuguese ships brought 10,000, Dutch ships 4,000, and Danish ships 2,000.

2. *Encyclopaedia Britannica* (Chicago: William Benton, Publisher, 1956), 23:594.

3. F. L. Cross and E. A. Livingston, eds., "Wilberforce, William," *The Oxford Dictionary of the Christian Church* (Oxford, England: Oxford University Press, 1983), 1479.

4. Durant, *Story of Civilization*, 11:368.

5. Ibid.

6. Ibid.

7. *Encyclopaedia Britannica*, 23:595.

8. Adapted from David J. Gyertson, ed., *Salt & Light: A Christian Response to Current Issues* (Dallas, Texas: Word Publishing, 1993), 12. I admit that some of these uses of the salt and light metaphors go beyond their biblical scope.

9. Suzy Platt, *Respectfully Quoted* (New York: Barnes & Noble, 1993), 230.

10. Justo L. Gonzalez, *The Story of Christianity* (1984, 1985; reprint, 2 vols. in 1, Peabody, Mass.: Hendrickson Publishers, Prince Press, 1999), 1:34-35.

11. Adapted from *The Rebirth of America* (Arthur S. DeMoss Foundation, 1986), 193.

12. Bella Fromm, *Blood and Banquets* (New York: Carol Publishing, 1990), 47.

13. Ibid., 79.

14. Bible Illustrator (Hiawatha, Iowa: Parsons Technology, 1990-1992).

15. Will Durant, *Caesar and Christ*, Vol. 3 (New York: Simon & Schuster, 1944, 1972), 665.

16. M. Rostovtzeff, *Rome*, ed. Elias J. Bickerman, trans. J. D. Duff (London, England: Oxford University Press, 1960), 324.

17. Clyde L. Manschreck, ed., *A History of Christianity* (Grand Rapids: Baker Book House, 1964), 2:530.

18. Kay Bonner Nee in *Witnesses to the Holocaust: An Oral History*; quoted in *The Book of Wisdom* (Sisters, Ore.: Multnomah Publishers, 1997), 319.

19. Manschreck, *History of Christianity*, 530-532.

20. James C. Livingston and Francis Shussler Fiorenza, *Modern Christian Thought*, Vol. 2, *The Twentieth Century*, 2nd ed. (Upper Saddle River, N.J.: Prentice Hall, 2000), 112-13, 119.

21. Manschreck, *History of Christianity*, 532-533.

22. John W. Alexander, ed., *Confessing Christ as Lord: The Urbana 81 Compendium* (Downers Grove, Ill.: InterVarsity Press, 1982), 198.

23. George Marsden, *Fundamentalism and American Culture: The Shaping of Twentieth-Century Evangelicalism: 1870-1925* (Oxford: Oxford University Press, 1980), 84.

24. Ibid.

25. Ibid., 85.

26. "The Holy Spirit in His Relation to City Evangelization," *The Holy Spirit in Life and Service*, ed. A. C. Dixon (New York: 1895), 129-130; quoted in Marsden, *Fundamentalism and American Culture*, 81.

27. Sermon preached around 1900; quoted in Marsden, 89.

28. Ibid., 91. He cites some other reasons for Evangelicals shunning works of compassion. There was a growing shift away from the view that Christ will return *after* the millennium (postmillennialism) to the view that He will return *before* the millennium (premillennialism). Postmillennialism assumes that the world will get better, which would require social works. Along with this shift, there was an increasing emphasis on the individual side of Christianity, that sanctification is a personal thing, not a matter of laws such as govern societies. (And if it is individual, then the condition of a whole society is not so important.)

29. Charles Caldwell Ryrie, *The Ryrie Study Bible* (Chicago: Moody Press, 1976, 1978), 405.

30. Ibid., 1579.

31. *Insight,* National Association of Evangelicals, Church Edition, December 1999.

32. *Special Report with Brit Hume*, Fox News, August 25, 2000. Tony Snow was filling in for Hume in an interview with Gary Bauer. Bauer was specifically referring to the Clinton administration.

33. John MacArthur, *The Christian and Government* (Panorama City, Calif.: Word of Grace Communications, 1986), 68.

34. It's hard to keep up with the abortion industry. For instance, in December 1999 it was revealed that the selling of baby parts had become a booming under-the-table business. During a two-year investigation by Life Dynamics, with the assistance of an industry insider, investigators were able to buy baby parts made available from abortions. Eyes were selling for

$75.00; skin for $100.00; brains for as much as $999.00 (prices vary based on length of gestation and condition of the parts). *Insight*, National Association of Evangelicals, Church Edition, December 1999, page 2. Senator Bob Smith (R-NH) gave this information to a congressional committee.

35. Harriet Beecher Stowe, *The Church and the Slave Trade*; quoted in *The Book of Wisdom* (Sisters, Ore.: Multnomah Publishers, 1997), 301.

36. Dr. & Mrs. Howard Taylor, *Hudson Taylor's Spiritual Secrets* (Chicago: Moody Press, 1935), 184.

37. Charles Dickens, *The Adventures of Oliver Twist* (New York: Charles Scribner's Sons, 1905), 376.

38. Ibid., 372.

CHAPTER 10
LIGHT—THAT ILLUMINATES DARKENED PATHWAYS

1. Ronald F. Youngblood, ed., *New Illustrated Bible Dictionary* (Nashville, Tenn.: Thomas Nelson Publishers, 1986, 1995). More detailed and theologically oriented tools include the *Evangelical Dictionary of Biblical Theology*, ed. Walter Elwell (Grand Rapids: Baker, 1996); Marvin R. Vincent's *Word Studies in the New Testament*, 4 vols. (Reprint, Peabody, Mass.: Hendrickson, n.d.); and *The New International Dictionary of New Testament Theology*, ed. Colin Brown, 3 vols. (Grand Rapids: Zondervan, 1976). In *Choices That Lead to Godliness* I explain some techniques for properly using some of these fine books as well as other resources.

2. *The Random House Dictionary* (New York: Random House, 1982), 637.

3. Youngblood, *New Illustrated Bible Dictionary*, 575.

4. KTLA, Los Angeles, Channel 5, February 19, 1996.

5. William Barclay, *The Gospel of John, Vol. 2* (Philadelphia, Penn.: Westminster, 1975), 177.

6. Will and Ariel Durant, *The Age of Napoleon*, Vol. 11, *The Story of Civilization* (New York: Simon & Schuster, 1975), 91.

7. Suzy Platt, ed., *Respectfully Quoted* (New York: Barnes & Noble, 1993), 292.

8. Charles Caldwell Ryrie, *The Ryrie Study Bible* (Chicago: Moody Press, 1976, 1978), 841.

9. Corrie ten Boom, *The Hiding Place* (Minneapolis, Minn.: Viking Press, 1971), 233.

10. John Calvin, *Institutes of the Christian Religion*, quoted in *The Book of Wisdom* (Sisters, Ore.: Multnomah Publishers, 1997), 159.

11. Robert C. Winthrop, *Life and Letters of John Winthrop, Vol. 2* (Boston: Ticknor and Fields, 1867), 19.

12. Walter B. Knight, *Knight's Treasury of 2,000 Illustrations* (Grand Rapids: Wm. B. Eerdmans Publishing Co., 1963), 202.

13. Karen Burton Mains, *Open Heart, Open Home* (Colorado Springs, Colo.: David C. Cook Publishing Co., 1976), 25.

14. [Edward] Everett Hale [1822-1909], quoted in *The Rebirth of America* (Arthur S. DeMoss Foundation, 1986), 223. A slightly different version appears in *Book of Wisdom*, 319, as quoted from "Lend a Hand." Apparently the source was a serial: "Lend a Hand: A Record of Progress and Journal of Organized Charity," cited in *Appleton's Cyclopedia of American Biography*, Vol. 3 (New York: D. Appleton & Co., 1887), 32.

CHAPTER 11
PATIENCE—IN GOD'S TIMING

1. Charles Caldwell Ryrie, *The Ryrie Study Bible* (Chicago: Moody Press, 1978), 1659.

2. Earl O. Roe, ed., *Dream Big: The Henrietta Mears Story* (Ventura, Calif.: Gospel Light Publications, 1990), 74.

3. Walter B. Knight, *Knight's Master Book of 4,000 Illustrations* (Grand Rapids: Wm. B. Eerdmans Publishing Co., 1956), 391.

4. Ronald F. Youngblood, ed., "Wait," *Nelson's New Illustrated Bible Dictionary* (Nashville, Tenn.: Nelson, 1995), 1299-1300.

5. William Gurnall, *The Christian in Complete Armour* (1655; reprint, Edinburgh, Scotland: The Banner of Truth Trust, 1986), 145.

6. Joe Wheeler, "The Man Behind Ben-Hur," *Focus on the Family* magazine (April 1998), 11. I want to express my appreciation to the ministry team at Focus on the Family for taking the time to dig into their archives and find information for me on the life of Gen. Lew Wallace.

7. Robert G. Gromacki, *Stand United in Joy: An Exposition of Philippians* (Grand Rapids: Baker Book House, 1980), 186, 187.

8. Isaac Watts, "O God, Our Help in Ages Past," *The New Church Hymnal* (Lexicon Music, 1976), 4.

EPILOGUE
WHAT IF YOU HAD NEVER BEEN BORN?

1. While I admire Helen Keller for inspiring thousands of people to do great things despite their limitations, I disagree with her religious beliefs. Her book *My Religion* endorsed the theology of Emanuel Swedenborg (1688-1772). He considered his authority to be greater than that of the apostles, claiming that his revelations came directly from Christ. He rejected the Trinity, the bodily resurrection of Christ, and many books of the Bible; he taught that the way to salvation is through obedience to the Ten Commandments.

2. Brian Leftow, in *God and the Philosophers*, ed. Thomas V. Morris (New York: Oxford University Press, 1994), 190.

3. Of course, like the rest of this book, statements about these matters do not constitute legal advice and should not be construed as such. To get legal advice, you should seek the help of a qualified professional.

4. John Greenleaf Whittier, "Maud Muller," in *The Poems of John Greenleaf Whittier* (New York: The Heritage Press, 1945), 6.

5 The man's identity was recently revealed after it was uncovered by diligent research done by civilians.

6. Ewen E. S. Montagu, "The Corpse That Hoaxed the Axis," *Reader's Digest*, November 1953; reprinted in *Secrets & Spies: Behind-the-Scenes Stories of World War II* (Pleasantville, NY: Readers Digest Association, 1964), 252-257. Condensed from the book *The Man Who Never Was* (Philadelphia, Penn.: J. B. Lippincott, 1954).